Contents

Introduction   **1**

I Basic Skills

1   Listening   **5**
Real Versus Pseudo-Listening
Blocks to Listening: Comparing; Mind Reading;
    Rehearsing; Filtering; Judging; Dreaming;
    Identifying; Advising; Sparring; Being Right;
    Derailing; Placating
Assessing Your Listening Blocks
Four Steps to Effective Listening: Active Listening;
    Listening With Empathy; Listening With Openness;
    Listening With Awareness
Total Listening
Listening for Couples

2   Self-Disclosure   **21**
Rewards of Self-Disclosure: Increased Self-Knowledge;
    Closer Intimate Relationships; Improved
    Communication; Lighter Guilt Feelings;
    More Energy
Blocks to Self-Disclosure
Optimal Levels of Self-Disclosure
Exercises: Assessing Your Self-Disclosure
Practice in Self-Disclosure

3   Expressing   **33**
The Four Kinds of Expression: Observations;
    Thoughts; Feelings; Needs

Whole Messages

Contaminated Messages

Preparing Your Message: Self-Awareness; Other
Awareness; Place Awareness

Practicing Whole Messages

Rules for Effective Expression: Messages Should Be
Direct; Messages Should Be Immediate; Messages
Should Be Clear; Messages Should Be Straight;
Messages Should Be Supportive

II Advanced Skills

4   **Body Language**   53

Body Movements: Facial Expression; Gestures; Posture
and Breathing

Spatial Relationships

5   **Paralanguage and Metamessages**   63

The Elements of Paralanguage

Changing Your Paralanguage

Metamessages: Rhythm and Pitch in a Metamessage;
Verbal Modifiers

Coping With Metamessages

6   **Hidden Agendas**   73

The Eight Agendas: I'm Good; I'm Good (But You're
Not); You're Good (But I'm Not); I'm Helpless,
I Suffer; I'm Blameless; I'm Fragile; I'm Tough;
I Know It All

Purpose of the Agendas

7   **Transactional Analysis**   81

Parent, Child, and Adult Messages: The Parent;
The Child; The Adult

Analyzing Your Communications

Kinds of Transactions: Complimentary Transactions;
Crossed Transactions; Ulterior Transactions

Keeping Your Communications Clean

8   **Clarifying Language**   93

Understanding a Model

Challenging the Limits of a Model

Challenging Distortions in a Model

Some Final Clarifications

MESSAGES

THE COMMUNICATION SKILLS BOOK

Second Edition

Matthew McKay, Ph.D.
Martha Davis, Ph.D.
Patrick Fanning

NEW HARBINGER PUBLICATIONS, INC.

To Jude Landis,
Nancy Kesselring
Ray and Kay Davis

Publisher's Note

This publication is designed to provide accurate and authoritative information in regard to the subject matter covered. It is sold with the understanding that the publisher is not engaged in rendering psychological, financial, legal, or other professional services. If expert assistance or counseling is needed, the services of a competent professional should be sought.

Copyright © 1995 New Harbinger Publications, Inc.
5674 Shattuck Avenue
Oakland, CA 94609

Cover design by SHELBY DESIGNS & ILLUSTRATES.
Text design by Tracy Marie Powell.

Distributed in the U.S.A. primarily by Publishers Group West; in Canada by Raincoast Books; in Great Britain by Airlift Book Company, Ltd.; in South Africa by Real Books, Ltd.; in Australia by Boobook; and in New Zealand by Tandem Press.

ISBN 1-57224-023-7 hardcover
ISBN 1-57224-022-9 paperback

Library of Congress Catalog Card Number: 95-69481

First Edition
Thirteen printings, from March 1983 through November 1994, totalling 94,500 copies.

Second Edition
First printing July 1995, 10,000 copies
Second printing October 1995, 10,000 copies
Third printing September 1996, 12,000 copies

9 **Culture and Gender** 107
   Other Cultures: Meaning; Pacing; Volume and
      Gesture; Space and Touch
   Gender: Rules of Awareness for Men; Rules of
      Awareness for Women; Awareness Exercises

III Conflict Skills

10 **Assertiveness Training** 121
   Your Legitimate Rights
   Identifying the Three Basic Styles of Communication:
      Passive Style; Aggressive Style; Assertive Style
   Assertive Goals
   Assertive Expression
   Assertive Listening
   Combining Assertive Expressing and Listening
   Responding to Criticism: Acknowledgment; Clouding;
      Probing
   Special Assertive Strategies: Broken Record;
      Content-to-Process Shift; Momentary Delay;
      Time Out; Assertive Skills Practice

11 **Fair Fighting** 143
   Unfair Fighting
   Identifying Unfair Fighting Styles
   Fair Fighting
   Fair Fighting Rules
   Your Script for Change

12 **Negotiation** 153
   Conflict
   Rules of Principled Negotiation: Separate the People
      From the Problem; Understand the People; State
      the Problem in Terms of Interests; List Options
   When the Going Gets Tough: Opponents Who Have
      All the Power; Hardliners Who Won't Cooperate;
      Opponents Who Play Dirty

IV Social Skills

13 **Prejudgment** 167
   The Limits of Perception
   Generalization of Expectations
   Perceptual Accentuation
   Stereotypes

Approval and Disapproval in Prejudgment
Parataxic Distortions
Perpetuating Illusions

14   Making Contact   **179**
The Fear of Strangers
Making Contact: Body Language; Icebreakers
The Art of Conversation: Questions; Active Listening;
      Self-Disclosure
Putting It All Together

V Family Skills

15   Sexual Communication   **195**
Myths of Sexual Communication
When Your Partner Refuses
Evaluating Your Sex Life
Guidelines for Effective Communication
Enhancing Your Sexual Communication: Sexual
      Vocabulary; Anatomy Lessons

16   Communicating With Children   **211**
Listening
Expressing: Specificity, Immediacy; Nonjudgment;
      Consistency; Disclosure
Joint Problem Solving
When To Let Go
When You Have To Say No
The Point Is . . .

17   Family Communications   **229**
Family Communication Disorders: Denial; Deletion;
      Substitution; Incongruent Messages
Family Pathology: Mind Reading; Alliances; Covert
      Manipulation Strategies
How To Keep Family Communications Healthy

VI Public Skills

18   Influencing Others   **245**
Ineffective Strategies for Influencing Change
Effective Strategies for Influencing Others: Positive
      Reinforcement; Negative Consequences
Your Plan for Influencing Change: Lisa's Plan for
      Influencing Change

19 Small Groups **253**
Types of Small Groups
Task-Group Roles: Members; Leaders
Blocks to Effective Task-Group Communication
Rules for Task-Group Effectiveness: Determine
    Purpose of Group; Know Your Own Mind; Listen;
    Contibute; Keep Your Cool
Leaders' Rules for Task-Group Effectiveness: State
    Group Purposes; Elicit Contributions; Determine
    Consensus; Keep Order; Maintain Group Morale;
    Choose the Appropriate Leadership Style

20 Public Speaking **265**
Purpose
Subject
Presentation
Organization
Audience Analysis
Style
Supporting Materials
The Outline
Delivery
Dealing With Stage Fright: The Week Before; An Hour
    Before; During Your Speech

21 Interviewing **279**
How Do You Interview?
Clarifying What You Want
Preparing To Conduct an Interview: Gathering
    Background Information; Preparing for an
    Informational Interview; Establishing Rapport;
    Directing the Flow of the Interview: Asking
    Questions and Responding to Answers; Closing;
    Debriefing After the Interview; Interviewer's
    Checklist
Preparing To Be Interviewed; Interviewee's Checklist;
    Making a Good First Impression; Anticipating and
    Responding to Questions in a Job Interview; Know
    Your Rights as an Interviewee: Illegal Questions
    and How To Respond to Them

Bibliography **301**

Index **305**

Introduction

Communication is a basic life skill, as important as the skills by which you make your way through school or earn a living. Your ability to communicate largely determines your personal happiness. When you communicate effectively you make and keep friends. You are valued at work. Your children respect and trust you. You get your sexual needs met.

If you're less effective at communicating, you'll find your life deficient in one or more areas: Work may be all right but your family shouts at the dinner table. Sex can be found but friendships never seem to work out. You bounce from job to job, your mate is often cool, but you have a great time with your old political buddies. You get a lot of laughs at parties but go home alone.

Effective communication makes life work. But where can you learn it? Parents are often dismal role models. Schools are busy teaching French and trigonometry. Often there's no one to show you how to communicate your wants, your anger, or your secret fears. No one shows you how to fight fair instead of blaming others, how to listen actively, or how to "check out" someone's meaning instead of mind reading.

These skills have been known and available for years. They can and should be taught right along with the three R's. Young adults, for example, should learn parent effectiveness skills in school before having children of their own—not years later when a teenage son is a truant or a daughter runs away. Colleges should provide core courses in the *skills* of communication in addition to the more traditional courses in communication theory.

This book gathers the most essential communication skills into one volume. They are presented in condensed form, but with sufficient examples and exercises so that you can begin practicing the skills you want to acquire. The book tells you what to do about communicating rather than what to think about it. Pure theory is omitted unless it contributes directly to your understanding of a particular communication skill.

Looking over the Table of Contents of this revised Second Edition, you will see that the emphasis on skills is reflected in the book's organization. The first three chapters cover Basic Skills. Everybody needs to know how to listen, how to disclose thoughts and feelings, and how to express what's really true.

The section on Advanced Skills contains six chapters that teach you about using and understanding body language, decoding paralanguage and metamessages, uncovering hidden agendas, applying Transactional Analysis to your communications, clarifying your own and others' language, bridging cultural and gender gaps.

The next section contains three chapters covering skills which are essential in conflict situations: assertiveness, fair fighting, and negotiating. The Social Skills section that follows contains two chapters on avoiding the pitfalls of prejudgment and making contact.

The section on Family Skills teaches you how to communicate with your sexual partner, your children, and with your whole family.

The final section offers four chapters about skills required for influencing others, for effective communication in small groups, when you are called upon to make a speech, and during interviews.

Obviously, you should read the basic and advanced skills chapters first, then go on to the specific chapters appropriate to your relationships and position in life. Not so obviously, you have to do more than read. If you merely read, you will miss the main point of this book—that communication is a *skill*. The only way to learn a skill is experientially. You have to *do it*. You actually have to perform the exercises, follow the suggestions, and make these skills your own through practice.

Just as you wouldn't expect to become a skilled woodworker after leafing through a back issue of *Popular Mechanics*, so you can't expect to become a glib, fascinating conversationalist after just perusing the chapter on making contact. Learning by doing applies to communication skills just as much as to woodworking, skiing, or playing a musical instrument. Skill requires knowledge. The knowledge is in this book. But you must put it to work in your everyday life.

I

Basic Skills

1

Listening

You're at a dinner party. Someone is telling anecdotes, someone is complaining, someone is bragging about his promotion. Everyone there is anxious to talk, to tell his or her story. Suddenly you get the feeling that no one is listening. While the talk goes on you notice that people's eyes wander. They are perhaps rehearsing their own remarks. It's as if they have secretly agreed: "I'll be an audience for you if you'll be an audience for me." The party may be a success, but people go home without hearing or knowing each other.

Listening is an essential skill for making and keeping relationships. If you are a good listener, you'll notice that others are drawn to you. Friends confide in you and your friendships deepen. Success comes a little easier because you hear and understand people: you know what they want and what hurts or irritates them. You get "lucky" breaks because people appreciate you and want you around.

People who don't listen are bores. They don't seem interested in anyone but themselves. They turn off potential friends and lovers by giving the message: "What you have to say doesn't matter much to me." As a result, they often feel lonely and isolated. The tragedy is that people who don't listen rarely figure out what's wrong. They change their perfume or cologne, they get new clothes, they work at being funny, and they talk about "interesting" things. But the underlying problem remains. They aren't fun to talk to because the other person never feels satisfied that he or she has been heard.

It's dangerous not to listen! You miss important information and you don't see problems coming. When you try to understand why people do things, you have to mind-read and guess to fill in the gaps in your listening skills.

Listening is a commitment and a compliment. It's a commitment to understanding how other people feel, how they see their world. It means putting aside your own prejudices and beliefs, your anxieties and self-interest, so that you can step behind the other person's eyes. You try to look at things from his or her perspective. Listening is a compliment because it says to the other person: "I care about what's happening to you, your life and your experience are important." People usually respond to the compliment of listening by liking and appreciating you.

Real Versus Pseudo-Listening

Being quiet while someone talks does not constitute real listening. Real listening is based on the *intention* to do one of four things:

1. Understand someone

2. Enjoy someone

3. Learn something

4. Give help or solace

If you want to understand someone, you can't help but really listen to them. When you're enjoying a conversation or you intend to learn something, listening comes quite naturally. When you want to help someone express his or her feelings, you are involved, listening. The key to real listening is wanting and intending to do so.

Unfortunately, a lot of pseudo-listening masquerades as the real thing. The intention is not to listen, but to meet some other need. Some of the typical needs met by pseudo-listening are:

1. Making people think you're interested so they will like you

2. Being alert to see if you are in danger of getting rejected

3. Listening for one specific piece of information and ignoring everything else

4. Buying time to prepare your next comment

5. Half-listening so someone will listen to you

6. Listening to find someone's vulnerabilities or to take advantage

7. Looking for the weak points in an argument so you can always be right, listening to get ammunition for attack

8. Checking to see how people are reacting, making sure you produce the desired effect

9. Half-listening because a good, kind, or nice person would

10. Half-listening because you don't know how to get away without hurting or offending someone

Exercise: Everyone is a pseudo-listener at times. Problems develop when real listening (the intention to understand, enjoy, learn, help) is happening a lot less than pseudo-listening. In general, the more real listening you do, the better your relationships feel. Use the following chart to assess the real versus the pseudo-listening you do with significant people in your life. Estimate the percentage of your listening that is *real* for each of the following:

WORK

Boss_____   _____%
Coworkers

_____   _____%

_____   _____%

_____   _____%

Subordinates

_____   _____%

_____   _____%

_____   _____%

RELATIVES

Mother   _____%

Father   _____%
Siblings

_____   _____%

_____   _____%

Others

_____   _____%

_____   _____%

HOME

Mate   _____%
Children

_____   _____%

_____   _____%

_____   _____%

Roommate____   _____%

FRIENDS

Best friend_____   _____%

Same-sex friends

_____   _____%

_____   _____%

_____   _____%

Opposite-sex friends

_____   _____%

_____   _____%

_____   _____%

_____   _____%

To use the information on your chart, ask yourself these questions:

1. Who are the people you listen to best?

2. Who are the people with whom you do more pseudo-listening?

3. What is it about these people that makes it easier or harder to listen to them?

4. Are there any people on the chart with whom you want to do more real listening?

Exercise: Choose one person you could relate to better. For one day, commit yourself to real listening. After each encounter, check your intention in listening. Were you trying to understand them, enjoy them, learn something, or give help or solace? Notice if you were doing any pseudo-listening, and what needs your pseudo-listening satisfied.

Habits form easily. If you continued this exercise for a week, attention to the quality of your listening would begin to be automatic.

Blocks to Listening

There are twelve blocks to listening. You will find that some are old favorites that you use over and over. Others are held in reserve for certain types of people or situations. Everyone uses listening blocks, so you shouldn't worry if a lot of blocks are familiar. This is an opportunity for you to become more aware of your blocks at the time you actually use them.

1. Comparing

Comparing makes it hard to listen because you're always trying to assess who is smarter, more competent, more emotionally healthy—you or the other. Some people focus on who has suffered more, who's a bigger victim. While someone's talking, you think to yourself: "Could I do it that well? . . . I've had it harder, he doesn't know what hard is. . . . I earn more than that. . . . My kids are so much brighter." You can't let much in because you're too busy seeing if you measure up.

2. Mind Reading

The mind reader doesn't pay much attention to what people say. In fact, he often distrusts it. He's trying to figure out what the other person is *really* thinking and feeling. "She says she wants to go to the show, but I'll bet she's tired and wants to relax. She might be resentful if I pushed her when she doesn't want to go." The mind reader pays less attention to words than to intonations and subtle cues in an effort to see through to the truth.

If you are a mind reader, you probably make assumptions about how people react to you. "I bet he's looking at my lousy skin. . . . She thinks I'm stupid. . . . She's turned off by my shyness." These notions are born of intuition, hunches, and vague misgivings, but have little to do with what the person actually says to you.

3. Rehearsing

You don't have time to listen when you're rehearsing what to say. Your whole attention is on the preparation and crafting of your next comment. You have to *look* interested, but your mind is going a mile a minute because you've got a story to tell, or a point to make. Some people rehearse whole chains of responses: "I'll say, then he'll say, then I'll say," and so on.

4. Filtering

When you filter, you listen to some things and not to others. You pay only enough attention to see if somebody's angry, or unhappy, or if you're in emotional danger. Once assured that the communication contains none of those things, you let your mind wander. One woman listens just enough to her son to learn whether he is fighting again at school. Relieved to hear he isn't, she begins thinking about her shopping list. A young man quickly ascertains what kind of mood his girlfriend is in. If she seems happy as she describes her day, his thoughts begin wandering.

Another way people filter is simply to avoid hearing certain things—particularly anything threatening, negative, critical, or unpleasant. It's as if the words were never said: You simply have no memory of them.

5. Judging

Negative labels have enormous power. If you prejudge someone as stupid or nuts or unqualified, you don't pay much attention to what they say. You've already written them off. Hastily judging a statement as immoral, hypocritical, fascist, pinko, or crazy means you've ceased to listen and have begun a "knee-jerk" reaction. A basic rule of listening is that judgments should only be made *after* you have heard and evaluated the content of the message.

6. Dreaming

You're half-listening, and something the person says suddenly triggers a chain of private associations. Your neighbor says she's been laid off, and in a flash you're back to the scene where you got fired for playing hearts on those long coffee breaks. Hearts is a great game; there were the great nights of hearts years ago on Sutter Street. And you're gone, only to return a few minutes later as your neighbor says, "I knew you'd understand, but don't tell my husband."

You are more prone to dreaming when you feel bored or anxious. Everybody dreams, and you sometimes need to make herculean efforts to stay tuned in. But if you dream a lot with certain people, it may indicate a lack of commitment to knowing or appreciating them. At the very least, it's a statement that you don't value what they have to say very much.

7. *Identifying*

In this block, you take everything a person tells you and refer it back to your own experience. They want to tell you about a toothache, but that reminds you of the time you had oral surgery for receding gums. You launch into your story before they can finish theirs. Everything you hear reminds you of something that you've felt, done, or suffered. You're so busy with these exciting tales of your life that there's no time to really hear or get to know the other person.

8. *Advising*

You are the great problem-solver, ready with help and suggestions. You don't have to hear more than a few sentences before you begin searching for the right advice. However, while you are cooking up suggestions and convincing someone to "just try it," you may miss what's most important. You didn't hear the feelings, and you didn't acknowledge the person's pain. He or she still feels basically alone because you couldn't listen and just *be* there.

9. *Sparring*

This block has you arguing and debating with people. The other person never feels heard because you're so quick to disagree. In fact, a lot of your focus is on finding things to disagree with. You take strong stands, are very clear about your beliefs and preferences. The way to avoid sparring is to repeat back and acknowledge what you've heard. Look for one thing you might agree with.

One subtype of sparring is the *put-down*. You use acerbic or sarcastic remarks to dismiss the other person's point of view. For example, Helen starts telling Arthur about her problems in a biology class. Arthur says: "When are you going to have brains enough to drop that class?" Al is feeling overwhelmed with the noise from the TV. When he tells Rebecca, she says, "Oh god, not the TV routine again." The put-down is the standard block to listening in many marriages. It quickly pushes the communication into stereotyped patterns where each person repeats a familiar hostile litany.

A second type of sparring is discounting. Discounting is for people who can't stand compliments. "Oh, I didn't do anything.... What do you mean, I was totally lame.... It's nice of you to say, but it's really a very poor attempt." The basic technique of discounting is to run yourself down when you get a compliment. The other person never feels satisfied that you really heard his appreciation. And he's right—you didn't.

10. Being Right

Being right means you will go to any lengths (twist the facts, start shouting, make excuses or accusations, call up past sins) to avoid being wrong. You can't listen to criticism, you can't be corrected, and you can't take suggestions to change. Your convictions are unshakable. And since you won't acknowledge that your mistakes are mistakes, you just keep making them.

11. Derailing

This listening block is accomplished by suddenly changing the subject. You derail the train of conversation when you get bored or uncomfortable with a topic. Another way of derailing is by *joking it off*. This means that you continually respond to whatever is said with a joke or quip in order to avoid the discomfort or anxiety in seriously listening to the other person.

12. Placating

"Right.... Right.... Absolutely.... I know.... Of course you are.... Incredible.... Yes.... Really?" You want to be nice, pleasant, supportive. You want people to like you, so you agree with everything. You may half-listen, just enough to get the drift, but you're not really involved. You are placating rather than tuning in and examining what's being said.

You've read the blocks, and you probably have an idea of which ones apply to you. In the space provided, list the blocks that seem typical of the ways you avoid listening.

_____

_____

_____

_____

Having identified your blocks, use the following chart to explore whom you are blocking. You can also find out which people or classes of people typically elicit certain blocks. For example, you may spar with your mother but derail your best friend, or you may placate and rehearse with your boss but do a lot of advising with your children.

Assessing Your Listening Blocks

Exercise: For significant people in your life, write in the listening blocks you typically use. Note that for many people you may use more than one block.

Person	Blocks
WORK	
Boss	_____
Co-workers	
_____	_____
_____	_____
_____	_____
Subordinates	
_____	_____
_____	_____
_____	_____
RELATIVES	
Mother	_____
Father	_____
Siblings	
_____	_____
_____	_____
Others	
_____	_____
_____	_____
_____	_____

Person	Blocks
Person	**Blocks**

Person	Blocks
HOME	
Mate	_____
Children	
_____	_____
_____	_____
_____	_____
Roommate	_____
FRIENDS	
Best friend	_____
Same-sex friends	
_____	_____
_____	_____
_____	_____
Opposite-sex friends	
_____	_____
_____	_____
_____	_____

Exercise: Look at your pattern of blocking. Are you blocking more at home or at work, with same-sex or opposite-sex friends? Do certain people or situations trigger blocking? Do you rely mostly on one kind of blocking, or do you use different blocks with different people and situations?

To help systematize your exploration of blocking, reserve a day to do the following five steps. Note that the goal of this exercise isn't to eliminate listening blocks, but to increase your awareness of how and when you engage in blocking.

1. Select your most commonly used block. _____

2. Keep a tally sheet: How many times did you use the block in one day? _____

3. With whom did you use the block most? _____

_____

4. What subjects or situations usually triggered the block?

_____

_____

_____

5. When you started to block, how were you feeling? (Circle
   everything that applies.)

BORED   ANXIOUS   IRRITATED   HURT   JEALOUS

FRUSTRATED   RUSHED   DOWN   CRITICIZED

EXCITED   PREOCCUPIED   ATTACKED   TIRED

(Other) _____

This awareness exercise can be repeated with as many blocks as
you care to explore. Keep track of only one block in any given day.

Exercise: After gaining more awareness, you may want to change some
of your blocking behavior. Reserve another two days for the following
exercise:

1. Select one significant person you'd like to stop blocking.

_____

2. Keep a tally sheet: How many times did you block them on
   day one?

_____

3. What blocks did you use? _____

4. What subjects or situations usually triggered the blocks?

_____

_____

_____

5. On day two, consciously avoid using your blocking gambits
   with the target person. Try paraphrasing instead (see the
   next section). Make a real commitment to listening. Notice

and write down how you feel and what happens when you resist blocking. (*Note:* Don't expect miracles. If you have a 50 percent reduction in blocking, that's success.)

Initially, you may feel anxious, bored, or irritated. You may find yourself avoiding one blocking gambit only to cook up another. The conversation may take uncomfortable turns. You may suddenly share and reveal things you previously kept to yourself. Be a scientist. Objectively observe what happens. Evaluate it. Does this feel better than the usual way you operate with the target person? If it doesn't, extend the exercise for a week. Notice how you gradually form the habit of checking how well you are listening.

Four Steps to Effective Listening

1. Active Listening

Listening doesn't mean sitting still with your mouth shut. A corpse can do that. Listening is an active process that requires your participation. To fully understand the meaning of a communication, you usually have to ask questions and give feedback. Then, in the give and take that follows, you get a fuller appreciation of what's being said. You have gone beyond passively absorbing; you are a collaborator in the communication process. Here are the ways to listen actively.

Paraphrasing. To paraphrase means to state in your own words what you think someone just said. Paraphrasing is absolutely necessary to good listening. It keeps you busy trying to understand and know what the other person means, rather than blocking. You can paraphrase by using such lead-ins as "What I hear you saying is.... In other words.... So basically how you felt was... Let me understand, what was going on for you was.... What happened was.... Do you mean ...?" You should paraphrase every time someone says something of any importance to you. Try it and you will reap five big dividends:

1. People deeply appreciate feeling heard.

2. Paraphrasing stops escalating anger and cools down crisis.

3. Paraphrasing stops miscommunication. False assumptions, errors, and misinterpretations are corrected on the spot.

4. Paraphrasing helps you remember what was said.

5. When you paraphrase you'll find it much harder to compare, judge, rehearse, spar, advise, derail, dream, and so on. In fact, paraphrasing is the antidote to most listening blocks.

If it's so great and solves so many listening ills, why doesn't everybody do it? Everybody should. But schools rarely teach basic life skills, and most people learn their listening skills by example. There are a lot of bad examples.

Exercise: To get practice paraphrasing, do the following exercise. Choose a friend who likes to try new things. Explain that you want to improve your listening skills. The friend's job is to tell you the story of something important that happened in his or her life. Basically, all your friend has to do is talk. Your job, at intervals, is to paraphrase what's just been said. Say in your own way what you've heard so far, and find out if you're getting it right. Every time you paraphrase, your friend gets to decide if you've really understood. The friend makes corrections in what you said, and you incorporate those corrections in a new attempt at paraphrasing. You keep at it, paraphrasing and correcting, until your friend is satisfied that he or she has been heard.

You may be surprised at how long it sometimes takes to clear up confusion and agree on what's been said. Misconceptions start very easily.

Clarifying. Clarifying often goes along with paraphrasing. It just means asking questions until you get more of the picture. Since your intention is to fully understand what's being said, you often have to ask for more information, more background. You have to know the circumstances. Clarifying helps you sharpen your listening focus so that you hear more than vague generalities. You hear events in the context of what someone thought and felt, the relevant history. Clarifying also lets the other person know that you're interested. It gives the message: "I'm willing to work at knowing and understanding you."

Feedback. Active listening depends on feedback. You've paraphrased and clarified what was said, and hopefully understand it. This is the point at which you can talk about your reactions. In a nonjudgmental way, you can share what you thought, felt, or sensed. This doesn't mean falling back into sparring or identifying as a reaction. It means sharing what happened inside you.

Now is a good time to check your perceptions. You watched the body language and listened to the tone of voice. You noticed things that seemed to betray what the other person felt. You may have also drawn conclusions about the content of the communication. To check perceptions, you transform what you saw and heard into a tentative description: "I want to understand your feelings—is this [*giving a description*] the way you feel?" "Listening to what you said, I wonder if [*your de-*

scription] is what's really happening in the situation." All this is done without approval or disapproval, with only a wish to see if your hunch is correct.

Feedback also helps the other person understand the effect of his or her communication. It's another chance to correct errors and misconceptions. It's also a chance for him or her to get a fresh and valuable point of view—yours.

There are three important rules for giving feedback. It has to be immediate, honest, and supportive. *Immediate* means as soon as you fully understand the communication (after paraphrasing and clarifying). Putting your feedback off, even a few hours, makes it much less valuable. *Honest* means your real reaction—not something out of *Who's Afraid of Virginia Woolf*. You don't have to cut somebody up to give your reaction. In fact, brutality is rarely honest. Your feedback should be honest *and* supportive. You can be gentle, saying what you need to say without causing damage or defensiveness. For example, "I get the feeling that there's something you're not telling me" is more supportive than "You're holding out on me." "I think there's a real possibility that you've made a mistake" is more supportive than "You've been a fool."

2. Listening With Empathy

There is only one requirement for listening with empathy: simply know that everyone is trying to survive. You don't have to like everyone or agree with them, but recognize that you do share the same struggle. Every second of the day you are trying to survive both physically and psychologically. Every thought, every choice, every movement is designed to preserve your existence.

The outrageous, the inconsiderate, the false, and the violent acts are all strategies to minimize pain (death) and hold on to life. Some people have better survival strategies than others. And some are plainly incompetent, making a mess of everything they touch. They don't live as long physically, and they die an early psychological death from chronic depression or anxiety.

Listening with empathy means saying to yourself, "This is hard to hear, but it's another human being trying to live." Ask yourself: "How did this belief or this decision, though it may ultimately fail, lower this person's anxiety or get some needs met?"

Your ability to listen naturally goes down when someone is angry, criticizes, or wallows in self-pity. If you find listening with empathy difficult, ask these questions:

1. What need is the [*anger, etc.*] coming from?

2. What danger is this person experiencing?

3. What is he or she asking for?

3. *Listening With Openness*

It's difficult to listen when you're judging and finding fault. All the information gets scrambled coming in, while you build a case to dismiss a person or his ideas. You have to listen selectively, filtering out everything that makes sense and pouncing on whatever seems false or silly. You collect and hoard the "stupidities" so you can share them later with a sympathetic audience.

Judgments can be very gratifying, but here's how you pay for them:

1. If your opinions have been proven false, you are the last to know.

2. You don't grow intellectually because you only listen to viewpoints you already hold.

3. You dismiss otherwise worthwhile people because you disagree with their ideas.

4. You turn people off because you spar and don't listen.

5. You miss important information.

Nearly everyone has trouble listening openly. You don't want to hear your sacred cows reduced to hamburger. You don't want to face certain facts about yourself. Nor do you want to believe that an unlikable person has said something worth thinking about. You naturally want to argue, to shout it down.

The fear of being wrong has vast proportions. That's because your opinions and beliefs are closely tied to self-esteem. Being wrong can equal being stupid, bad, or worthless. It would be a great step forward if beliefs and opinions could be seen as temporary hypotheses—held until disproved or modified. Rather than building your self-esteem on being right, you might reform your picture of yourself into that of one who, above all, wants to find the truth.

Listening with openness is a skill you can learn. The following exercise, called a *reversal*, should be tried with someone you trust. Select an old disagreement that isn't too explosive. Each of you state your side of the argument. Now reverse, and argue for the opposite position. Do it convincingly, really pushing the other person's point of view. Try to win the debate from the other side. Don't stop until you feel immersed in the viewpoint you once opposed. At the end, share with each other what you experienced.

Obviously, you can't practice reversals in most situations. What you can do, as an exercise in openness, is become an anthropologist. Imagine that the individuals that you're talking to hail from another planet or country. They have different customs, religion, ways of think-ing. And you are an anthropologist trying to understand it all. Your job is to find out how their point of view makes sense, to see how it fits their world view, their history, their particular social system.

The most important rule for listening with openness is to hear the whole statement, the entire communication, before judging. Premature evaluations don't make sense because you don't have all the informa-tion.

4. Listening With Awareness

There are two components to listening with awareness. One is to compare what's being said to your own knowledge of history, people, and the way things are. You do this without judgment, simply making note of how a communication fits with known facts.

The second way you listen with awareness is to hear and observe congruence. Does the person's tone of voice, emphasis, facial expres-sion, and posture fit with the content of his or her communication. If someone is telling you that his father has just died, but smiles and leans back comfortably with his hands laced behind his head, the message doesn't make sense. There is no congruence. If body, face, voice, and words don't fit, your job as a listener is to clarify and give feedback about the discrepancy. If you ignore it, you're settling for an incomplete or confusing message.

If you want to practice noticing incongruity, watch some TV come-dies. Much of the humor is based on the mismatch of expression and content.

Total Listening

People want you to listen, so they look for clues to prove that you are. Here's how to be a total listener:

1. Maintain good eye contact.

2. Lean slightly forward.

3. Reinforce the speaker by nodding or paraphrasing.

4. Clarify by asking questions.

5. Actively move away from distractions.

6. Be committed, even if you're angry or upset, to understanding what was said.

Listening for Couples

Perhaps the most important application for your listening skills is when you communicate to your partner. A process called *reciprocal communication* provides a structure in which you can really hear each other. Here's how it works. When you're discussing a topic that is a conflict area for you, take turns being the speaker and the listener, switching places after five minutes.

When you're the speaker:

1. Explain your point of view briefly and succinctly.

2. Avoid blaming and name calling. Don't accuse and don't focus on your partner's failings.

3. Talk in terms of yourself and your experience. Focus on what you want and what you feel.

When you are the listener:

1. Give your full attention so that you can really understand your partner's feelings, opinions, and needs.

2. Don't disagree, argue, or correct anything your partner says.

3. You can ask questions to clarify an issue, but not to debate and make counterpoints.

After the speaker describes his or her side of the issue for five minutes, the listener summarizes, using the paraphasing skills discussed earlier. If the listener's summary leaves out something important, or the listener has misunderstood, the speaker can clarify and reexplain until he or she feels completely heard.

When the first round of expressing and listening is over, it's time to switch places. The speaker becomes the listener, and vice versa. Follow exactly the same instructions until the second speaker feels thoroughly understood.

Reciprocal communication can be used with virtually any problematic issue. Its main virtues are that it slows down communication so that conflicts are less likely to escalate while it promotes clarity about the needs and feelings of each partner.

2

Self-Disclosure

Self-disclosure may be as scary to you as skydiving without a parachute. You hold back because you anticipate rejection or disapproval. But you miss a lot. Self-disclosure makes relationships exciting and builds intimacy. It clarifies and enlivens. Without self-disclosure, you are isolated in your private experience.

You can't help disclosing yourself. You do it whenever you're around other people. Even if you ignore them, your silence and posture are disclosing something. The question isn't whether to disclose yourself, but how to do it appropriately and effectively.

For the purposes of this chapter, self-disclosure is simply *communicating information about yourself*. Contained in that short definition are some important implications. First of all, communication implies another human being on the receiving end of your disclosure. Introspection and writing about yourself in a journal or diary won't pass as self-disclosure. Communication also implies disclosure by nonverbal language such as gestures, posture, and tone of voice. Nonverbal language tends to include a lot of unintentional slips.

Information in the definition implies that what is disclosed is new knowledge to the other person, not a rehash of old themes and stories. The information can take the form of facts you have observed and are pointing out, feelings you had in the past or are experiencing now, your thoughts about yourself or others, and your desires or needs in the past or present.

The key word in the definition is *yourself*. This means your true self. Self-disclosure is not a cloud of lies or distortions, or an attractive mask.

To better understand this "self that is being disclosed, imagine that your entire being is represented by a circle, divided into quadrants like this:

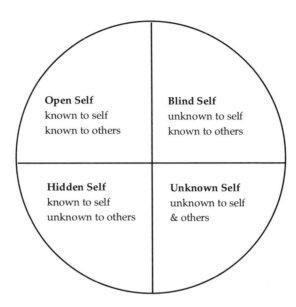

Open Self
known to self
known to others

Blind Self
unknown to self
known to others

Hidden Self
known to self
unknown to others

Unknown Self
unknown to self
& others

(Adapted from the Johari Window, presented in Luft, Joseph. *Group Process: An Introduction to Group Dynamics.* Palo Alto, CA: National Press Books, 1984.)

The first quadrant is your Open Self. It contains all your conscious actions and statements. The second is your Blind Self, which is comprised of things others can find out about you that you are unaware of: habits, mannerisms, defense mechanisms, flight strategies. The third quadrant is your Hidden Self. This includes all your secrets—everything you think, feel, and desire that you keep to yourself. The fourth quadrant is your Unknown Self. Since this self is by definition unknown, we can only assume its existence and give it names like the unconscious or subconscious. Dreams, drug trips, and mystical experiences are the strongest evidence for the existence of the Unknown Self.

These are not rigid compartments. Observations, thoughts, feelings, and wants are constantly moving from one area to another as you go about your daily routine. Everything you see and hear and touch in the outside world is taken into the Hidden Self. Some is forgotten, which may mean that it goes down into the Unknown Self. Some experiences contribute to your continuing unconscious habits, and thus move into your Blind Self. Some things you remember but never reveal, just leaving them in the Hidden Self. And some things that you notice you pass on to others, moving them into the Open Self. When you have an insight about how you operate in the world, you move it from the Blind to the Hidden Self. Sharing the insight with someone moves it into the Open Self.

The movement that this chapter studies is the shift of information about your observations, feelings, thoughts, and needs from the Hidden to the Open Self. This is self-disclosure. If you are good at self-disclosure, your Open Self quadrant is large compared to the other quadrants. The larger your Open Self, the more likely you will be to reap the rewards of self-disclosure.

Rewards of Self-Disclosure

Accurately revealing who you are is hard work. Sometimes you think, "Why struggle to explain? Why risk rejection?" And yet the need to be close to others, to let them inside, keeps reemerging. Some of the things that make self-disclosure worth the trouble are:

Increased Self-Knowledge

It's paradoxical but true that you know yourself to the extent that you are known. Your thoughts, feelings, and needs often remain vague and clouded until you put them into words. The process of making someone else understand you demands that you clarify, define, elaborate, and draw conclusions. Expressing your needs, for example, gives them shape and color, adds details, and points up inconsistencies and possible areas of conflict that you need to resolve.

Closer Intimate Relationships

Knowledge of yourself and the other person is basic to an intimate relationship. If you are both willing to disclose your true selves, a synergistic deepening of the relationship develops. If one or both of you keep large parts withheld, the relationship will be correspondingly shallow and unsatisfying.

Improved Communication

Disclosure breeds disclosure. As you make yourself available to others, they are encouraged to open up in response. The range of topics available for discussion broadens, even with those who are not particularly intimate with you. The depth of communication on a given topic deepens too, so that you get more than mere facts and opinions from others. They become willing to share their feelings, their deeply held convictions, and their needs.

Lighter Guilt Feelings

Guilt is a hybrid emotion composed of anger at yourself and fear of retribution for something you have done, failed to do, or have thought. Guilt is often unreasonable and always painful. One thing that can relieve the pain a little is disclosure. Disclosing what you have done or thought lightens the guilt feeling in two ways: (1) You no longer have to expend energy to keep the transgression hidden. (2) When the thing you feel guilty about is disclosed, you can look at it more objectively. You can get feedback. Here is an opportunity to examine whether the guilt is justified, or whether your rules and values are too strict, too unforgiving.

Disclosure as first aid for guilt is institutionalized in several forms: Catholics confess, Protestants witness, AA members declare themselves alcoholics, and those in therapy relive traumatic events. But you don't need a priest or a therapist to experience the healing effects of disclosure. A good friend will do.

More Energy

It takes energy to keep important information about yourself hidden. Suppose you quit your job and go home to your family as usual, making no mention of your impending poverty. Here's what happens: you don't notice that your wife has a new haircut, that your favorite dinner is on the table, or that the bathroom has been painted. In fact, you're so concerned with keeping your secret, you can barely notice anything. You are silent, withdrawn, grouchy. Nothing is fun. Life is a burden. All your energy is drained. Until you unburden yourself, you are a walking corpse.

When a conversation seems dead, boring, and hard to keep going, ask yourself if there's something you're withholding. Unexpressed feelings and needs tend to simmer. They build up inside you until you lose spontaneity and your conversation takes on all the liveliness of a funeral oration. That's one way to tell if you should reveal a secret: if withheld feelings or needs keep cropping up to deaden your relationship.

Blocks to Self-Disclosure

Since self-disclosure is so rewarding, why doesn't everybody tell everybody else everything all the time? In fact, there are some powerful sources of resistance to self-disclosure that often keep you huddled in your Hidden Self.

There is a societal bias against self-disclosure. It isn't considered "nice" to talk about yourself too much, or to discuss your feelings or needs outside a narrow family circle.

You often don't disclose yourself out of fear: fear of rejection, fear of punishment, fear of being talked about behind your back, or fear that someone will take advantage of you. Someone might laugh, or say no, or leave. If you reveal one negative trait, they will imagine you're all bad. If you reveal something positive, you might be accused of bragging. If you take a stand, you might have to do something about it—vote, contribute, volunteer, or get involved in other people's troubles. Finally, you may be afraid of self-knowledge itself. You instinctively know that by disclosing you will come to know yourself better. You suspect that there are some unpleasant truths about yourself that you would rather not be aware of.

Optimal Levels of Self-Disclosure

Some people are just more extroverted and forthcoming about themselves than others. Their Open Selves are relatively larger:

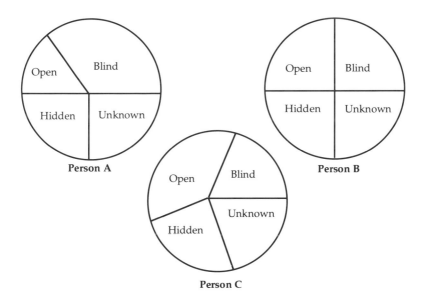

Actually, how much you reveal of yourself is not a fixed quantity. You may have a constant tendency to be more open or reserved than the next guy, but within your range of openness you fluctuate depending on your mood, whom you're talking to, and what you're talking about. The following diagrams represent the same person in different conversations:

Talking to traffic cop

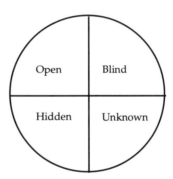

Talking to casual friend

Research in self-disclosure confirms what common sense suggests. You are more open with your mate, certain family members, and your close friends. You are more willing to disclose your preferences in clothes and foods than your financial status or sexual preferences. In some moods you don't want to tell anyone anything. As you age from seventeen to fifty you'll probably increase your average level of self-disclosure, and become more reserved after fifty.

Healthy self-disclosure is a matter of balance, of learning when to tell what to whom. Generally speaking, the more information you consistently move into the Open Self, the better your communication will be. The more you keep hidden or remain blind to, the less effective your communication will be. Beware of extremes. If your Open Self is too large, you'll be a garrulous, inappropriate blabbermouth; if too small,

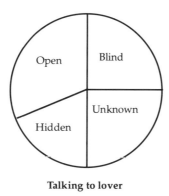

Talking to lover

you'll be closed and secretive. If your Blind Self is too large, you'll be oblivious to how you appear in the world. Unknown to you, you'll get a reputation as a bully, a "space cadet," a "tight wad," and so on. If your Blind Self is too small, you'll be an over-analyzed self-awareness addict. If your Hidden Self is too large, you will be withdrawn and out of reach; if too small, you will be untrustworthy—no secret will be safe with you.

Exercises

Assessing Your Self-Disclosure

This exercise will show you how you disclose yourself to significant people in your life. Reach each item on the left and then indicate how you have talked about it to your mother, father, best friends, and mate. If your parents are dead or you can't think of anyone to fill the friends or mate categories, leave those columns blank.

Use this rating scale:

0   Have told the other person *nothing* about this aspect of me.

1   Have talked in *general terms* about this. The other person knows some of the facts, but not the complete message.

2   Have told the other about this *completely*, including my observations, thoughts, feelings, and needs.

X   Have *lied* or misrepresented myself regarding this aspect. The other person has a false picture of me.

	Mother	Father	Mate	Child	Best Female Friend	Best Male Friend

Tastes and Interests

1. My favorite foods and beverages and food dislikes. _____
2. My likes and dislikes in music. _____
3. My favorite reading matter. _____
4. The kinds of movies and TV shows I like. ___
5. The style of house, and the kinds of furnishing I like best. _____
6. The kind of party or social gathering I like best. _____

Attitudes and Opinions

1. What I think and feel about religion. _____
2. My views on the question of racial integration in schools. _____
3. My personal views on drinking. _____
4. My personal views on sexual morality. _____
5. My personal standards of beauty and attractiveness in women. _____
6. The things I regard as desirable for a man to be. _____

Work (or studies)

1. What I enjoy most. _____
2. What I enjoy least. _____
3. What I feel are my shortcomings and handicaps. _____
4. What I feel are my special strong points. ___
5. How I feel that my work is appreciated by others. _____
6. My ambitions and goals in my work. ___

	Mother	Father	Mate	Child	Best Female Friend	Best Male Friend
Money						
1. How much money I make at my work, or get as an allowance. _____						
2. Whether or not I owe money; if so, how much and to whom. _____						
3. Whether or not I have savings, and the amount. _____						
4. Whether or not others owe me money; the amount, and who owes it to me. _____						
5. Whether or not I gamble, and how much. _____						
6. All of my present sources of income. _____						
Personality						
1. The aspects of my personality that I dislike. _____						
2. The feelings I have trouble expressing or controlling. _____						
3. The facts of my present sex life—how I get sexual gratification; any problems; with whom I have relations. _____						
4. Whether or not I feel I am attractive to the opposite sex. _____						
5. Things in the past or present that I feel ashamed and guilty about. _____						
6. What I fear most. _____						
Body						
1. My feelings about the appearance of my face. _____						
2. How I wish I looked. _____						
3. My feelings about different parts of my body—legs, hips, waist, weight, chest or bust, etc. _____						
4. Whether or not I now have any health problems. _____						
5. My past record of illness and treatment. _____						
6. Whether or not I now make special effort to keep fit, healthy, and attractive. _____						

Notice which categories seem easier to talk about—the ones with 1's and 2's. Notice what items you consistently remain quiet or lie about. How much energy are you devoting to keep that stuff hidden?

Notice to whom you talk and from whom you are hiding. Are there any obvious patterns along family lines? Along sexual lines?

Make a note of the topics or people you want to concentrate on, and keep them in mind for the next exercise.

Practice in Self-Disclosure

This exercise will give you practice in disclosing. It proceeds in three easy stages from telling a few facts about yourself to revealing your current thoughts, feelings, and needs.

1. Information. In this part of the exercise you deal with facts only. Choose an acquaintance and tell him or her about your job, your last vacation, or some interesting experience you've had. Stick to the facts of when, where, what, who, and so on. Don't include any of your feelings or opinions. When you are comfortable with disclosing facts, go on to step two.

2. Thoughts, feelings, and needs regarding the past or future. Facts are only part of the story. The next step in practicing self-disclosure is to include thoughts, feelings, and needs. Refer to the assessment exercise to find topics for this step. You can talk about your tastes in music, your religious convictions, your ambitions at work, your finances, what you're especially proud of, your health, and so on. Tell someone you trust about your chosen topic. Besides just the facts, tell him or her what you think about the matter, how you feel about it, and what needs or wants you have regarding it.

Don't try to talk with this person about what you feel or think right now. Practice only on topics that relate to the past (recent or remote) or future. When you are comfortable with this step, go on to step three.

3. Here-and-now communications. This is the most difficult type of self-disclosure because you have to take the risk of sharing with this person what you think, feel, and need right now.

For example, you can talk about how you're feeling attracted to the other person, how his or her responses are affecting you, how you're holding something back, how you're slanting your story to make you look good, how you want the conversation to come out, what you need right now, how relaxed or nervous you're feeling, and so on. This is the most complete and satisfying mode of self-disclosure, and is explored at length in the chapter on expressing.

To get into here-and-now communications gradually, select one thing to concentrate on for a week. For example, you might practice giving feedback on how conversations are affecting you. Go slowly. Scare yourself a little bit, but not so much that you give up talking about the here-and-now.

3

Expressing

Sam:	"Do we have to go down to the P.T.A. meeting tonight?"
Jane:	"Why, does it bother you?"
Sam:	"It's just the same old thing. I don't know."
Jane:	"Did something happen last time?"
Sam:	"It's nothing. Sometimes the speakers are interesting, but I don't know . . . and Mrs. Williams is running it now."
Jane:	"You don't like how she's handling it?"
Sam:	"She's all right. She's so . . . organized. Forget it, let's get a move on if we're going."

Sam is in for another deadly evening. Mrs. Williams will carry on like General Patton. A speaker will drone about "multicultural awareness." If Sam had been able to express himself, he might have persuaded Jane to skip a night, or to help him push for changes in the meeting format. As it is, Jane has no idea what's irking him and can't respond to his needs.

This chapter is about expressing yourself when it counts and to the people who matter to you. It doesn't tell you how to assertively ask your butcher for a good cut of meat. But it does tell you how to make clear and complete statements about your inner experience.

The Four Kinds of Expression

Your communications to other people can be broken down into four categories: expressing your observations, thoughts, feelings, and needs. Each category requires a different style of expression, and often a very different vocabulary.

Observations

This is the language of the scientist, the detective, the TV repairman. It means reporting what your senses tell you. There are no speculations, inferences, or conclusions. Everything is simple fact. Here are some examples of observations:

1. "I read in the *Enquirer* that an ice age is due to start within five hundred years."

2. "My old address was 1996 Fell Street."

3. "She plans to wear a chiffon dress with white ruffled collar."

4. "I broke the toaster this morning."

5. "It was a very hot day when I left Kansas. A slight wind riffled the fields and a thunderhead was beginning to form up north."

All of these statements adhere strictly to what the person has heard, read, or personally experienced. If Sam had been able to talk about his observations at the P.T.A. meeting, he might have pointed out that the meetings invariably went overtime, that the speakers were selected by Mrs. Williams without consulting the group, and that certain parent-teacher problems were never discussed.

Thoughts

Your thoughts are conclusions, inferences drawn from what you have heard, read, and observed. They are attempts to synthesize your observations so you can see what's really going on and understand why and how events occur. They may also incorporate value judgments in which you decide that something is good or bad, wrong or right. Beliefs, opinions, and theories are all varieties of conclusions. Here are some examples:

1. "Unselfishness is essential for a successful marriage." *(belief)*

2. "I think the universe will keep exploding and collapsing, exploding and collapsing, forever." *(theory)*

3. "He must be afraid of his wife; he always seems nervous around her." *(theory)*

4. "Log Cabin is the only syrup worth buying." *(theory)*

5. "You were wrong to just stop seeing her." *(value judgment)*

If Sam had been able to express his thoughts about the P.T.A. meeting, he might have said that Mrs. Williams was dominating and grandiose. He might have suggested that she was deliberately squelching conflicts because she was friendly with the school administration.

Feelings

Probably the most difficult part of communication is expressing your feelings. Some people don't want to hear what you feel. They get bored or upset when feelings come up. Some people are selectively receptive. They can hear about your post-divorce melancholy, but not about your fear of death. Anger is the most discouraged feeling because it's threatening to the listener's self-esteem.

Since people are often threatened or frightened by emotion, you may have decided to keep many feelings to yourself. Yet how you feel is a large part of what makes you unique and special. Shared feelings are the building blocks of intimacy. When others are allowed to know what angers, frightens, and pleases you, two things happen: They have greater empathy and understanding and are better able to modify their behavior to meet your needs.

Examples of some feeling statements are:

1. "I missed Al and felt a real loss when he left for Europe."

2. "I feel like I let you down, and it really gnaws at me."

3. "I sit alone in the house, feel this tingling going up and down my spine, and get this wave of anxiety."

4. "I light up with joy when I see you. I feel this incredible rush of affection."

5. "I'm checking my reactions, and I feel stunned and a little angry."

Note that feeling statements are not observations, value judgments or opinions. For example, "Sometimes I feel that you are very rigid," has nothing to do with feelings. It's just a slightly buffered judgment.

If Sam had expressed his feelings to Jane, he might have told her that he felt bored at the meetings and that he was angry at Mrs. Williams. He also might have discussed his worries that the school has serious curriculum inadequacies and his frustration that nothing was being done about it.

Needs

No one knows what you want, except you. You are the expert, the highest authority on yourself. However, you may have a heavy injunction against expressing needs. You hope friends and family will be sensitive or clairvoyant enough to know what you want. "If you loved me, you'd know what's wrong" is a common assumption. Since you feel it's bad to ask for anything, your needs are often expressed with a head of anger or resentment. The anger says "I'm wrong to ask, and you're wrong to make me have to."

Trying to have a close relationship in which you don't express your needs is like driving a car without a steering wheel. You can go fast, but you can't change directions or steer around chuckholes. Relationships change, accommodate, and grow when both people can clearly and supportively express what they need. Some typical need statements are:

1. "Can you be home before seven? I'd love to go to a movie."

2. "I'm exhausted. Will you do the dishes and see that the kids are in bed?"

3. "I need a day to myself this weekend. Can we get together Sunday night?"

4. "I need to reserve time with you so we can sit down and work this out."

5. "Could you just hug me for a while?"

Needs are not pejorative or judgmental. They don't blame or assign fault. They are simple statements about what would help or please you.

Returning to the Sam and Jane story, Sam might have told Jane that he really needs rest and wants to spend time with her alone. "Let's light the fire and snuggle up tonight."

Whole Messages

Whole messages include all four kinds of expressions: what you see, think, feel, and need. Intimate relationships thrive on whole messages. Your closest friends, your mate, and your family can't know the real you unless you share all of your experiences. That means not leaving things out, not covering up your anger, not squelching your wants. It means giving accurate feedback about what you observe, clearly stating your inferences and conclusions, saying how it all makes you feel, and if you need something or see possibilities for change, making straight-forward requests or suggestions.

When you leave something out, it's called a *partial message*. Partial messages create confusion and distrust. People sense something is missing, but they don't know what. They're turned off when they hear judgments untempered by your feelings and hopes. They resist hearing anger that doesn't include the story of your frustration or hurt. They are suspicious of conclusions without supporting observations. They are uncomfortable with demands growing from unexpressed feelings and assumptions.

Not every relationship or situation requires whole messages. Effective communication with your garage mechanic probably won't involve a lot of deep feeling or discussion of your emotional needs. Even with intimates, the majority of messages are just informational. But partial messages, with something important left out or obscured, are always dangerous. They become relational boobytraps when used to express the complex issues that are an inevitable part of closeness.

You can test whether you are giving whole or partial messages by asking the following questions:

1. Have I expressed what I actually know to be fact? Is it based on what I've observed, read, or heard?

2. Have I expressed and clearly labeled my inferences and conclusions?

3. Have I expressed my feelings without blame or judgment?

4. Have I shared my needs without blame or judgment?

Contaminated Messages

Contamination takes place when your messages are mixed or mislabeled. For example, you might be contaminating feelings, thoughts, and observations if you said to your daughter, "I see you're wearing that old dress again." What you really needed to say were three very distinct things:

1. "That dress is a little frayed and still has the ink spot we were never able to get out." (*observation*)

2. "I don't think it's nice enough for a Sunday visit to Grandpa's." (*thought*)

3. "I feel anxious that your grandfather will think I'm not a very good parent if I let you wear a dress like that." (*feeling*)

Contaminated messages are at best confusing and at worst deeply alienating. The message "I see your wife gave you two juicy oranges for lunch" is confusing because the observation is contaminated by need. The need is only hinted at, and the listener has to decide if what he heard was really a covert appeal. The message "While you were feeding your dog, my dinner got cold" is alienating because what appears to be a simple observation contains undercurrents of anger and judgment ("You care more about your dog than me").

Contaminated messages differ from partial messages in that the problem is not merely one of omission. You haven't left the anger, the conclusion, or the need out of it. It's there all right, but in a disguised and covert form. The following are some examples of contaminated messages:

1. "Why don't you act a little human for a change?" In this message need is contaminated with a value judgment (thought). A whole message might have been, "You say very little, and when you do it's in a soft, flat voice (*observation*). It makes me think that you don't care, that you have no emotions (*thought*). I feel hurt (*emotion*), but what I really want is for you to talk to me (*need*)."

2. "Every year you come home to visit with a different man. I don't know how you move from one to another like that." Said in an acid tone, this would be an observation contaminated with a value judgment (*thought*). The whole message might be "Each year you come home with someone else (*observation*). I wonder if it creates a sort of callousness, a shallow affection (*thought*). I worry, and also feel disappointed when I start liking your friend and never see him again (*feeling*). I hope you'll make a commitment to a life partner (*need*)."

3. "I know what your problem is, you like to get paid but you don't like to work." This is an example of feeling contaminated with a value judgment (*thought*). The whole statement might be "You've been late six times in the last two weeks (*observation*). It makes me think that you're trying to work as little as possible (*thought*). The lateness irritates me (*feeling*) and I want you to be late no more than once a month (*need*)."

4. "I need to go home . . . another one of those headaches." Said in an angry voice at a party, this is an example of feelings contaminated with need. The person really wants to say "I've been standing by myself (*observation*). You don't seem to care or draw me into conversation (*thought*). I get to feeling hurt and angry (*feeling*). I want you to involve me in things or I don't want to be here (*need*)."

5. "You eat your breakfast without a word, you get your hat, you leave, you get home, you mix a drink, you read the paper, you talk about golf and your secretary's legs at dinner, you fall asleep in front of the TV, and that's the way it is." In this case, observation is contaminated with feelings. It seems like a straightforward recital of events, but the speaker really wants to say "I'm lonely and angry, please pay attention to me."

The easiest way to contaminate your messages is to make the content simple and straightforward, but say it in a tone of voice that betrays your feelings. "I want to stop interviewing people, we have enough already" can be said in a matter-of-fact or very annoyed voice. In one case it's a clear statement of need. In the other, need is contaminated with unacknowledged anger. The secret of avoiding contaminated messages is to separate out and express each part of the communication.

Preparing Your Message

Self-Awareness

The only way you can be sure to give whole messages, and to avoid partial and contaminated ones, is to examine your own inner experience. What you are observing, thinking, feeling, and wanting? What is the purpose of this communication? Is the stated purpose the same as your real purpose? What are you afraid of saying? What do you need to communicate?

Awareness may include a bit of a rehearsal, particularly while getting used to whole messages. You run things over in your mind until each part of the message is clear and distinct. You separate what you observe and know from what you surmise and believe. You contact your feelings and find a way to say them. You arrive at a nonthreatening way to express your need.

Other Awareness

A certain amount of audience analysis should precede any important message. If your friend just lost a job, he may not be receptive to a diatribe about your low rate of pay. What kind of shape is the other person in? Is he or she rushed, in pain, angry, or able to listen?

Other awareness also means keeping track of the listener's response while you're talking: facial expressions, eye contact, and body language. Is he or she asking questions, giving feedback, or sitting like a lump in the chair?

Place Awareness

Important messages are usually delivered when two people are alone, in a nondistracting environment. Talking where you can be overheard discourages whole messages. Partial and contaminated messages increase as you feel the need to compress and sanitize your comments for public consumption. Here are some general rules for finding the right environment to talk:

1. Find some privacy.

2. Find a place where you won't be interrupted.

3. Find a place that's congenial and physically comfortable.

4. Find a place that's quiet, with few distractions.

Practicing Whole Messages

In the following exercise, try making a whole message out of each statement. Write it using first person sentences ("I noticed that you've been very quiet. . . .").

1. "I see you're getting uptight again." (This is in an annoyed voice, which covers a certain amount of anxiety and hurt. His wife has been silent for thirty minutes following his late arrival home.)

OBSERVATIONS:

THOUGHTS:

FEELINGS:

NEEDS:

2. "Should we be talking like this?" (Between new lovers who've suddenly launched into fantasies of kids and marriage. The speaker is anxious that her partner may feel pressured, and may withdraw.)

OBSERVATIONS:

THOUGHTS:

FEELINGS:

NEEDS:

3. "A person runs out of time, something just changes in them." (A man trying to explain why he quit his job. Passed over for promotion, he was depressed and fearful of getting older without finding satisfying work. He's trying to get his fourteen-year-old daughter to understand.)

OBSERVATIONS:

THOUGHTS:

FEELINGS:

NEEDS:

4. "I'm here, aren't I?" (Said to the boss, after being asked how he felt having to work overtime. He's missing his ten-year-old's play, and wants to be home in time to help with the cast party.)

OBSERVATIONS:

THOUGHTS:

FEELINGS:

NEEDS:

5. "I know, I know, you don't have to tell me," (After being reminded of upcoming finals for the fourth time. A sixteen-year-old is feeling over-controlled by her parents.)

OBSERVATIONS:

THOUGHTS:

FEELINGS:

NEEDS:

Here are examples of whole messages for the above statements. See how yours compare.

1. "You haven't said anything since I got home, and I assume you're angry. When you withdraw like that I get angry too. I'd rather talk about it than do this."

2. "We're fantasizing about a lifetime together after two weeks. I'm worried that one of us may get scared and withdraw. Does it feel okay to you to do this?"

3. "I'd been passed over for a long time and didn't really like what I was doing anyway. I don't think it's healthy to grow old someplace doing work you don't like. I was getting depressed and wanted to take a chance on finding something that really felt good. It's hard and I need your support."

4. "I'm missing my ten-year-old's play. I should be there. It's frustrating. But I do want to be home by nine to help with the cast party."

5. "You've reminded me four times, and I get the impression you think I'm stupid or irresponsible. I feel watched and it makes me angry. Let me handle this myself and we can talk about it if I mess up."

The ability to make whole rather than partial or contaminated messages is a skill. It is acquired with practice. This this exercise:

1. Select a friend or family member whom you trust.

2. Explain the concept of whole messages.

3. Arrange a time to practice.

4. Select something you want to talk about, something that was important enough to affect you emotionally. It can be something in the past, or something going on right now; something involving others; or something directly related to the person you practice with.

5. Talk about your chosen subject, using the four components of a whole message: Talk about what happened and what you observed; describe what you thought and concluded; say

something about how it all made you feel; and describe your needs in the situation.

6. When you finish, your partner should repeat back in his or her own words each part of the message.

7. You should correct anything that he or she didn't get quite right.

8. Reverse the whole process, and let your partner describe an experience using whole messages.

Now make an agreement with your partner that every significant communication between you will involve whole messages. Commit yourself to practicing whole messages for two weeks. Always be sure to give each other feedback about what was heard and what was left out of the message. At the end of two weeks, evaluate your experience. The goal is for whole messages to become automatic. Eventually you can expand your exercise program to include other significant people. The exercises will sharpen your awareness so you can rapidly look inside yourself for the information necessary to make whole messages.

Rules for Effective Expression

Messages Should Be Direct

The first requirement for effective self-expression is knowing when something needs to be said. This means that you don't assume people know what you think or want.

Indirectness can be emotionally costly. Here are a few examples. One man whose wife divorced him after fifteen years complained that she had no right to call him undemonstrative. "She knew I loved her. I didn't have to say it in so many words. A thing like that is obvious." But it wasn't obvious. His wife withered emotionally without direct expression of his affection. A woman who had been distressed by her child's performance in school stopped nagging when his grades went up. She was surprised to learn that her son felt unappreciated and wanted some direct approval. A man who had developed a chronic back problem was afraid to ask for help with gardening and household maintenance. He suffered through these tasks in pain and experienced a growing irritation and resentment toward his family. A fifteen-year-old retreated to her room when her divorced mother became interested in a new man. She complained of headaches and excused herself whenever the boyfriend arrived. Her mother, who once told the children they would always come first, assumed that her daughter was just embarrassed and would soon get over it.

These are all examples of people who have something important to communicate. But they don't know it. They assume others realize how they feel. Communicating directly means you don't make any assumptions. In fact, you should assume that people are poor mind readers and haven't the faintest idea what goes on inside you.

Some people are aware of the times when they need to communicate, but are afraid to do so. Instead they try hinting, or telling third parties in hope that the target person will eventually hear. This indirectness is risky. Hints are often misinterpreted or ignored. One woman kept turning the sound down on the TV during commercials. She hoped her husband would take the hint and converse a little at the breaks. Instead he read the sports page until she finally blew up at him. Third party communications are extremely dangerous because of the likelihood that your message will be distorted. Even if the message is accurately delivered, no one wants to hear about your anger, disappointment, or even your love secondhand.

Messages Should Be Immediate

If you're hurt or angry, or needing to change something, delaying communication will often exacerbate your feelings. Your anger may smoulder, your frustrated need become a chronic irritant. What you couldn't express at the moment will be communicated later in subtle or passive-aggressive ways. One woman was quite hurt at the thought of not being invited to Thanksgiving at her sister's house. She said nothing, but broke a date they had to go to the planetarium and "forgot" to send a Christmas card.

Sometimes unexpressed feeling is gunnysacked to the point where a small transgression triggers a major dumping of the accumulated rage and hurt. These dumping episodes alienate family and friends. A hospital ward secretary had a reputation with peers for being dangerous and volatile. For months she would be sweet, considerate, and accommodating. But sooner or later the explosion came. A slight criticism would be answered with megatons of gripes and resentments.

There are two main advantages to immediate communication: (1) Immediate feedback increases the likelihood that people will learn what you need and adjust their behavior accordingly. This is because a clear relationship is established between what they do (for example, driving too fast) and the consequences (your expressed anxiety). (2) Immediate communication increases intimacy because you share your responses now. You don't wait three weeks for things to get stale. Here-and-now communications are more exciting and serve to intensify your relationships.

Messages Should Be Clear

A clear message is a complete and accurate reflection of your thoughts, feelings, needs, and observations. You don't leave things out. You don't fudge by being vague or abstract. Some people are afraid to say what they really mean. They talk in muddy, theoretical jargon. Everything is explained by "vibes" or by psychological interpretations. One woman who was afraid to tell her boyfriend she was turned off by public petting said that she felt "a little strange" that day and thought that her parents' upcoming visit was "repressing her sexuality." This ambiguous message allowed her boyfriend to interpret her discomfort as a temporary condition. He never learned her true needs.

Keeping your messages clear depends on awareness. You have to know what you've observed, and then how you reacted to it. What you see and hear in the outside world is so easily confused with what you think and feel inside. Separating these elements will go a long way toward helping you express yourself clearly.

Here are some tips for staying clear:

1. Don't ask questions when you need to make a statement. Husband to wife: "Why do you have to go back to school? You have plenty of things to keep you busy." The statement hidden in the question is "I'm afraid if you go back to school I won't see you enough, I'll feel lonely. As you grow in independence I'll feel less control over the direction of our lives."

Wife to husband: "Do you think we need to make an appearance at your boss's barbeque today?" Imbedded in the question is the unexpressed need to relax and putter in the garden. By failing to plead her case clearly, her husband can either miss or safely ignore her needs.

Daughter to father: "Are we going to have a little three-foot tree this year?" What she thinks but doesn't say is that she likes the big trees seen at friends' houses—the ones full of lights and tinsel around which the family gathers. She wishes that her family did more things together, and thinks Christmas decorating would be a good place to start.

Father to son: "How much did that paint job cost?" He really wants to talk about the fact that his son lives above his means, and then borrows from Mom without any intention of paying back. He's worried about his son's relationship to money and angry because he feels circumvented.

2. Keep your messages congruent. The content, your tone of voice, and your body language should all fit together. If you congratulate someone on getting a fellowship, his response is congruent if the voice, facial gestures, and spoken messages all reflect pleasure. Incongruence is apparent if he thanks you with a frown, suggesting that he doesn't really want the compliment.

Incongruence confuses communication. Congruence promotes clarity and understanding. A man who spent the day in his delivery truck arrived home to a request that he make a run to the supermarket. His response was, "Sure, whatever you want." But his tone was sarcastic and his body slumped. His wife got the message and went herself. But she was irritated by the sarcastic tone and later started a fight about the dishes. A model asked soothingly to hear about her roommate's "boyfriend in trouble." But while the story unfolded, her eyes flitted always to the mirror and she sat on the edge of her chair. Her voice said, "I care," but her body said, "I'm bored, hurry up."

3. Avoid double messages. Double messages are like kicking a dog and petting it at the same time. They occur when you say two contradictory things at once. Husband to wife: "I want to take you, I do. I'll be lonely without you. But I don't think the convention will be much fun. Really, you'd be bored to death." This is a double message, because on the surface the husband seems to want his wife's company. But when you read between the lines, it's evident that he's trying to discourage her from coming.

Father to son: "Go ahead, have a good time. By the way, I noticed your report card has some real goof-off grades. What are you doing about them?" This is a rather obvious double message, but the effect is confusing. One message undercuts the other, and the son is left unclear about his father's real position. The most malignant double messages are the "come close, go away" and "I love you, I hate you" messages. These communications are found in parent-child and lover relationships, and inflict heavy psychological damage.

4. Be clear about your wants and feelings. Hinting around about your feelings and needs may seem safer than stating them clearly. But you end up confusing the listener. Friend to friend: "Why don't you quit volunteering at that crazy free clinic?" The clear message would be: "I'm afraid for you struggling in that conflict-ridden place. I think you are exhausting yourself, and I miss the days when we have time to spend an afternoon together. I want you to protect your health and have more time for me."

Husband to wife: "I see the professors and their wives at the faculty party, and I shudder at some of the grotesque relationships." The real message that couldn't be said was "When I see that terrible unhappiness, I realize what a fine life we have and how much I love you."

Mother to daughter: "I hope you visit Grandma this week." On the surface this seems straightforward, but underneath lurks the guilt and anxiety she feels about Grandma's loneliness. She worries about the old woman's health and, without explaining any of this, badgers her daughter to make frequent visits.

Two lovers: "I waited while you were on the phone and now our dinners are cold." The underlying statement is "I wonder how much you care about me when you take a phone call in the middle of dinner. I'm feeling hurt and angry."

5. Distinguish between observations and thoughts. You have to separate what you see and hear from your judgments, theories, beliefs, and opinions. "I see you've been fishing with Joe again" could be a straightforward observation. But in the context of a longstanding conflict about Joe, it becomes a barbed conclusion. Review the section on contaminated messages for more discussion of this issue.

6. Focus on one thing at a time. This means that you don't start complaining about your daughter's Spanish grades in the middle of a discussion about her boyfriend's marijuana habits. Stick with the topic at hand until both parties have made clear, whole messages. If you get unfocused, try using one of the following statements to clarify the message: "I'm feeling lost . . . what are we really talking about?" or "What do you hear me saying? I sense we've gotten off the track."

Messages Should Be Straight

A straight message is one in which the stated purpose is identical with the real purpose of the communication. Disguised intentions and hidden agendas destroy intimacy because they put you in a position of manipulating rather than relating to people. You can check if your messages are straight by asking these two questions: (1) Why am I saying this to this person? (2) Do I want him or her to hear it, or something else?

Hidden agendas are dealt with at length in another chapter. They are usually necessitated by feelings of inadequacy and poor self-worth. You have to protect yourself, and that means creating a certain image. Some people take the *I'm good* position. Most of their communications are subtle opportunities to boast. Others pay the *I'm good but you aren't* game. They are very busy putting everyone down and presenting themselves, by implication, as smarter, stronger, more successful. Agendas such as *I'm helpless, I'm fragile, I'm tough,* and *I know it all* are good defensive maneuvers to keep you from getting hurt. But the stated purpose of your communication is always different from your real purpose. While you are ostensibly discoursing on intricate Middle East politics, the real purpose is to show how knowledgeable you are. We all succumb to little vanities, but when your communications are dominated by one such agenda, you aren't being straight.

Being straight also means that you tell the truth. You state your real needs and feelings. You don't say you're tired and want to go home if you're really angry and want more attention. You don't angle for compliments or reassurance by putting yourself down. You don't say you're anxious about going to a couples therapist when actually you feel angry about being pushed to go. You don't describe your feelings as depression because your mate prefers that to irritation. You don't say you enjoy visiting your girlfriend's brother when the experience is one step below fingernails scraping on the chalkboard. Lies cut you off from others. Lies keep them from knowing what you need or feel. You lie to be nice, you lie to protect yourself, but you end up feeling alone with your closest friends.

Messages Should Be Supportive

Being supportive means you want the other person to be able to hear you without getting blown away. Ask yourself, "Do I want my message to be heard defensively or accurately? Is my purpose to hurt someone, to aggrandize myself, or to communicate?"

The Fair Fighting chapter explores step-by-step methods of working through anger. However, if you prefer to hurt your listener with your messages, use these six tactics:

1. Global labels. Stupid, ugly, selfish, evil, assinine, mean, disgusting, worthless, and lazy are a few of the huge list of hurtful words. The labels are most damaging when used in a "You're a fool, a coward, a drunk," and so on format. Making your point that way creates a total indictment of the person, instead of just a commentary on some specific behavior.

2. Sarcasm. This form of humor very clearly tells the listener that you have contempt for him. It's often a cover for feelings of anger and hurt. The effect on the listener is to push him away or make him angry.

3. Dragging up the past. This destroys any chance of clarifying how each of you feels about a present situation. You rake over old wounds and betrayals instead of examining your current dilemma.

4. Negative comparisons. "Why aren't you generous like your brother?" "Why don't you come home at six like other men?" "Sarah's getting A's and you can't even get a B in music appreciation." Comparisons are deadly because they not only contain "you're bad" messages, but they make people feel inferior to friends and family.

5. Judgmental "you messages." These are attacks that use an accusing form. "You don't love me anymore." "You're never here when I need you." "You never help around the house." "You turn me on about as much as a 1964 Plymouth."

6. Threats. If you want to bring meaningful communication to a halt, get out the big guns. Threaten to move out, threaten to quit, threaten violence. Threats are good topic changers, because instead of talking about uncomfortable issues, you can talk about the hostile things you plan to do.

Communicating supportively means that you avoid "win/lose" and "right/wrong" games. These are interactions in which the intention of one or both players is "winning" or proving the other person "wrong" rather than sharing and understanding. Your intention in communication will guide you toward a predictable result. Real communication produces understanding and closeness, while "win/lose" games produce warfare and distance. Ask yourself, "Do I want to win or do I want to communicate? Do I want to be right or do I want mutual understanding?" If you find yourself feeling defensive and wanting to criticize the other person, that's a clue that you're playing "win/lose."

Win/lose interactions can be avoided by sticking rigidly to the whole-message structure. You can also get around the win/lose pattern by making clear observations on your process. "I'm feeling pretty defensive and angry right now, and it looks like I've fallen into the old win/lose syndrome."

II

Advanced Skills

4

Body Language

You can't "not communicate" with others. Without saying a word, you reveal your feelings and attitudes. Your smile says, "I'm happy," your frown and crossed arms say, "I'm mad," and your drumming fingers and explosive sighs say, "I'm impatient—get moving." Even when you try to show nothing, your closed-off stance and refusal to speak say, "I don't want to talk about it. Leave me alone."

There are two ways you communicate nonverbally: (1) body movements such as facial expressions, gestures, and posture, and (2) spatial relationships, such as how much distance you put between yourself and the other person.

Understanding body language is essential because over 50 percent of a message's impact comes from body movements. Albert Mehrabian has found that the total impact of a message breaks down like this:

7 percent	verbal (words)
38 percent	vocal (volume, pitch, rhythm, etc.)
55 percent	body movements (mostly facial expressions)

Another reason to pay close attention to body language is that it is often more believable than verbal communication. For example, you ask your mother, "What's wrong?" She shrugs her shoulders, frowns, turns away from you, and mutters, "Oh . . . nothing, I guess. I'm just fine." You don't believe her words. You believe her dejected body language, and you press on to find out what's bothering her.

The key to skillful nonverbal communication is congruence. Nonverbal cues usually occur in congruent clusters—groups of gestures and movements that have roughly the same meaning and agree with the meaning of the words that accompany them. In the example above, your mother's shrug, frown, and turning away are congruent among themselves. They could all mean "I'm depressed," or "I'm worried." However, the nonverbal cues are not congruent with her words. As an astute listener, you recognize this incongruency as a signal to ask again and dig deeper.

In another situation you may find a lack of congruence among the nonverbal cues themselves. A salesperson may be standing close to you, shaking your hand with a warm, firm grip, and smiling. However, he refuses to meet your eyes. These conflicting nonverbal cues are often a sign of conflicting feelings or incomplete communications. Perhaps while he's talking to you the salesperson is hoping that you won't ask about the guarantee. Or maybe he has his eye on the boss or on another customer who just walked into the store.

Awareness of incongruence in your own nonverbal messages can make you a much more effective communicator. For example, you might have a good idea for improving morale at work, but you hang back at meetings, slouch in your chair, fold your arms protectively, and keep your eyes downcast. Verbally you might be saying, "I've got a great idea," but your body says, "Please ignore me."

As you become aware of your own nonverbal cues, you will discover that your body language provides a wealth of information about your unconscious feelings and attitudes. For instance, in an awkward social situation you might notice that your arms are folded and your fingers are wrapped tightly around your biceps. You realize that you are nervous and defensive. With this increased awareness of your internal state, you can move to reduce your tension, rather than just continue tensing up.

You'll also discover that nonverbal communication always occurs in a context. A particular gesture or expression may have different meanings in different contexts. Covering your mouth as you watch a car smash into the back of your parked car will communicate your horror. You may use the same gesture during a tedious lecture to express your boredom. Or you could use this gesture with a policeman as you say, "Oh no, Officer, I was only going the legal speed limit," reflecting your uncertainty or perhaps your untruthfulness. Sometimes the context is difficult for others to ascertain. As you walk from your house to the car, you cover your mouth and then hurry back to your house. Only you know the full context of this situation: you forgot your keys or left the gas on.

Body Movements

Social kinesics, or body communication, is largely learned. Gestures are passed from one generation to the next without any special training. A boy learns to walk bowlegged like his rancher father and a girl learns to laugh and cover her mouth like her mother. Many gestures are restricted to a specific peer group, others are typical of a particular region or culture, and some body movements are universal.

While there are more similarities between cultures in body language than there are in verbal language, the differences are sufficient to create considerable confusion. For example, maintaining steady eye contact while answering the question of someone in authority is a sign of sincerity in our culture. For a Puerto Rican to maintain eye contact under similar circumstances would be a sign of disrespect. Hence a respectful Puerto Rican might be judged untrustworthy by an American.

Within a culture there is room for much individual variation. For instance, you may indicate annoyance by quick, jerky movements, while your partner may express annoyance by frowning, folding arms, and standing rigidly at attention. Tuning into each other's unique way of expressing feelings and attitudes helps communication.

Body movements serve several communication purposes. Besides indicating attitudes and conveying feelings, body movements can serve as *illustrators* and *regulators*. Illustrators are nonverbal movements that accompany and illustrate verbal communication. You say to the butcher, "I want that one," and point to the T-bone steak. You nod your head up and down to indicate yes and shake it from side to side to indicate no. You use your hands to draw a picture in the air of something you are discussing. You imitate the movement you are verbally describing or move in a way that underscores the significance of a particular word or phrase.

Regulators are nonverbal cues that monitor or control the speaking of another individual. As you listen you nod your head, indicating to the speaker that you understand and want him or her to keep talking. You lean or look away to communicate that you want the speaker to stop talking. You raise your eyebrows in disbelief, suggesting that the speaker needs to defend a position. The sensitive speaker modifies his or her conversation in the direction indicated by the listener's regulators.

Facial Expression

The face is the most expressive part of the body. The next time you're reading a magazine, look at some photos of people in action. Use your hands to cover up everything but their faces. What kind of information do you get from the face alone? What kind of information do you lose?

You'll probably find that, although you can't tell what the people are doing, you can still identify feelings and attitudes. Try covering up everything but the eyes and see if you can still sense feelings and attitudes. Try it with everything but the mouth area covered. You'll see that some emotions can be interpreted reliably by looking only at the eyes and mouth. But the more of the face you cover, the harder it is to identify emotions and attitudes.

When observing facial expressions, you will also want to note if the eyebrows are raised or lowered, the forehead is wrinkled or smooth, and the chin is set or flaccid. How flushed or pale the skin is can also provide useful information.

As an experiment, try using different facial expressions in your daily interactions with people. For instance, smile and look directly at people you normally would not give the time of day to. Stare vacantly into space as you address your best friend. Tell an amusing story with a straight face. Tell the same story again with animated facial expressions. Deliver a very serious message with a broad smile. Deliver it again with a serious facial expression. In each case, note how you feel and the reaction you get from other people. What differences do you notice between when you are being congruent and when you are being incongruent?

Gestures

Arms and hands. You have probably known people who "talk with their hands." Even when they are on the phone, they unconsciously use regulating and illustrating gestures that are lost on their listener. People scratch their heads in puzzlement, touch their noses in doubt, rub their necks in anger or frustration, tug on their ears when they want to interrupt, wring their hands in grief, and rub their hands in anticipation. They will put their hands on their knees to indicate readiness, on their lips to indicate impatience, lock their hands behind their back as a signal of self-control, lock their hands behind their head as a statement of superiority, stick their hands into their pockets to hide their meaning, and clench fists as a sign of anger or tension. They will extend their arms out in front of them with palms up to indicate sincerity, and then shrug their shoulders in this position as if to say, "How should I know?" or "I just couldn't help it." They'll cross arms in front of their chest when feeling defensive or unwilling to communicate openly. They use their arms and hands to create nonverbal emblems that translate directly into words or phrases such as "Peace" or "Up yours."

Legs and feet. When you sit with your legs uncrossed and slightly apart, you communicate openness. When you straddle a chair, you are indicating dominance. When you put one leg over the arm of a chair, you are suggesting indifference. Sitting with one ankle over the other knee or sitting with ankles crossed can be a sign of resistance. Sitting with one leg crossed over the other and swinging or kicking it back and forth is often a sign of boredom, anger, or frustration. Agreement is most likely when all limbs are uncrossed. The direction in which the legs and feet are pointed is often the direction in which the individual feels most interest.

To experience how much you rely on body movements to communicate, try telling a story without using gestures. You may have to plant your feet firmly on the floor and hold your hands behind your back. After talking for a few minutes, allow yourself to use body movements and notice the difference it makes. Note how you felt when you couldn't illustrate your points with your hands. How do you imagine your communication was affected? Ask your listener what differences he or she noticed.

You can use another exercise to experiement with regulators. When a friend is talking, use different gestures to indicate nonverbally that you want your friend to:

1. go on talking

2. speed up

3. slow down

4. get to the point

5. expand on a point

6. defend a point

7. stop and let you talk

8. stop and end the conversation

Posture and Breathing

Slumped posture can be a sign of feeling "low," fatigue, a sense of inferiority, or of not wanting to be noticed. Some sensitive tall people will slump so as not to tower over and intimidate shorter people. Erect posture is generally associated with higher spirits, greater confidence, and more openness than slumped posture. Leaning forward tends to suggest openness and interest. Leaning away suggests lack of interest or defensiveness. A tense, rigid posture tends to be a sign of defensiveness, while a relaxed posture indicates openness.

Breathing is another important indicator of feelings and attitudes. Rapid breathing can be associated with excitement, fear, irritability, extreme joy, or anxiety. A pattern of holding your breath, alternating with short gasps for air, is a sign of anxiety of built-up tension. Shallow breathing in the upper chest often indicates thinking that is cut off from feelings. Deep breathing into the stomach is more likely to be associated with feelings and action.

You can find out a lot about people by watching and imitating their breathing for a few moments. It is probably easiest to follow a person's pattern of breathing by focusing on his or her collar as it rises and falls. Notice the speed and depth of the breathing, then imitate it with your own for a few minutes. As you do so, notice what changes occur in your own body. What feelings come up for you? Often people find that in the process of imitating they take on the feelings of the other person.

In the course of everyday events you can pause at times to notice how you are breathing and feeling. Experiment with varying your breathing pattern. For instance, if your breathing is shallow and you are feeling tired or depressed, try breathing more rapidly and deeply for a few minutes and observe what happens. If your breathing is very rapid and you feel anxious or annoyed, try slow, deep breaths for a few minutes. Changing how you breathe will often change how you feel.

Exercise. Observe on TV or in your everyday life how people use body movements to convey meaning. At first, concentrate on facial expressions. Then look at arm and hand gestures. Notice what they're doing with their feet, balance, and posture. Watch their breathing for a while.

Notice how much meaning can be understood from each movement considered by itself. Then take into account the context in which the movement occurs. What is going on in the interaction that defines the meaning of a body movement?

Notice how body movements tend to occur in clusters. Are these groups of movements congruent? Do they mean the same thing? Or is one part of the body sending a different message from the rest?

Finally, is the nonverbal message conveyed by the body the same as the verbal message? Are there any jarring incongruities that indicate anxiety, anger, withheld communication, or outright lying? What feelings and attitudes are missing from the verbal message but conveyed by the nonverbal part?

Spatial Relationships

Proxemics is the study of what you communicate by the way you use space. How far you stand from a person you're talking to, how you arrange the furniture in your home, and how you respond to others invading your territory are important nonverbal statements.

The father of proxemics was Edward T. Hall, an anthropologist who described four distinct zones that people unconsciously use as they interact with others: (1) intimate distance, (2) personal distance, (3) so-

cial distance, and (4) public distance. Imagine that each person is sur-
rounded by four concentric bubbles of personally defined space. The
bubbles are largest in front of the individual and smallest at their sides
and back. Each zone also has a "close" and a "far" subphase. Generally
speaking, the greater the distance between two people interacting, the
less intimate their relation.

Intimate distance has a close subphase of actually touching, and a
far subphase of 6 to 18 inches from the body. This is the zone for lovers,
close friends, and children holding onto their parents or each other.
Nonintimates usually feel embarrassed or threatened if circumstances
force them to share this space without nonverbal barriers to protect
themselves. Observe on a crowded bus or elevator how people avoid
eye contact and draw away or tense up if touch is unavoidable. If eye
contact is made, it is brief and often combined with a polite, nonintru-
sive smile.

Personal distance has a close subphase of 1 1/2 to 2 1/2 feet,
which is a comfortable zone for talking at a party. You can still easily
touch your partner, whereas in the far subphase of 2 1/2 to 4 feet, you
can discuss something relatively privately without risking touch. In the
far subphase, you are literally keeping your partner at arm's length.

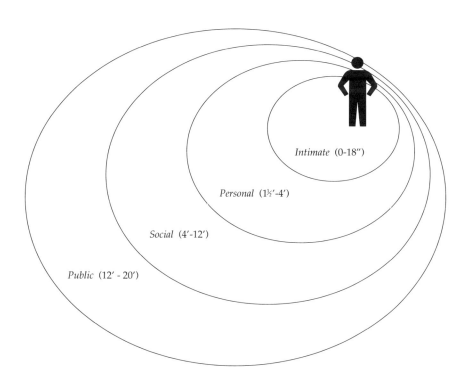

Social distance has a close subphase of 4 to 7 feet, in which you are most likely to transact such interpersonal business as talking to a client or service person. This subphase is often used manipulatively to indicate dominance. A supervisor will stand over a seated employee at this distance as an indication of her higher status. The far subphase of 7 to 12 feet is most frequently used for formal business or social interactions. The president of the company will often sit behind a desk that gives him about this much distance from his employees, so that he can convey his superior status even when looking at an employee from a sitting position. This distance is also useful in an open office setting, where it allows employees to continue working without feeling rude for not interacting with co-workers nearby. At home a husband and wife could sit at this distance from one another as they read, watch TV, and occasionally chat.

Public distance has a close subphase of 12 to 20 feet which is usually used for relatively informal gatherings such as a teacher working with a classroom of students or a boss talking with a group of employees. The far subphase of 20 feet or more is reserved for politicians and celebrities.

The four zones vary greatly from culture to culture, and people from different cultures often misinterpret one another for lack of an understanding of their differently defined zones. For instance, the personal zone of Latins is much closer than that of Anglo Americans. A conversation between acquaintances from these two distinct cultures can start at one end of a room and end at the other, as the Latin tries to move closer to the personal zone where he feels most comfortable, and the Anglo American draws away, feeling uncomfortable in his intimate zone. The Latin invariably goes away thinking that Anglos are standoffish, and the Anglo leaves with the perception that Latins are pushy.

Individual variations in the size of these zones for members of the same culture can also lead to discomfort when the wrong people slip into the wrong zone. Hall's model of four zones should be used only as a general guide.

The old double standard between the sexes may still apply to how they interact spatially. A woman can usually move into a man's space more easily than into another woman's, perhaps because there is the possibility of flirtation with the man. But if a man were to do the same to a woman, the woman is more likely to read the intrusion as a sign of disrespect. The same message is sent by a boss who stands in an employee's intimate zone, thereby indicating the boss's superiority.

Spatial zones are routinely ignored when people are thought of as objects. It is permissible to invade the personal space of a nonperson. Patients often become nonpersons while doctors and nurses discuss their cases in front of them as though they were not there. Similarly, white bigots might discuss their racist views in front of an African-American waiter, or men might tell lurid sexual jokes in front of their female colleagues. In each case, the other person's humanness is not respected. Treating a person as a nonperson can also be achieved by staring at them as though they are an object, or by not talking to them when they would ordinarily be part of the conversation.

Territory is similar to personal space. It is a place you have staked out as your own and where you feel safe. In your territory you can relax and not have to worry about constant intrusion. Your territory may be your home, your office, your favorite chair, or for a few hours the spot on the beach where you unfold your towel to sunbathe. The instinct to take and defend territory is well known among animals, and humans are no exception. From street gangs to nations, people react strongly in defense of their territory when they feel it is being invaded.

Exercises. Stand in the middle of an empty space and have someone walk slowly toward you. Tell the person to stop as soon as you begin to feel uncomfortable. Instruct him or her to move forwards and backwards until you are at a comfortable distance. This is your body's buffer zone. Does this zone change when you have different people walk toward you and stand at the point at which you feel comfortable? Can you explain any differences?

Experiment with invading someone's buffer zone. For instance, stand "too close" in a waiting line, elevator, or bus. Observe the person's response to you. (Do this exercise with caution, preferably with members of your own gender.)

A few times during each day, take note of the distance between yourself and the people with whom you are speaking. Are the zones you are in consistent with your relationships with the other people? If not, can you explain?

5

Paralanguage and Metamessages

Paralanguage is the vocal component of speech, considered apart from the verbal content. It includes pitch, resonance, articulation, tempo, volume, and rhythm. Through paralanguage you unintentionally betray your moods and attitudes. No matter what you say, the sound of how you say it will reveal a great deal about who you are and what you feel.

When you *intentionally* alter your rhythm or pitch for emphasis, or include special verbal modifiers, you may be sending *metamessages*. Metamessages add another level of meaning to a sentence, often a disapproving one. The statement "*We* like you, of course," is very different from "We like you." By emphasizing "we" and adding "of course," the meaning has been subtly changed to imply that others don't feel the same way and that your personal charm may be somewhat doubtful. A few innocuous words and a change in rhythm are all it takes to make this metamessage.

The Elements of Paralanguage

Pitch. As you tighten your vocal cords you raise the pitch of your voice. Intense feelings of joy, fear, or anger make your voice go up. When you are depressed, tired, or calm, the muscles of your vocal cords relax. The pitch of your voice goes down. Though your pitch varies in normal conversations, it will move toward the extremes when you're expressing intense feelings.

Resonance. The shape of your vocal cords and chest determine resonance. Resonance refers to the richness or thinness of your voice. A man with heavy vocal cords and a large chest is likely to have a deep, full voice. A woman with tight, thin vocal cords is apt to have a thin, high voice. With some practice, both pitch and resonance can be controlled—as singers and public speakers regularly do. Deep chest tones communicate firmness, self-assurance, and strength. Thin, high-pitched voices suggest insecurity, weakness, and indecisiveness.

Articulation. How carefully do you enunciate your words? Do you speak in so relaxed a manner that many of your sounds are slurred together, or do you say each syllable precisely? Different levels of articulation are appropriate in different situations. A slight slur or drawl may add to an atmosphere of comfort or intimacy. But slurred words would be inappropriate in a board meeting, where clear, decisive speech is expected.

Tempo. The tempo or speed at which words are spoken reflects emotions and attitudes. Fast talkers convey excitement and can be expressive and persuasive. Speaking too fast, however, can make the listener nervous. Rapid speech can also signal insecurity. A slow, hesitant speaker may give an impression of laziness or indifference. To another listener, the slow speaker may sound sincere, thoughtful, and interested.

The speed at which you speak often reflects the region of the country where you grew up. People from New York City speak more rapidly than those from Arkansas, and people raised in large cities generally tend to speak faster than those from the country. Fast talkers and slow talkers often feel frustrated when they converse. The fast talker feels uncomfortable with long pauses and often will attempt to finish the sentences of slow talkers for them. The slow talkers have difficulty keeping up and may eventually give up trying to communicate.

Volume. On the positive side, loud volume is usually associated with enthusiasm and confidence. Negative connotations include aggressiveness, an over-inflated ego, or an exaggerated belief in the importance of a message. A person of higher status often raises the volume of his or her voice over that of a subordinate. A loud voice says, "I'm in command, you do what I tell you to do." A soft voice says, "Don't attack me, I know my place, I know I'm helpless."

In everyday settings a soft voice is often heard as a sign of trustworthiness, caring, and understanding. It can also indicate a lack of confidence, a feeling of inferiority, or a sense that the message is unimportant. But as an extreme version of the soft voice, a whisper accentuates communication. A whisper can imply special intimacy, meaning—"This is just between the two of us." It can also convey sadness, fear, or awe.

Rhythm. Rhythm determines which words will be emphasized in a sentence. In the question "What time is it?" the emphasis is normally on the word "time." If you were to place the emphasis on "what," you would upset the rhythm. Notice the change in meaning as you vary the rhythm in the following sentence:

Am *I* happy!

Am I happy?

The sentence changes from an exuberant statement of fact to a message of doubt and uncertainty by a switch in emphasis between two words.

Just as every song has its particular rhythm, so does every language. As a baby you imitated the language rhythms of the adults around you before you could speak words. Later, as you began using words, you would simply fit them into the familiar rhythms. By now, rhythm patterns are so natural for you that you rarely pay any attention to them. But despite its invisibility, rhythm is extremely important. The words you choose to emphasize in a sentence ("*Am* I happy?" versus "Am *I* happy!") make a vital difference in the meaning of a statement. The section on metamessages will show how rhythm and pitch are used to communicate broader meanings than the verbal content of a sentence.

Changing Your Paralanguage

If you did not vary your pitch, resonance, volume, tempo, or rhythm as you spoke, you would sound like a robot. Others would experience your speaking style as monotonous and tune you out. They would assume that you were bored with what you were saying. To assess your own paralanguage and learn what it says about you, make a tape recording of your voice as you carry on a normal conversation. Wait at least 24 hours before listening to the replay so you can be more objective. Also, if you haven't heard your voice on tape before, you should listen to it for a while until the novelty wears off and your recorded voice sounds relatively natural to you. As you listen to yourself on tape, ask yourself the following questions:

1. Does your voice reflect what you want to say?

2. Is your voice congruent with the words you speak?

3. Is there something about your voice that you dislike?

If you discover something about your paralanguage that you want to change, practice again with the tape recorder. Speak or read on tape, varying your voice and always keeping in mind how you want to sound. Play the original tape recording of your voice for a friend to get some feedback on your voice quality. Experiment with any changes he or she suggests.

Cindy, a cocktail waitress, found that her customers were often a little light on tips. She made a tape and found that her voice had a monotonous, high-pitched, flat, nasal-sounding tone. She also noticed that she spoke so fast and slurred so many words that she was hard to understand. Her voice reminded her of her maiden aunt, who was 30 years older than Cindy and incredibly boring. Cindy began a regime of voice exercises (see the three exercises that follow) and read into the tape recorder for five minutes each day for a month. While she was reading, she focused on deep, slow breathing and relaxation of her vocal cords. Over time she noticed an improvement in her resonance, and greater variations in pitch, speed, and rhythm. Cindy's tips didn't improve much, but attractive customers did begin asking her out on dates.

The Body-Vocal Stretch. Your body is the instrument you use to produce your voice. To increase your range of pitch, resonance, and volume, you need to loosen up your body. If you speak too softly, if your resonance is too thin, or if your pitch is unpleasantly high, low, or monotonous, this exercise will help you gain greater range. It will open up your throat and upper chest as well as exercise your vocal cords.

Begin by yawning—widely and loudly. Open your mouth as wide as you can and empty your lungs of air. Then inhale deeply. As you yawn, let your voice travel up and down the tonal scale. After a few minutes, try speaking while yawning.

Volume Modulation. How loud is loud enough? If you speak too loudly or too softly, this exercise will help you modulate your volume. It allows you to connect your visual sense with your vocal sense so that you can choose an appropriate volume for each situation.

Focus your attention on an object near you and say *"Touch"* slowly and precisely. Imagine your voice going out and touching that object. Then look at a more distant object and say *"Touch"* louder. Again imagine your voice actually touching that object. Let your eyes find other items in the room to "touch." Find out how far away you can "touch" an object with your voice. With practice, you will be able to sense when the volume of your voice is falling short of or over-shooting another person.

Articulation and Tempo. If people have difficulty understanding you because you speak too rapidly, mumble, or otherwise distort your words, this exercise in articulation is for you. It will help you to slow down and enunciate your words in normal, everyday conversations.

Recite something you know by heart, such as a favorite saying, poem, nursery rhyme, or even your phone number and address. Say it over and over again, out loud. Speak s-l-o-w-l-y. Draw out all the vowel sounds to three or four times their normal duration. Exaggerate all the consonants so that hard words such as *b, p, k,* and *t* explode from your lips.*

Metamessages

Many statements have two levels of meaning. One level is the basic information being communicated by a series of words. The second level, or metamessage, communicates the speaker's attitudes and feelings. The metamessage is largely communicated by rhythm, pitch, and verbal modifiers.

Consider the sentence "You're late tonight." If the word "late" is emphasized with a slightly rising inflection, the sentence communicates surprise. It may also imply a question about the cause of the delay. If the word "you're" is emphasized, the metamessage is irritation.

Metamessages are a source of much interpersonal conflict. On the surface, a statement may seem reasonable and straightforward. But underneath, the metamessage communicates blame and hostility. Consider the statement "I'm trying to help." If the verbal modifier "only" is inserted, and given the emphasis of a rising inflection, the metamessage becomes very different. "I'm *only* trying to help" communicates hurt feelings and defensiveness. The message is now an attack.

It's hard to defend against the anger and disapproval expressed in negative metamessages. The attack is often so subtle that you aren't aware of exactly how you've been hurt. For example, John has just moved out of a college dormitory into his own apartment. When his mother visits she remarks, "Of course, it *is* your first apartment." By adding the modifier "of course" and emphasizing the verb "is," the metamessage becomes "This place isn't very nice, but what can you expect from a novice homemaker?" John feels irritated for the rest of her visit, but has no idea of how he has been put down.

You can learn to recognize your own metamessages and deal with the negative metamessages of others. The trick is to be aware of how a metamessage is constructed. Step one is to listen for rhythm and pitch.

Rhythm and Pitch in a Metamessage

A sentence in which each word gets equal emphasis is unlikely to contain a metamessage. But by accentuating one or more of the words, the speaker communicates a great deal about his or her emotional state. For example, examine the sentence "Just a minute." When every word has equal emphasis, the sentence is a simple request. When the words

---

* The three exercises in this section were provided by John Argue, dramatic voice teacher.

"just" or "minute" are emphasized, the message is annoyance or impatience.

Now consider the sentence "I'm not going home with you." Depending on which word receives rhythmic emphasis, the sentence will have a very different metamessage. "*I'm* not going home with you" has the metamessage "Somebody else might, but not me." When "home" is emphasized, the message is "I might go somewhere with you, but not home." If the word "you" is emphasized, the metamessage reads "I might go home with someone, but certainly not with you." The same words have very different meanings depending on your emphasis.

Many compliments have hidden metamessage barbs in them. The simple sentence "You're sweet" changes considerably, depending on rhythm and pitch. When "you're" is emphasized with a rising inflection the metamessage is surprise, perhaps distrust. The statement reads, "You're being sweet, but that's an unusual occurrence." When "sweet" is emphasized, the message is clearly appreciation or affection. A sarcastic, cutting metamessage is achieved by giving both words a strong emphasis and "sweet" a falling inflection.

Some metamessages function as warnings. Consider the phrase "in my opinion." If the word "opinion" is emphasized, you get the message that it's okay to disagree. When "my" is strongly emphasized, the message is "Listen, but don't contradict me."

Pitch and rhythm are an important component of sexual metamessages. The boss's secretary is wearing an attractive, tight-fitting sweater. He remarks, "That's quite a nice . . . *sweater* you have on." The words are the same, but the metamessage is a covert sexual invitation.

Verbal Modifiers

Verbal modifiers are special words that add nuances of meaning to a sentence. The following is a list of words often used as verbal modifiers:

Certainly	Sure
Only	Just
Merely	Still
Naturally	Again
Now	Slightly
Lately	Supposedly

Some phrases like "of course," "come on," "I'm sure," or "I guess" show up frequently in metamessages. In general, any word that denotes quantity (either a lot or a little) can be crafted into a sarcastic metamessage: "You're *a little bit* on the messy side" or "I got *slightly* wet waiting for you."

In the column on the left are a series of sentences that include verbal modifiers. The column on the right contains the metamessage implied by each modifier.

It's *only* a game.	There's something wrong with you. You're taking this too seriously.
You *sure* have been tired lately.	There's something wrong with you or you're up to no good.
I was *just* being frank.	There's something wrong with you if you can't take honesty.
Naturally, you'll want to come.	There's something wrong with you if you don't want to come.
Are you *still* here?	You shouldn't be here.
I was *merely* making a point.	There's something wrong with you if you can't be reasonable.
You *certainly* are quiet.	You're too quiet and it bugs me.
Come on, let's relax.	There's something wrong with you and you're annoying me.
You tried your best, *I'm sure*.	I'm not so sure you tried your best.
Now what do you want?	You ask for too much. You're trying my patience.

The verbal modifiers usually create an undertone of irritation and disapproval. Go back and read the sentences in the left-hand column without the modifiers. Notice that they turn back into simple statements of fact. Gone are the covert barbs and the implied rejection.

Coping With Metamessages

The basic function of metamessages is to say something covertly that you're afraid to say directly. Since a metamessage attack is covert, there is little chance of overt retaliation. Here are two simple steps for coping with an attacking metamessage:

1. Repeat the message over in your own mind, listening to rhythm and pitch, noticing any verbal modifiers.

2. Say what you think the metamessage is out loud, and ask if that's what the person really thinks or feels.

The second step is absolutely necessary. If you don't check your interpretation out, you're stuck in a position of mind-reading the other person's intent. You'll act as if the assumed metamessage is true, without ever knowing for sure. Checking it out is also a good way of teaching metamessagers to talk straight. When you call them on their covert attack, they are more likely to be direct with you. The thoughts and feelings hidden in the metamessage can then be looked at openly and honestly.

Harry, who often worked late, knew how to deal with metamessagers. When a co-worker remarked, "I guess *you're* staying late *again* tonight, Harry ran the statement over in his mind. He noticed the emphasis and rising inflection on the word "you're." He also noticed the verbal modifier "again." Harry still couldn't decide whether the statement was critical ("Your diligence makes us all look bad") or sympathetic ("Please take care of yourself"). He decided to repeat back the negative metamessage to check out his perceptions. "I wonder if it irritates people that I work late, like I'm showing them up or something?" To his relief, Harry found that the comment had been made out of genuine concern.

Sometimes it requires real tenacity to get the speaker to acknowledge a metamessage. Lisa's father was famous for his subtle sarcasm. When he asked, "Are you *still* interested in that . . . *young* man?" Lisa heard the message for what it was: a disapproving put-down. She ran the message over in her mind to verify what she heard. She recalled the emphasized verbal modifier "still." She recalled the pause, and the heavy emphasis on "young."

Lisa: Dad, was there something about him you didn't like?

Dad: I suppose he's the usual sort of man one sees these days.

Lisa: Dad, I have the feeling from what you said that you didn't like him very much. You thought I was foolish to go out with him.

Dad: He's all right, I guess.

Lisa heard how the "I guess" modified the sentence to give the impression that there was a great deal of doubt about her boyfriend's worth. She decided to specify exactly what she had heard.

Lisa: Dad, when you asked me if I was still going out with him, you gave a lot of emphasis to the word "still." The way you referred to him as "that . . .

young man" also gave me the feeling that you felt
that there was something foolish about him and our
relationship.

Dad: I don't know him, but I guess he does bother me.

Lisa is finally getting down to brass tacks with her dad. In a few moments they will be talking openly about his negative feelings. If she can remain undefensive, Lisa will really have the opportunity to hear and directly respond to her dad's point of view. The need for metamessage attacks will be over.

6

Hidden Agendas

On the bus you overhear: "Every night he's got his nose to the TV while I'm still cleaning up. I could break a leg and he'd just sit there. He says he works all day. He doesn't know what work is. I've got the shopping, the constant care of kids, three meals, the cleaning up. When I complain, he says, 'Take time to relax.' But when I do a job, I have to do it right. I guess I'm too good."

You invite a couple to dinner. The man sits upright at the table like he's at a podium. He begins by holding forth on politics. The subject changes to the economy and he argues for the gold standard. The subject is sports and he proves that baseball is dying. The subject is child rearing and he describes the seven developmental stages. The subject is ecology and he pronounces on the ozone layer. Your dinner is one long lecture.

You've known people like this. Their stories and remarks all have the same theme, the same hidden agenda. The point is to prove that they are good, smart, blameless, invulnerable, and so on.

Hidden agendas are excellent defensive maneuvers if you don't feel very good about yourself. They protect you from rejection by creating a desired impression. Over and over, they help you make a case for your essential value as a person.

Hidden agendas are death on intimacy. Nobody gets to see the real you. What they get are carefully selected stories and calculated remarks. They hear how brave, helpless, or fragile you are. You can usually tell if you are using hidden agendas by listening to yourself. Do your anecdotes all make the same point? Are you always trying to prove something?

The Eight Agendas

The following is a list of the eight major hidden agendas. As you read, notice which ones may apply to you.

1. I'm Good

You are the hero of all your stories. Each anecdote highlights the attributes you value most. If you want people to know about your wealth or power, your stories tell them. If you want the word out about your strength or generosity, your stories do that for you. A frequently encountered *I'm Good* agenda is the "caring and sensitive person." This role is played as if you were on the stage—you create an undeniably fine character, but not your authentic self. You have to prove your caring constantly by a gesture, a recollection, a sensitive remark.

Here are some typical *I'm Good* messages:

I'm honest	I'm successful
I'm hard working	I'm powerful
I'm courageous	I'm strong
I'm loyal	I'm wealthy
I'm generous	I'm self-sacrificing
I'm ambitious	I'm adventurous

Everyone is a little phoney, but the *I'm Good* agenda is more than that. It's a life's work. It's a way of distorting yourself so that only very selected parts get seen. It means you don't trust anyone with the parts of yourself that are less than wonderful.

There are two big disadvantages to the *I'm Good* agenda. It's hard to get close to people because they only know you through your *I'm Good* stories. And people get bored. They get tired of seeing the same mask, hearing the same theme over and over. They listen for a while, then go away.

2. I'm Good (But You're Not)

In this agenda, you prove that you're all right by showing how bad everyone else is. "Everyone's stupid, incompetent, selfish, unreasonable, lazy, frightened, or insensitive but me." Every story is a variation of this theme. You're always the one who does it right, who reasons clearly, who really cares. One nurse often complained, "I'm always willing to stop and answer a light even if it's not my patient. I'll help another nurse lift someone who's heavy, but do you think I can get anyone to help me? Not on your life."

There are several versions of *I'm Good (But You're Not)*. One is the "implied criticism." You point out how hard you've worked or how much you've compromised—with the implication that the other person is lazy or rigid. Another version of this agenda is a game that Eric Berne calls *Courtroom*. This involves spouses who are each trying to prove how awful the other is. The *Courtroom* judge is usually played by a next door neighbor, a therapist, or one of the children. Berne has also identified *If It Weren't For You*, a game for spouses who blame each other for restricted, joyless lives.

I'm Good (But You're Not) can give a boost to your self-esteem, but you pay a price. Your family and friends feel threatened and put down by you, and they soon begin defensive maneuvers of their own.

3. *You're Good (But I'm Not)*

The simplest version of this agenda is flattery. More complex forms involve a kind of worship of smart, beautiful, or strong people. The worship often means putting yourself down by comparison. "You do that so well; I'm all thumbs." "I wish I had your gumption and guts; I'm too afraid of blowing it." "I've never had a head for business; I look at what you've done and think how clever you are." This one-down position is sometimes used to extract favors or strokes. *You're Good (But I'm Not)* can be a token to buy low-grade relationships. Sometimes it's a strategy to ward off anger and rejection. After all, how can you really get angry at someone who's already putting themselves down? The agenda is also useful to block uncomfortable demands and expectations. Nobody's going to expect much of an incompetent.

You're Good (But I'm Not) can be the agenda of the depressed person. The basic statement is "I'm wrong, bad, damaged, stupid, boring, or unlovable. Take pity on me." The alcoholic, the chronic gambler, and the philandering spouse may also emphasize an "I'm no good" position as a way to head off rejection and also as an excuse not to change.

4. *I'm Helpless, I Suffer*

This is the agenda of the victim. The stories focus on misfortune, injustice, abuse. The stories are about someone who's stuck, who tries but can't escape, who endures without hope of remedy. The person is implicitly saying, "Don't ask me to do anything about all this pain; I'm not responsible."

Berne has described several games which depend on the *I'm Helpless* agenda. *Ain't It Awful* is played by people who want to complain about their spouses. The injustices they suffer always seem beyond solution. *Why Don't You. . . Yes But* is ideal for maintaining helplessness. This is a game for two. The second person makes a series of suggestions that the helpless person shoots down, one after another. The helpless person is vindicated in the end by proving nothing will work, that his suffering is beyond his ability to control.

A classic *I'm Helpless, I Suffer* game is *Why Does This Always Happen To Me?* One man, who'd gotten a little break from his ulcer symptoms, complained of a reoccurrence after he got stuck in traffic without his antacids. "This always happens. I feel a little better and then some crazy thing comes up to set me back. Somebody puts pepper on my salad or sales take a plunge at work. It never fails." The *I'm Helpless, I Suffer* agenda is ideal for avoiding scary new solutions, or for accepting pain that otherwise suggests the need for a major life decision. "I'm ugly, ill, too nervous" will often help put off change indefinitely.

A past-tense version of this agenda can dominate the early phase of courtship. Horror stories are traded back and forth about the previous spouse or lover. A bond of sympathy is built on the old hurts, the former years of immobility and pain.

5. I'm Blameless

This is the agenda of choice when things go wrong. You've heard people with a thousand excuses for their failures. You've watched them cast about for something or someone to blame. The basic position is: "I didn't do it." Painful marriages often breed *I'm Blameless* agendas. Each spouse looks for proof that the fault lies elsewhere. "She didn't give enough." "He never was home." "The children took all our time." "If we hadn't moved to Long Island. . . ." "It was different after she quit her job."

One of the games played from the *I'm Blameless* position is *See What You Made Me Do.* You ask for suggestions or advice, you follow the advice, then blame your advisor for everything that went wrong. It's like taking out a kind of psychological insurance that you'll never have to be responsible for anything.

6. I'm Fragile

The basic statement from the *I'm Fragile* position is "Don't hurt me." The statement is made by telling stories about how you have been betrayed and wounded in the past. You make it clear that you need protection, that you cannot hear the whole truth. You speak in a soft voice and your vulnerability is often quite attractive. "How did you do at school today? Oh. You know, it really upsets me when I hear about you playing alone without any friends." "Everything that goes on with you is important to me, dear. But why do you have to tell me things that upset me?" "Please don't cry, I'm getting another one of my head-aches." "My parents always fought about money, let's not get into that."

7. I'm Tough

You muscle your way through life, both psychologically and physically. You are a student who carries 40 units freshman year and holds down a full-time job. You are a superwoman who works forty hours a week, raises four kids, bakes bread, does all the cleaning and cooking, and heads up the March of Dimes campaign in the neighbor-hood. You are the workaholic man who has a high-paying stressful job and spends twelve-hour days on the weekend replacing all the plumb-ing by himself.

With this agenda, a typical communication is often a harried list-ing of things you have done or are in the process of doing. You recite your schedule and overwhelm the other person with news of where you've been, details of your current labors, and a litany of all the places you have to rush off to as soon as the conversation is done. Your un-derlying message is that you are stronger and work harder, faster, and longer than anyone else. The payoff is admiration and assurance that you won't be criticized. People won't ask you for much because you are so busy. You are in control, in charge, and, most importantly, above reproach. With this agenda you don't slow down, you collapse.

I'm Tough is also the position of the hard, the dangerous, and the sometimes violent. In this posture, gesture and speech combine to create a studied invulnerability. The message is "Don't attack me, or I'll cut you up." For some people, *I'm Tough* is a masculine ideal. But the sole purpose of the agenda is to ward off hurt and protect a very fragile self-esteem. The only thing that is really "hidden" is the vulnerability of those who use it. Inside the wall of defenses is a person very afraid of rejection, very unsure of his or her worth.

8. I Know It All

This is the agenda of the endlessly lecturing dinner guest in the beginning of the chapter. The purpose of this communication is not to inform or entertain, but to prove how much you know. *I Know It All* can take the form of moralizing or teaching. You are the perpetual in-structor, comfortable only behind the imaginary lectern. People don't get too close. This agenda works best with younger people, who may be impressed or intimidated. But peers soon learn that they can't be heard or appreciated, except as an audience. The real function of *I Know It All* is to prevent you from reencountering early experiences of shame at not knowing and not being adequate.

Purpose of the Agendas

The agendas serve two functions. The first is to build up and preserve an existential position, a basic stance in the world. The agenda becomes your individual strategy for coping with core feelings of inadequacy. You deal with those feelings by asserting your worth in the *I'm Good* agenda, or borrowing some worth by denigrating others with *I'm Good (But You're Not)*. You protect your vulnerability with *I'm Tough, I'm Fragile*, or *I Know It All*.

The second function of your agendas is to promote ulterior motives and needs. If you need a friend but don't know how to get one, you might flatter someone with *You're Good (But I'm Not)*. You can solicit comfort and assistance from the *I'm Helpless, I Suffer* position. You can excuse your failures with *I'm Blameless*. Consider the accusation, "I'm trying to save our marriage, and you're not." It communicates the existential position of blamelessness and simultaneously promotes the ulterior motives of producing guilt and forcing change.

There is no doubt that the agendas are adaptive and serve a purpose, but ultimately your maneuvers isolate you. In the end they wall you off from the relief of being known and accepted for what you are.

Counting. For one day, count the number of times you use your agendas. Keep track of your stories, reminiscences, and remarks. Carry a file card with a list of the eight agendas and make a hatch mark each time you use one.

Now make an assessment. If the agendas are a major influence on your interactions, try keeping track a second day. This time, write down the name of everyone you talk to. Next to the name write a percentage— how much of what you said was influenced by agendas. One woman who did this exercise found that 80 percent of her communication with her boss was a mixture of *I'm Good* and *I'm Blameless* agendas. Conversations with co-workers were about 30 percent *I'm Good*. At home there were no agendas with her children, but 20 percent of her contact with her husband was *I'm Good (But You're Not)* (they had a discussion about his neglect of the lawn).

Deciding. If you did the exercise, you're beginning to notice your agendas. Should an important relationship be dominated by agendas, you may want to take additional action. Here are four suggestions:

1. Let the person in question know about your agenda. "I know I'm always telling you stories of my heroics, but I'm trying to take a break from that." "I notice I'm always telling you how I'm down on someone, I'm going to try looking on the bright side." "I always seem to make myself out as helpless, but I don't think it's really me."

2. Keep track of your agendas with the target person ("There I go again.")

3. Reward yourself with something nice when you block an impulse to use the old agendas.

4. If you are stuck on one agenda, mentally rehearse a new position. Here are some examples:

Agenda	Your New Position
I'm Good	"I'm a mixture of strengths and weaknesses. I can shape both sides of myself."
I'm Good (But You're Not)	"I don't have to tear you down to make me good. I'm no longer in the business of comparing."
You're Good (But I'm Not)	"I can get attention with my strengths and abilities. I don't need to make excuses."
I'm Helpless, I Suffer	"My life is a balance of pleasure and pain, hope and sadness. I can share each side of myself."
I'm Blameless	"Nobody's perfect. Decisions I make sometimes affect things that go wrong."
I'm Fragile	"It scares me a little when someone is upset, but I can listen to it."
I'm Tough	"I can take care of myself. I can relax and people will still like me. I can be safe without scaring people."
I Know It All	"I can listen, can be interested, can ask questions. There are interesting things to learn and discover."

Notice that these new positions are in the form of simple self-instructions. They are like mantras that you can say over and over to yourself in situations that traditionally elicit your agendas. You can even turn them into personal mottos, taping them to your bathroom mirror or to the inside of your briefcase.

7

Transactional Analysis

Parent, Child, and Adult Messages

Transactional Analysis was introduced by Eric Berne in the early 1960s as a way of examining communication. Berne suggested that every human being has three ego states: a parent, an adult, and a child. In any given day you will probably spend some time in each ego state, and each will affect how you behave. Your communication style will vary markedly depending on whether you are functioning from the parent, adult, or child position.

The Parent

Your internal parent is a huge collection of rules, moral dictums, and how-to-do-it instructions that your parents provided you. These rules and instructions are recorded on a tape inside you, probably during your first five years, and they continue to play throughout your entire life. The parent tapes include everything you ever heard your parents say, every pronouncement, every favorite adage. "Don't be lazy. . . . Don't brag. . . . Never let anyone make a fool of you. . . . A marriage lasts forever. . . . Always finish everything on your plate. . . . Never trust wealthy people. . . . All politicians are criminals. . . . Avoid risks. . . . Strangers are dangerous. . . . Don't walk under ladders." These rules were all important as a child because you had no way of predicting danger and no knowledge of the ways of the world. As a child you didn't know what "hot" meant or what a burn did to the skin, so there were strong rules to govern your behavior with the stove.

Parental rules also provided "how-to" information. They gave you instructions on how to shake hands, how to eat at the table, how to fill a glass, how to make conversation, and how to navigate in your neighborhood. The rules helped you cope with your first social encounters and gave you confidence as you stepped tentatively into the world.

In many ways, the parent tapes are good and helpful. They provide a structure for your life. Some parent tapes have a supportive, caring quality. Like a good teacher, they remind you of the right way to do something, but without coercion or attack. If your parents were strict and rigid, however, then the parent inside you may be equally strict and unforgiving. Your internal parent may have a punitive, rejecting voice that leaves you feeling hemmed in and controlled by absolute rules.

You can usually tell when you are talking from your parent position because you use words like *always, never, stop,* and *don't.* Your communications are full of commands and value judgments. The punitive parent, in particular, will use judgmental words like *disgusting, stupid, ridiculous,* and *idiotic.* The supportive parent may describe things as *perfect, wonderful,* or *excellent.* Functioning from your parent, you tend to discuss problems in terms of what "ought to" and "should be" done. Ought and should statements are a real tip-off that you're in your parent state.

The Child

Just as your parents are still inside you, so also is the child that you were. Your child consists of all your urges to know, to feel, to touch, and to experience a new world. Your child is hungry for discovery and sensation. But your child is also a product of all the disapproval, punishment, and negative feelings brought on by confrontations with parental mandates. A child concludes very early, "I'm not okay." It decides this because inexplicable frightening episodes of disapproval continually mar its existence.

Your child is the part of you where your emotions reside: your attractions, your love, your delight, and also your fear, your anger, and your feelings of not being okay left over from the turmoils of growing up. Your child is full of healthy appetites and at the same time raw and wounded from the inevitable parental rejections.

When you are communicating from a child position there is usually a great deal of energy: tears, pouting, temper tantrums, and whining. Your child is also the source of exuberance, giggling, and sexual excitement. Your child uses phrases like "I hate, I wish, why do I have to." It can't stand being told it isn't okay, and retreats into hurt and anger when it senses rejection.

The Adult

There is a part of you that has to juggle the intense feelings and needs of the child and the rules and mandates of the parent. This is your adult. Your adult is like a computer, a data processing center that sorts through and keeps you aware of what's going on inside and outside of you. The adult has to make decisions. To do so, it examines the conditions of the outside world and makes predictions about likely outcomes. On the inside, the adult listens to the advice of the parent and hears out the needs and reactions of the child.

The focus of Transactional Analysis is to strengthen the adult. Sometimes the adult is overwhelmed or "contaminated" by the child or parent. You can tell when your adult has succumbed to your child because you tend to act on intense feelings and impulses without examining them. Your feelings overwhelm you. You may express them by whining, complaining, having crying jags or tantrums. Spending sprees and ill-advised sexual adventures are also indications that your impulsive child has gotten the upper hand. When your adult is contaminated by your parent, the result is usually a large supply of unquestioned prejudices. You have strict, unexamined beliefs. You are straitjacketed in rules that you have no permission to evaluate. Often you communicate with an attacking, blaming style.

The healthy adult knows the needs of the child and is aware of the rules of the parent. But it can function independently. It communicates and makes decisions without blocking out or giving up control to either of them.

Communications that come from your adult position are direct and straight. Your adult describes, it asks questions, it assesses probabilities; it evaluates the known and the unknown, the true and the false. It has opinions rather than judgments or beliefs. It is aware, but the awareness has no emotional charge.

Analyzing Your Communications

The skill of Transactional Analysis is learning to identify whether you are talking from your parent, adult, or child. If you are talking from a hurt, angry place while your son is having a tantrum, it probably means that your child is involved too. If you're making stern threats and warnings, it probably means that your parent has gotten activated. Thomas Harris, in his book *I'm OK You're OK*, suggests these rules for analyzing your communications:

1. Learn to recognize your child, its vulnerabilities, its fears, and its primary ways of expressing these feelings.

2. Learn to recognize your parent, its rules, injunctions, fixed ideas, and primary ways of expressing these commands.

Harris's rules mean that you have to develop an ear for the language characteristically used by your parent and child. Once you are sensitive to the child and the parent in yourself, you can more easily recognize these ego states in other people. They will use language similar to yours an expressing their punitive parent. Their child will be angry, frightened, and impulsive, just as yours is.

The following exercises are designed to help you get practice in identifying parent, adult, and child statements. For the purpose of these exercises, the focus will be on the punitive rather than the supportive parent. The punitive parent creates most of your interpersonal conflicts; it is therefore enormously important to learn to recognize punitive parent statements. The child who appears in these exercises is the not-okay (adaptive) rather than the healthy (natural) child.

Exercise: Identify the following statements as those of parent, child, or adult:

1. I won't go, forget it. That's it, that's final, no way.   _____

2. You're just lazy. There's no other word for it.   _____

3. Get a move on, we're late.   _____

4. You've been here three hours and haven't accomplished thing one.   _____

5. I'll need some help with the packing when you're free.   _____

6. Why do I always have to go to the store?   _____

7. Don't mope around. Straighten up, get on with life.   _____

8. Please, let's eat out tonight.   _____

9. You call that makeup? You look like a dead carp.   _____

10. One of us can get more dip for the party.   _____

Answer key: 1. child   2. parent   3. parent   4. parent   5. adult
6. child   7. parent   8. child   9. parent   10. adult

Exercise: Write the following statements from the parent, adult, and child positions.

1. John wants to tell Susan that he'd like her to call if she's going to be late. How would he express his need from the three ego states?

Parent: _____

Adult: _____

Child: _____

2. Sylvia wants to tell Ramone that she's lonely when he goes to political meetings at night. How can Sylvia express her feeling from each of the three ego states?

Parent: _____

Adult: _____

Child: _____

3. David wants to ask his boss for a raise.

Parent: _____

Adult: _____

Child: _____

4. How would each of the three ego states tell the butcher that the meat was tough?

Parent: _____

Adult: _____

Child: _____

5. Ron wants to tell Enid that it frightens him when she expresses her anger through coldness.

Parent: _____

Adult: _____

Child: _____

Answer key: Compare your parent, adult, and child statements with these.

1. *Parent:* If you can't be punctual, at least have the courtesy to call. *Adult:* When you're going to be late, Susan, I'd appreciate it if you'd call. *Child:* Why do I have to wait for you all the time? At least you could call.

2. *Parent:* It's thoughtless and uncaring to go to all those late meetings while I'm left alone. *Adult:* I'm lonely in the evenings when you're out at meetings. *Child:* Can't you see how lonely I am at night?

3. *Parent:* You're paying a ridiculously low wage. I want a raise. *Adult:* I'm asking for a raise. The figure I had in mind was. . . . *Child:* I wish I could get a bit more money. Do you think I could?

4. *Parent:* It's outrageous to sell meat like that. It's a rip-off. *Adult:* The last meat I bought here was pretty tough. *Child:* I hate it when I get tough meat. My meal was ruined.

5. *Parent:* Your coldness is a stupid, ugly way to act. *Adult:* Enid, you seem to get cold when you're angry. The coldness frightens me. *Child:* Why do you have to get cold like that? Why do you do it to me?

Exercise: Change the following child statements to adult statements.

1. I wish you'd leave me alone.

_____

2. Do you think we could be home by ten?

_____

3. I hate cooking!

_____

4. Why do I have to do everything?

_____

5. Why do you get to read the front page first?

_____

Answer key: Compare your statements with these. 1. I'd like to be alone now. 2. I need to be home by ten. 3. I prefer not to cook. 4. I'm overworked and tired. 5. I'd like to read the front page first today.

Exercise: Change the following parent statements to adult statements.

1. That's a sloppy way to make a bed.

_____

2. What's the matter with you, buying that ridiculous tea set?

_____

3. Get back to work!

_____

4. You're sure tight with money.

---

5. Don't sit on the coffee table!

Answer key: Compare your statements with the following. 1. I'd prefer it if the bed was tucked in neatly. 2. What prompted you to buy that tea set? 3. It's time to return to work. 4. I'd prefer it if we had a different policy about money. 5. The coffee table won't support your weight.

You'll notice from the exercises that the punitive parent commands, accuses, and attacks. This ego state is easily recognizable by the critical, evaluative language. The not-okay child complains, pouts, and functions as a victim. The adult makes clear statements without blaming and without whining complaints.

Kinds of Transactions

Complimentary Transactions

Complimentary transactions can be defined as messages that are sent or received by the same ego state for each of the participants. Person A's messages are sent by the same ego state that person B is addressing. And B's messages are sent by the same ego state that A is addressing. In Type One complimentary transactions, the same ego states communicate with each other (Figure 1).

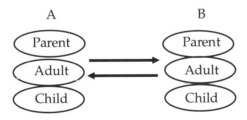

Figure 1

Adult communicates with adult, parent with parent, and child with child.

In a Type Two complimentary transaction, each person is in a different ego state, but each addresses messages to the other's current state (Figure 2).

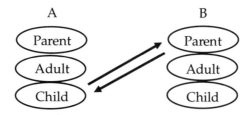

Figure 2

A typical example is the child addressing the parent and the parent therefore responding to the child.

A: Let's buy the couch anyway.

B: Now you know we can't afford it, we can barely make the rent.

Complimentary transactions can usually go on indefinitely because they don't create conflict. For example, when people address each other's parents, they are usually in agreement.

A: Workmen all do shoddy work nowadays.

B: It's disgusting, they certainly do.

When people are addressing each other's child, there is also agreement.

A: I hate it when we have to go right home from school.

B: It's awful, we miss out on all the fun.

Crossed Transactions

Crossed transactions occur when you address an ego state that the other person isn't in. Some crossed transactions cause conflict and others solve conflict. Figure 3 shows how crossed transactions can precipitate conflict.

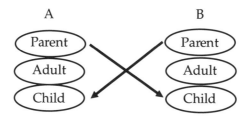

Figure 3

In Figure 3 parent A punitively addresses child B, while parent B attacks child A. Here's how it might sound:

A: Why don't you stop bringing food into the bedroom?

B: Why don't you cook a dinner worth eating once in a while, so I don't have to snack all night?

Both A and B are using their punitive parent voices to attack the vulnerable child in the other. The result is that the child in each of them is wounded while they escalate the hostilities.

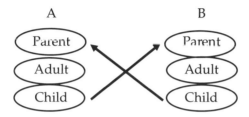

Figure 4

Figure 4 shows child A complaining to parent B, while child B complains to parent A. Here's how it could sound:

A: I hate French movies, why do we have to go to French movies all the time?

B: If you don't like them, then I see no point in going to the movies with you anymore.

Figure 5 shows cross transactions that can short circuit conflict.

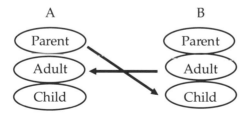

Figure 5

In diagram 1 parent A is punitively addressing child B. However, adult B responds to adult A to cut off the conflict. Here's how it might sound:

A: Why don't you stop wasting time with those endless TV sit-coms and read a good book?

B: I prefer to look at the TV tonight.

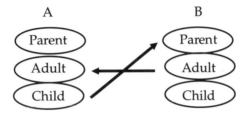

Figure 6

Figure 6 shows child A whining to parent B. B, however, refuses to engage in conflict, and uses an adult-adult communication. Here's how it sounds:

A: Why do I have to take out the garbage all the time? Why don't you do it? I hate taking out the garbage.

B: Each of us has a job. I'd like you to take out the garbage as soon as possible.

When someone addresses your child with a punitive parent, or addresses your parent with a complaining child, the only way to stop the conflict is to function in the adult position. Here is an exercise to help you get some practice.

1. *Punitive parent to your child:* You're always in a lousy mood after work. *Your adult-adult response:*

---

2. *Child to your parent:* Why can't we ever go dancing like other couples? *Your adult-adult response:*

---

3. *Punitive parent to your child:* Your desk is a complete mess. No wonder you can't find anything. *Your adult-adult response:*

---

4. *Child to your parent:* I hate it when you don't pay attention to me. *Your adult-adult response:*

---

5. *Punitive parent to your child:* You're talking a lot of nonsense. *Your adult-adult response:*

Answer key: Compare your statements with these. 1. I do feel tired after work. I didn't know I was upsetting you. 2. I'm not much of a dancer, but there are other things we might go out to do. 3. I'm comfortable with my desk the way it is. 4. I wasn't aware that you needed my attention right now. 5. They may be nonsense to you, but they are my opinions.

Ulterior Transactions

This third class of transactions is the basis of what Eric Berne called games. In ulterior transactions there are more than two ego states involved at the same time. For example, when communication is ostensibly adult-adult, there might be ulterior and sometimes nonverbal messages between an adult and child (see Figure 7).

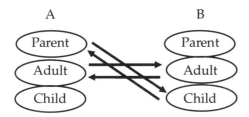

Figure 7

Salesperson A says, "This is better, but you can't afford it." Car-buyer B says, "That's the one I'll take then." The transaction operates at the adult level, but the salesperson has provided a hook for the buyer's child. He is covertly addressing the child with the challenge, "You can't afford it." The child responds, "Oh yes I can."

You can keep track of ulterior transactions by asking yourself: "What am I trying to get this person to do. . . . What covert feeling am I trying to express?" The game *Now I've got you, you son of a bitch* is an example of how a hidden need to express hostility becomes an opportunity for an ulterior transaction. During a minor contract violation, adult A says, "You've done wrong." Adult B says, "I guess you're right." But an ulterior communication is also going on between parent and child. The parent of person A says, "I've been hoping you'd make a slip." Child B says, "I guess I'm gonna get it now." Parent A responds, "Yes, and I'm really going to blast you." The ulterior transaction progresses while the adult communication is apparently focused on working out the contract.

Keeping Your Communications Clean

The following are basic Transactional Analysis rules for effective communication:

1. Know the ego state from which you are communicating.

2. Know the ego state to which you are sending your message.

3. Be sensitive to the child in others, protect that child, and recognize the "not-okay" burden that it must carry.

4. Protect your own child. Keep it safely tucked away when others are angry and attacking.

5. Don't use your punitive parent to communicate. No one wants to hear it, and people are likely to react by trying to hook your child with not-okay attacks. When appropriate, use your supportive parent, or rely on your adult.

6. Solve problems and conflicts with your adult only. Listen to your parent and listen to your child, but communicate using your adult when resolving issues.

7. Give your adult time to process data. Count to ten if necessary in order to analyze the communication. Your own parent or child may be clamoring inside you to get on stage and make a statement. It's important to sort out what really needs to be said from the impulsive statements your parent and child may demand that you make.

8

Clarifying Language

No two people experience the world in the same way. Everyone has his or her own particular picture or model of the way things are. If you were raised in a low-income farming community, your model of the world is likely to contrast sharply with the model held by someone raised in Beverly Hills. Whether you were born nearsighted or with 20/20 vision, whether you're an orphan or a rabbi's son, whether A's came easy or you had to labor for a D+, you form a model of the world that fits your experience.

A model of the world helps you make sense of what happens. It tells you what's really important, what should be noticed or ignored, why people do things, what choices are best for you. It says who you are in relationship to other people. For example, the person who has to study to get D's might place enormous importance on intelligence and tend to see others as brighter and more confident. The same person might also value hard work and see most people as lazy, just coasting on natural talents.

You don't experience the world directly. You experience your subjective representation of it. What you see, hear, and feel is converted into a thought or an interpretation. Your "idea" of the world becomes your reality.

It is therefore your model of the world, and not the world itself, that determines what choices you see as open and what limitations you think constrain you. You use your model to guide you in making the best choices you can. No matter how odd it may seem to others, each person's behavior makes sense when considered within the context of the choices generated by his or her model.

It is not unusual for people to mistake their models of the world for the real world, thereby limiting their choices. You limit your choices when your model is full of very strict rules about what you can and cannot do. Or your model is full of absolutes: "I'm always going to have trouble with math." "My mother-in-law will never like me." "Everybody enjoys a party." You might limit your choices by simply mind-reading rejection: "She thinks I'm stupid." "He thinks I'm too quiet." "They know I work too slow." A limited model that restricts or distorts reality results in a limited life.

Your model of the world also determines how well you listen and communicate. Consider the following dialogue:

Sarah: I can't wait till we're married, we can really start building a home together.

Jim: Yes, and we'll have the security to do things we haven't been able to do.

Sarah: No more apartments, a real house, a place you can move around in.

Jim: One of us could go back to school, or make a career change, and the other one would back him up.

Sarah: A real living room where people can sit quietly and talk. I want to feel like a couple, I want to have couples over.

Jim: There are so many possibilities, we can go anywhere together, do anything.

Sarah: Yes, but I still want a house that has enough room for children.

Jim: Yes, sure. We'll have kids when we're ready, but there's so much we can do now.

Jim and Sarah have a very different model of marriage. Sarah sees marriage as settling down, building a home, making a social network with other couples, and preparing for children. Jim sees marriage as an opportunity to take risks that wouldn't otherwise be possible. Because they aren't able to listen to each other's different personal model of the world, Sarah and Jim are in for a big surprise.

Many relationships are made up of Jim-and-Sarah dialogues. People use the same words, but the words mean something different. Marriage, family, love, selfishness, duty, fairness, and loneliness are words that can have particular, idiosyncratic meanings to each person. Someone says, "I feel exhausted." You say to yourself, "I know what exhausted means, it's a feeling of being very tired, worn down from too much work." The speaker, however, may have a completely different model of what exhaustion is. The word might stand for pent-up rage, confusion, or a sense of powerlessness.

A way of clarifying language so that each person's model of the world can be communicated has been developed by Richard Bandler and John Grinder. In their book, *The Structure of Magic I,* Bandler and Grinder adapted many of the concepts of transformational grammar into a set of linguistic information-gathering tools that you can use to explore and expand personal models. They describe certain universal language patterns that do one of three things:

1. Keep people from understanding your model.

2. Keep your model of the world limited.

3. Keep your model of the world distorted.

Understanding a Model

Most people talk in ways that make it very difficult for others to fully understand their experience. Because someone else's model of the world remains hidden, it's tempting and easy for you to assume that you both see things the same way. The facts are that different people draw on very different experiences and that words very rarely mean exactly the same thing to others that they mean to you. Four important language patterns prevent people from really understanding each other: (1) deletion, (2) vague pronouns, (3) vague verbs, and (4) nominalizations.

Deletion refers to material that has been completely left out of a sentence. You don't know exactly what the speaker means, but you fill in the blanks with your own set of assumptions. You can deal with deletions by asking for the information that is missing. For example, when the speaker says, "I'm happy," you can ask her, "About what?" or "About whom?" The following are statements that contain deletions and examples of questions you can use to clarify them.

Statements	*Questions*
I'm confused.	About what? About whom?
I'm ready.	What are you ready to do?
My mood is better.	About what? Better than what?
I want help.	What kind of help do you want?

Ann is the worst.	Worst what? The worst compared to whom?

Exercise: To get more practice with clarifying deletions, write down questions that challenge the deletions in the following statements.

Statements	*Questions*
I'm sad.	_____
The empire was destroyed.	_____
James is too good.	_____
I just don't know what to do.	_____
Alice is the most talented.	_____

Vague Pronouns. Confusion and misinterpretation are the usual results when a speaker relies on vague pronouns. Here are some examples:

Statements	*Questions*
It's unbelievable.	What is unbelievable?
It's unfair.	What is unfair?
They say asbestos causes cancer.	Whose research shows that asbestos is cancer-causing?
It's going wrong.	What is going wrong?
That's a hard way to find happiness.	What am I doing that makes happiness unlikely?

Exercise: Write down questions that uncover the missing references in the following statements.

Statements	*Questions*
They aren't listening to me.	_____
This is easy!	_____
It was sensational.	_____
This can't go on this way.	_____
It looks wrong to me.	_____

Vague Verbs. Some verbs such as tickle, yawn, and blink are much more specific than others such as move, touch, and see. If someone said to you, "I grew a lot last year," you might wonder to yourself, "Well, how did you grow? Are you two inches taller? Did you put on weight? Overcome your hangups?" By challenging a speaker with the question "How did you grow last year?" you get clarification of the other person's experience and model of the world. The following are statements containing vague verbs, with questions that challenge them.

Statements	Questions
She *makes* me so mad!	In what way does she make you mad?
My parents *pushed* me to become a doctor.	What did your parents do to push you toward medicine?
He just *faded* away.	How did he leave? Where did he go?
We just had to *keep moving*.	How did you keep moving?
I *love* the Rodin.	Specifically what was it about the Rodin that you liked?

Exercise: Write questions challenging the statements with vague verbs:

Statements	Questions
You frustrate me!	_____
They liked your work.	_____
She seemed to miss us.	_____
I feel like I'm running down.	_____
We were a little angered.	_____

Nominalizations are abstract nouns that give the false impression of being concrete things or events. "The problem," "our relationship," "this discussion," and "your guilt" are examples of nominalizations.

There are two ways to create a nominalization. One way is to use extremely vague nouns that don't clearly denote anything that people can agree on. If other people talk about "your guilt," they may have a very good idea of what they mean. But you may have a very different model of how guilt operates in your life.

The second way to create nominalizations is to turn verbs into nouns. "Let's make a decision" is an example of this sort of nominalization. A more dynamic, understandable sentence would read, "Let's decide on how many shade trees to plant." By turning the noun "decision" into the verb "decide," you make a sentence that requires more specific information. The indefinite "decision" to be made is replaced by the specific thing to be decided.

Nominalizations are easy to distinguish from other nouns. Visualize a green wheelbarrow. Now imagine putting a young tree, a little girl, or a couple of sacks of cement in the wheelbarrow. These are all nouns. Now try putting guilt, problems, or relationships in the wheelbarrow. As you can see, nominalizations are not persons, places, or things; they are too abstract to visualize. When a speaker uses a static nominalization, you can get them to turn it into a dynamic process word by doing one of two things: (1) Demand a specific definition of the nominalization, or (2) ask a question using the nominalization as a verb. For example, if someone says that he or she wants more attention, you could demand a definition of attention by asking, "Specifically, what kind of attention do you need?" If someone tells you, "I'm feeling a lot of disapproval," you can turn the nominalization into a verb by asking, "How am I disapproving of you?" The following are statements with nominalizations and questions that challenge them:

Statements	*Questions*
Our *relationship* seems strained.	How are we relating that you're feeling strained?
Work is nothing but *problems*.	Exactly what kind of problems have been plaguing you?
The day was full of *rejection*.	How were you rejected during the day?
The *excitement* is gone.	What excited you that isn't happening now?
There are no *solutions*.	In what ways have you tried to solve the problem?

Exercise: Write down questions which clarify the nominalizations.

Statements	*Questions*
He's a success.	_____
I want guidance.	_____
It is all a misunderstanding.	_____
I felt a lot of anger.	_____
A strange sadness came over me last night.	_____

Challenging the Limits of a Model

There are three important language patterns that artificially restrict your experience: (1) absolute, (2) imposed limits, and (3) imposed values.

Absolutes are over-generalizations typified by words such as *always, never, all, none, everyone,* and *no one.* You can challenge a speaker's absolutes by exaggerating them with your tone of voice and by adding even more absolutes. When a speaker says, "My mother's always late," you can reply, "She's *always* and *forever* late?" Another way to challenge someone who makes a statement containing an absolute is to ask him if he's ever had an experience that contradicts his generalization. "Can you think of even one time when your mother was punctual?" The following are statements containing absolutes and questions to challenge them:

Statements	Questions
I'm always in pain.	You're *absolutely always* in pain?
Nobody cares about me.	There's *not a single* person on earth who cares about you? *Not even one?*
I never win.	There has *never been* an instance when you won?
She's always brusque with me.	She's *always* brusque with you? Do you ever recall her being cordial?

Exercise: Write down questions challenging the following statements containing absolutes.

Statements	Questions
I can never get a date.	_____
I'm always the last one to be served.	_____
Everybody says he's right.	_____
All the good ones are married.	_____
Everyone at the party thought I was foolish.	_____

Imposed. Limits are words or phrases that suggest that you have no choice. Examples of such words are *can't, must, have to, should, ought, it's necessary,* and *it's impossible.*

Imposed limits fall in two categories. The *I can't* and *it's impossible* category defines reality in such a way that certain options are absolutely excluded. The *must, should,* and *have to* category often carries the weight of a moral imperative. "Should" statements are extremely limiting because they imply that you're a bad person if you break the rules that the statements impose.

Many people hem themselves in with unquestioned limits. You might overhear a man say, "I can't speak in front of any kind of crowd." His model of the world says that such experiences are out of the question, completely beyond his capability. You can challenge his imposed limits by asking either "What would happen if you did speak to a large crowd?" or "What stops you from speaking to a large crowd?" The first question propels the speaker into the future to imagine the possible consequences of his actions, and the second forces the speaker into the past to discover the experience on which his fear is based.

Shoulds and moral imperatives can be challenged in the same way. A friend remarks, "I have to finish my work before I can relax." You might challenge that imposed limit by asking, "What would happen if you didn't finish your work before relaxing?" The following are statements containing imposed limits and questions that challenge them.

Statements	Questions
I'd like to go, but I can't.	What stops you from going?
You must not say things like that.	What will happen if I say things like that to you?
I have to do what my boss says.	What would happen if you didn't do what your boss says?
I'd like to go but I can't.	What stops you from going?
I can't cook.	What about cooking is too difficult for you?

Exercise: Write down questions that challenge the following imposed limits:

Statements	Questions
I can't get very far with my homework.	_____

I can't wait for her any longer. _____

You have to get a more
mature attitude.   _____

You must think of their
feelings.   _____

You ought to spend your
time doing something
really productive.   _____

Imposed values. When people state a generalization about the world, they make a judgment based on their personal model. Essentially they are taking values that they find appropriate to themselves and applying them to other people. You can tell that you are encountering imposed values when you hear people using global labels: stupid, money-hungry, corrupt, gutless, ugly. People who rely on this language pattern are typically unaware that there is any legitimate, alternative viewpoint. Challenging such statements forces the speaker to own his or her personal opinions, and at the same time acknowledge that the rest of the world has its own values and opinions. When the speaker says, "All modern art is a waste of paint," you can ask, "For whom is all modern art a waste of paint?" The following are statements containing imposed values, and questions that challenge them:

Statements	*Questions*
That's a worthless piece of junk.	For whom is it worthless?
Communism is evil.	To whom does communism seem evil?
Walking out was the wrong thing to do.	For whom was walking out wrong?
Sex therapy is stupid.	For whom is sex therapy foolish or ineffective?

Exercise: Write down questions challenging the following statements containing imposed values.

Statements	*Questions*
Rock and roll is just noise.	_____
Jogging is the best form of exercise.	_____

Fanaticism is dangerous.   _____

Anger is an unnecessary
emotion.   _____

Politicians are fools.   _____

Challenging Distortions in a Model

When your personal model of the world is distorted, it cuts you off from considering other alternatives and your experience becomes severely impoverished. Three language patterns that distort reality are (1) cause and effect errors, (2) mind reading, and (3) presuppositions.

Cause and effect errors result from the belief that one person can cause another to experience some emotion or inner state and that the second person has no choice about how he or she will respond. When you challenge this belief, you are asking whether this causal connection does indeed exist, and whether the second person does have any alternative ways of responding. For example, if your mother says, "I'm anxious because you're leaving," you can challenge her statement with "How does my leaving make you anxious?" The point is to gently remind her that she is responsible for her own feelings and that she generates her own responses to events. The following are statements that contain cause and effect errors, and questions that challenge them:

Statements	*Questions*
You make me sad.	How did I make you sad? What am I doing that you get sad about?
Your baby gives me a headache.	Gives you a headache? Did my baby actually make your head hurt?
Your silence makes me angry.	How does my silence anger you? What is it about my silence that irritates you?
The work bored me.	What was it about the work that you found boring?

Exercise: Write down questions challenging the statements containing cause and effect errors:

Statements	Questions
I'm tense whenever you're near me.	_____
He infuriates me.	_____
Your procrastination frustrates me.	_____
Your judgmental attitude ties me in knots.	_____
You make me tired.	_____

Mind reading refers to the belief that one person can know what another is thinking or feeling without direct communication with that person. It distorts your model of the world because it invariably leads you to form beliefs that are simply untrue. Mind reading depends on a process called projection—the expectation that people feel and react in the same way as the mind reader. The mind reader doesn't watch or listen closely enough to notice that others are actually experiencing the world differently. The challenge for the language pattern involving mind reading is: "How do you know such-and-such?" Speakers then have the opportunity to become aware of and question assumptions that they previously took for granted. The following statements contain mind-reading errors and questions to challenge them:

Statements	Questions
My co-workers think I'm lazy.	How do you know that your co-workers think you're lazy?
My husband knows what I want.	How do you know that your husband is aware of what you want?
He only married her for her money.	What makes you feel that he only married her for her money?
Please don't be mad at me.	What gives you the impression that I'm mad at you?

Exercise: Write down questions challenging the following statements containing mind-reading errors.

Statements	Questions
Tony doesn't like me.	_____

You think that I don't care
about the kids.   _____

I think that you're
pretty anxious.   _____

You're expecting too much
of me.   _____

When she talks fast like that,
she's angry.   _____

Presuppositions are parts of a statement that must be true in order for
the whole statement to be valid. "Since you got so jealous the last time
we went dancing, let's not go again." The conclusion of this statement,
'let's not go again," can only be valid if the assumption that "you got
jealous" is true. To challenge this statement, you could ask, "In what
way did I seem to you to be jealous?" The following are statements that
contain presuppositions and the questions which challenge them.

Statements	*Questions*
If Tom would only listen to me, then I would tell him how I really feel.	How does Tom seem not to listen to you?
If you really loved me, you'd spend more time with me.	In what ways do I seem not to really love you?
I'm in serious trouble, so I need an immediate appointment.	In what way is the trouble serious?
Your dog menaces my children, either lock him up or put him to sleep.	How does my dog seem to menace your children?
She's not much of a mother and the children suffer for it.	What does she do that indicates she's a poor mother?

Exercise: The following statements contain presuppositions. Write
down opposite each statement a question that would challenge the assumption it makes.

Statements	*Questions*
If you're going to be greedy, let's stop playing cards.	_____

Since he's so cheap I won't
ask him for a loan.   _____

I wouldn't work overtime if
they didn't really need me.   _____

If Stella weren't so lazy,
she would have gotten
better grades.   _____

If you cared more, you'd
keep the lawn nice.   _____

The list of language patterns presented in this chapter was adapted from Bandler and Grinder's *Meta-Model*. Some of the terms were changed to promote simplicity and ease in memorization. Additional challenges were also included.

Some Final Clarifications

The clarifying techniques you've learned in this chapter shouldn't be used excessively. Constantly demanding clarification of the casual remarks others make would be obnoxious. But the techniques *should* be used when someone's statement doesn't make sense, is vague, or misses some vital piece of information. Consistent use of absolutes, mind reading, and other language patterns indicates that the speaker's model is limited or distorted, and you should judiciously use clarifying techniques. Be gentle. Explore or challenge with an attitude of interest rather than hostility.

How do you know when a speaker's statement is incomplete? You may feel puzzled, you may see an incomplete or fuzzy picture, or the statement may not sound right. Any of these signals indicate that something's missing, that you need more pieces to fit the puzzle together. Clarifying techniques keep you from jumping to your own conclusions and help to get you back in tune with the speaker. Rather than filling in the holes with your own model, you're really trying to understand the speaker's.

Exercise: Have a friend make statements that contain one of the language pattern errors. Challenge each statement with an appropriate question. Initially, your friend should make several statements in a row containing the same type of error. Later he or she can make statements with language pattern errors in random order.

Summary Chart

Language Pattern Error	Example of Error	Clarifying Questions
Understanding a Model		
Deletions	I'm disgusted!	About what or whom?
Vague Pronouns	They say a housing shortage is coming.	Who says that?
Vague Verbs	Bill made me lose.	How exactly did Bill make you lose?
Nominalizations	I'm feeling regret.	What are you regretting?
	The marriage is empty.	What about the marriage makes you feel empty?
Challenging the Limits of a Model		
Absolutes	I'm always left out.	Absolutely, always? Can you recall ever being included?
Imposed Limits	You can't succeed.	What would happen if I did? What or who would stop me from succeeding?
	You must visit her.	What would happen if I didn't?
Imposed Values	Conservatives are idiots.	To whom are conservative beliefs idiotic?
Challenging Distortions in a Model		
Cause and Effect Errors	You've made me very unhappy.	Could I make you feel that way? What have I done that you've been unhappy with?
Mind reading	I can tell that Sally is jealous of me.	How do you know that Sally is jealous of you?
Presuppositions	If Jean were a more efficient worker, she wouldn't have been fired.	How specifically was Jean an inefficient worker?

9

Culture and Gender

Technology and global commerce are making the world a smaller place. Fluid immigration patterns are making your home town's population more diverse. In times like these, it's important to be aware that different cultures communicate differently. Many communication problems are caused by conflicting cultural assumptions, not by actual disagreement or ill will.

Your nationality, religion, race, class, language, and gender all contribute to a particular world view that colors everything you say, do, and hear. This chapter will shed some light on your own cultural and gender biases and help you understand others better.

To highlight differences, this chapter necessarily contains generalizations about members of different cultural groups and about men and women. Please forgive the stereotypes, and remember that exceptions always exist—there are quiet Italians, forthright Japanese, cooperative men, and competitive women.

Other Cultures

Anthropologist Edward Hall makes a helpful distinction between *low context* and *high context* cultures.

The United States, Canada, Europe, Israel, and Australia are examples of low-context cultures. Individuals from these parts of the world prefer a direct, literal style of interaction, and people are expected to say more or less exactly what they mean. Low-context cultures value self-expression skills such as clarity, fluency, and brevity. Speakers often seek to convince and persuade their listeners.

The Orient, the Arab world, and much of Africa are examples of high-context cultures. The prefered style of interaction is an indirect one in which meaning is carried less by the literal meaning of the words and more by contextual clues such as the place, time, and situation and the relationships between the speakers. High-context cultures value harmony, subtlety, sensitivity, and tact more than clarity. Speakers often seek to connect with their listeners.

Differences between low and high context cultures cause conflicts of meaning, pacing, volume, gesture, space, and touch.

Meaning

To the Japanese, a profuse apology is an expression of goodwill, part of a pattern of mutual self-depreciation that sets the tone for a discussion between equals. To Americans, an apology is an admission of guilt that puts the speaker in a one-down position. It's easy for Japanese to think that Americans are tactless oafs and for Americans to think that Japanese are passive and insecure.

Koreans are very formal. They value preserving status and class distinctions more than strict accuracy of meaning. They choose different words depending on whether they are talking to an inferior or a superior. Westerners often consider Koreans stiff and unfriendly, while Koreans consider Westerners crude, pushy, and insensitive.

When an Arab says "No thanks" to your offer of a lift back to his office, he may actually mean "Maybe . . . ask me again." Arabs tend to be more elaborate in speaking. The acceptance of an offer for a ride or a second helping at a meal is expected to go on for several interchanges. Only when he says "Oh no, absolutely not. By God, I just couldn't . . . I forbid it" can you be sure that he really means no.

Pacing

Cultures have different standards for how fast you should talk, how much you should talk, how long you should pause between ideas, and how long you should wait after someone finishes talking before you say something.

Among speakers of English, intellectual New York Jews are noted for a very fast style. They talk quickly, rarely pause, overlap each other, interrupt, finish each other's sentences, and ask "machine gun" questions faster than they can be answered. Because they speak English faster than most, Jewish New Yorkers are often stereotyped as loud, pushy, and rude.

On the other end of the continuum, Native Americans and Swedish Americans are noted for talking slowly, using few words, allowing long pauses, and seldom interrupting. Because they speak English slower than most, Native Americans and Swedish Americans are often stereotyped as dour and taciturn.

Volume and Gesture

Italians and Greeks tend to have loud discussions, with lots of arm waving and other gestures, in which each side staunchly defends a position against the other side. This is a style of conversation-by-argument that is invigorating and entertaining if you were born to it. But to staid northern Europeans or Asians, this style seems contentious and violent.

Space and Touch

Every culture has a different size of "comfort zone" and unspoken rules about appropriate touching. Your comfort zone is the range between "too close" and "too far" in which you feel comfortable talking to people. You might be comfortable staying six feet away from a business associate, three feet from a friend, and mere inches from an intimate.

For example, Latins like to be closer to strangers than North Americans do. A Mexican mother talking about her son's broken arm to an Anglo emergency room nurse might find herself moving closer to get within comfortable range. But this feels too close to the nurse, and so she retreats half a step, creating a gap which the Mexican tries to shrink by moving closer, which again makes the Anglo uncomfortable, and so on. The mother thinks "She's avoiding me" and the nurse thinks "She's pushy." Neither is right and neither knows why.

In some cultures, it's okay to touch somebody's arm to make a point, and in other cultures this same gesture is considered rude. In some cultures, straight men routinely kiss or hold hands with each other in public, while in other cultures that same behavior means that you're gay.

Gender

You can live a lifetime without having to negotiate a treaty with a Korean diplomat or close a million-dollar deal with a Japanese executive. But you have to deal with members of the opposite sex every day. The most common and potentially hurtful cultural clashes occur between men and women.

Deborah Tannen, author of *That's Not What I Meant!* and *You Just Don't Understand*, makes this point repeatedly: that the differences between female and male communication styles are cultural differences. Boys and girls grow up in different cultures. Tannen and others have studied how girls and boys communicate at all ages, from preschool to adulthood, and it's clear that men and women grow up in radically different cultures.

From the time they learn to talk, girls and women:

1. Seek connection

2. Relate symmetrically as equals

3. Prefer interdependence and cooperation

4. Decide by consensus

5. Yearn for intimacy

6. Want approval of peers

7. Speak up more in private

8. Share problems

9. Focus on details of feelings

10. Mix personal and business talk

11. Ask for help, advice, and directions

12. Give empathy and sympathy

13. Want to understand problems

On the other hand, boys and men:

1. Seek status

2. Relate asymmetrically as rivals

3. Prefer independence and autonomy

4. Decide by force, persuasion, or majority rule

5. Yearn for "space"

6. Want the respect of their peers

7. Speak up more in public

8. Keep problems to themselves

9. Focus on details of fact

10. Stick to business

11. Don't ask for help, advice, or directions

12. Give advice and analysis

13. Want to solve problems

You can argue for hours about whether these differences are innate or learned, whether they arise from nature or nurture. But few deny that the differences exist. And these differences can cause you more trouble than those between black and white, north and south, rich and poor.

What can you do about it? Men can train themselves to be more sensitive, to express feelings, and to curb their natural competitive impulses. Women can practice being more assertive, more direct, and more solution oriented.

The purpose of these efforts is not to produce men who talk like women and women who talk like men. The goal is awareness. Awareness enables you to interpret and understand the opposite gender's dialect. It allows you to avoid having stereotypical reactions when you're in conflict with the opposite gender. And it helps you to make allowances for stereotypical behaviors you encounter.

Rules of Awareness for Men

1. Make connection first. When you get home, greet your partner with a kiss and hug instead of going straight for the TV, the computer, or the refrigerator. If you're arguing and having trouble getting your point across, check to see if your partner is feeling separate, disconnected, or alone. Tell her, "Even though we're fighting right now, I still love you, and I know you love me. That doesn't change."

In a social setting, see if the lines of connection have polarized into the in-group and the out-group, or men versus women. Repair the breach with comments like "Let's not let this ruin our friendship" or "Wouldn't you agree that men and women are sincerely doing the best they can, just trying to met their needs?"

In a business setting, see whether your female colleague is feeling isolated, cut off from the team. To repair the connection, say things like "Despite our different positions on this, I think we're agreed on the overall goal and the importance of working together as a team."

2. Seek a common level. When dealing with women, take a break from dominance, rivalry, and competition. Enjoy the discussion for the mutual discoveries you make rather than strive to make winning points. Equality and cooperation are more important to women than who wins every round. Try to see things eye to eye, and feel things heart to heart.

3. Cooperate. Suggest doing things together, even if you'd rather do them by yourself. For many women, a task done cooperatively over an hour's time is a pleasure, whereas the same task done alone in thirty minutes is just a chore.

4. Decide by consensus. Men like to vote on things, decide by majority rule, and get on with it. Women like to take more time and discuss things thoroughly until everybody agrees on a plan of action. Develop patience. Remind yourself that she's not "talking it to death," she's building consensus, finding ways to cooperate, building bridges, nurturing connections.

5. Hang in there. Do you ever feel like your partner is smothering you? Always pushing for more togetherness? Crowding into your space? When you feel smothered, remind yourself that she probably isn't trying to control and contain you. She's pursuing you because she wants more intimacy. The more you retreat and demand "space," the more she will be frustrated in her need for intimacy and be tempted to redouble the pursuit. Learn to tolerate just a little more contact than initially feels comfortable. And when you do need time to yourself, say so—don't just withdraw or use harsh words to push her away.

6. Express appreciation. Whenever a woman does something that you appreciate, say so out loud. Remember that women want the approval and esteem of others, without being hung up on questions of status and prestige. For example, if a man and a woman receive the same pay raise and a sincere "well done" from the boss, the woman is likely to rate the boss's statement as most gratifying for the approval it confers, while the man is likely to count the pay raise as most gratifying for the increased status it confers.

7. Chat. Women complain that men are silent oafs who can ride with them for two solid hours in the car without saying a word. Men complain that women are always chattering away about nothing. That's because women talk to maintain a sense of connection and intimacy, while men tend to talk to convey information, period.

So when she asks you a leading question, answer it fully. Tell her what you're thinking or feeling, even if your thoughts seem obvious or irrelevant. What you say doesn't have to be profound—a string of trivialities can be a kind of glue that maintains the connection between you.

8. Share your problems. Let women know what's bothering you. It's not an admission of weakness. They will think more of you, not less. And they don't tend to pester you with advice and unrealistic solutions, the way some men will.

9. Include feelings. If you want to become twice as interesting to women as you are now, start answering their question "How are you?" with a true statement of how you're feeling. Instead of saying "I'm fine, everything's okay," try something like "Well, I've been depressed lately. My work's not going smoothly, and I'm worried about my kids."

10. Mix personal and business talk. Reveal a little more of your personal life at work or school or church. You don't have to spill your guts—just be willing to share a few details about your home situation, your opinions, your feelings, or your outside interests.

11. Ask for help and advice. This is not an admission of weakness or inferiority. Think of it as a way of sharing the burden of problems and gathering information on other unique points of view.

12. Listen with empathy. When a woman starts talking to you, shut up for a while. Make eye contact. Nod and say "I see" or "I understand," even if doing so feels weird at first. Imagine what it's like to be this woman and try to experience her problems from her point of view. Paraphrase what you think you heard, to make sure you are getting the full picture. Ask questions for clarification.

13. Offer understanding instead of advice. Men love to fix things. At the first hint of a problem, they go into a problem-solving mode. For a man, solving a problem means you're competent and smart, and it makes the problem go away so that you don't have to deal with it anymore.

Often a woman doesn't want a solution, just understanding. If you try to solve her problem for her, she gets frustrated. Stifle the urge to fix things quickly and just listen for a while. Try to hear the feelings behind the complaint. Offering an understanding ear will usually work better than jumping in with clever advice.

Rules of Awareness for Women

1. Notice who's on top. When you're talking in a group with several men, notice who is jockeying for position, who is trying to impress, who is comparing, who is trying to get the biggest laugh or garner the most support for his position. Being aware of any ongoing struggles for status will help you make more sense out of male conversation. It will help you participate with more skill, because you'll know whom your remarks are supporting or opposing, whose status you are enhancing or threatening, and how your own status is likely to be viewed in the group.

This isn't to say that all male conversation is about status, but you need to be able to recognize chest thumping when you run across it.

2. Make your position clear. Men like to know where you stand, even if you disagree with them. Having ideas and sides defined clearly and maintaining their status and autonomy are more important to them than cozy feelings of connectedness. State your opinions, feelings, and needs clearly, and you'll stand a better chance of getting men's respect and cooperation. Remember that a certain amount of friendly rivalry feels comfortable and natural to most men.

3. Act independently. Some couples can work together cooperatively, collaborating on every detail of a new business venture, a garden, a wedding, the kids' summer camp plans, or a remodeling project. But sooner or later you'll want to do something your partner just isn't interested in doing with you. When that happens, be prepared to act independently. Don't waste time and effort nagging him to help.

Men like being in complete control and doing things by themselves. They tend to respect and appreciate women who can do the same.

4. Vote on it. If you want to win the respect and gratitude of men in a small-group setting, try saying this: "Why don't we cut the discussion short and just vote on it?"

Men like to make decisions quickly and don't care as much as women do about everyone coming to agree on a common solution.

5. Protect his "space." Be sensitive to your partner's need for "space." Carefully observe where the boundaries are. Notice how close you can get before he starts feeling pursued. If he withdraws, remember that he's most likely choosing autonomy rather than rejecting you. Talk plainly about your need for more closeness, rather than make repeated forays into his space. Men take words and actions literally and will respond to a direct request more readily than they will pick up on symbolic behavior.

When you feel disconnected and taken for granted, remind yourself that men don't naturally think about buying little gifts and giving spontaneous hugs. It takes a huge effort for most men to make the nurturing gestures that come naturally to women.

6. Express respect. Men often want respect more than approval or agreement. If you can honestly say to a man "I don't agree with you, but I respect your conviction," you stand a good chance of eventually bringing him around to your side or achieving a workable compromise.

Bear in mind that "respect" in this context refers to genuine admiration of someone's virtues, or an appreciation of everybody's human dignity. Except as necessary for survival, no one should have to express the kind of "respect" that is based on fear of someone in a position of power.

7. Speak up more in public. Overcome your reluctance and make your points more often and more forcefully in public. There is good feminist politics—and you'll also reap some real interpersonal and self-esteem rewards.

8. Cultivate silence. Although many women enjoy talk for its own sake, fewer men are into chatting. Learn to appreciate the company of your own unuttered thoughts. Don't fall into the trap of assuming that because your male companion is silent, he is depressed, distant, or uninterested in you. It's very likely that he's silent because there is no relevant information that he feels compelled to convey to you.

Men congregate around tasks. They rarely just sit and talk to each other or to women. If you want a man to talk to you, look for a task that you can do together: planting a garden, painting a bedroom, reorganizing a bookshelf.

9. Focus on the facts. When the mechanic tells you what's wrong with the car, when the insurance agent calls about the flood coverage, when the painter explains his estimate—pay attention to the details. Write everything down. Ask for explanations of unfamiliar terms. Forget the emotional overtones, forget whether you like these people or you think they like you, and *zero in on the facts*. Then when your husband or boyfriend or father or brother wants to know what's what, you can tell him without sounding like his idea of a "typical scatterbrained female."

10. Stick to business. At work, at school, at church, or at club meetings, try sticking to business more of the time. Talk less about your personal life and more about the matter at hand. The men in the group will appreciate it, and the group will probably get more done.

11. Ask for help, advice, directions. Men love to fix things, give their opinions, and tell you where to go. So when you need and want help, you might as well ask for it.

Here's a conflict so common it's a cliche: you're riding in a car with a man driving, he's lost, but he doesn't want to ask for directions. This is the time for you to say "Why don't you pull over at that convenience store? I'd like a cup of coffee, and while I'm in there, I can ask for directions." That way, he's not stopping for directions, he's stopping for coffee. And he can wait in the car while you bravely risk humiliation and ask for directions. (But remember to get all the details straight, or you'll have another typical male-female argument.)

12. Ask for empathy. On the other hand, if you want your partner to listen to you with empathy and compassion, to really understand how you feel, ask him for exactly that. Otherwise, he may flood you with a lot of unwanted advice, reacting in a stereotypical "Mr. Fixit" mode.

13. Focus on joint problem solving. Show an "I can figure this out" attitude. Work together with your partner to brainstorm many possible solutions to a problem. Look at the probable outcomes of each solution and pick the best one. Decide on a first step and when to do it. Objectively evaluate the results later. This systematic approach will work much better than complaining to your partner and waiting for him to come up with a solution.

Awareness Exercises

Changing your pattern. Pick a conflict situation that comes up for you with someone of the opposite gender. Step one is to write out a bit of dialogue that is typical of the problematic interaction. Just put down the usual sort of thing that you say and the other person says back. Here's a dialogue that Jim remembered having with his wife.

Rema: Are you concerned with what the teacher told us about Billy?

Me: Not really.

Rema: He's so anxious about everythingv. He's terrified to make a mistake.

Me: Hc's okay. Just tell him you expect at least one mistake on everything he does.

Rema: Come on! You're just brushing this off. I'm serious. Don't you see he's heading for trouble?

Me: Just *insist* on him screwing up a little. Tell him he has to spell some stuff wong. Or maybe forget to do his homework one night.

Rema: That's ridiculous. I'm worried. There's some way he doesn't feel secure.

Me: What can I tell you? Just relax. Don't worry about him. We should give him a quota, that he has to make X number of mistakes a week.

Rema then explodes

Step two is to review the thirteen ways men and women display differect patterns of communication and decide which ones are most clearly exemplified by the dialogue you've just written. When Jim looked at his dialogue and reviewed the different communication styles for men and women, he saw that his pattern of advice giving was probably at odds with Rema's need for support and shared concern. Jim also realized that he was secretly worried about his son as well—not so much that Billy was anxious about mistakes, but that he seemed timid and effeminate. Here was a second gender difference in communication styles. Jim tended to keep his concern to himself and leave Rema with the impression that she was the only one who worried.

The third step is to rewrite your part of the diaglogue using the communication style of the opposite gender. Jim tried to figure out what he could say differenlty if he stopped keeping problems to himself and stopped giving advice. Here's how Jim rewrote his dialogue.

Rema: Are you concerned with what the teacher told us about Billy?

Me: Yes, I'm a little worried about Billy.

Rema: He's so anxious about everything. He's terrified to make a mistake.

Me: That's true. But what worries me most is how timid he is, how he donsn't stand up for himself.

Rema: So you're worried too?

Me: I guess I am. I can see that what the teacher said really shook you up. It's kind of disturbing when someone else sees that he has a problem.

Jim saw that giving up his problem-solving mode would allow him to express his concern and validate Rema's feelings. He would also be able to share his worry instead of keeping everything to himself.

The fourth step is to change one or two of your communication patterns in real life. Jim decided he was going to try to share more of what he felt with Rema and cut out all advice giving unless asked. The next time Rema brought up a problem, he carefully avoided suggesting solutions. He acknowledged how upsetting the problem was instead of trying to fix it. And he made an effort to share his own relevant feelings and concerns.

The "as if" exercise. This challenging but extremely valuable exercise requires you to spend one entire day communicating "as if" you were the opposite gender. The first step is to go back to the rules of awareness for men and women. Look at the suggested guidelines for your gender and mark the ones that are *least* typical of your communication patterns. To act "as if" you were the opposite gender will require you to pay the most attention to these marked items. For example, if you marked "cooperate" and "decide by consensus" at least typical of your communication style, these items would be the main focus for your "as if" day. You'd be trying to share tasks, rather than doing them yourself. You'd be building agreement for all parties involved, finding ways to cooperate, and looking for common needs and concerns.

As another example, if your least typical patterns were "make your position clear" and "focus on the facts," your "as if" day would have you focusing on details of fact, while stating your positions and opinions more directly.

At the end of your "as if" day, evaluate your communications with the opposite gender. Were the outcomes different? Was there less conflict? Did you feel more appreciated? Or did you feel less comfortable, less authentic? If you weigh the positive outcomes of your new communication patterns versus the cost, which side of the scale tips heaviest? Was the reward worth the effort? Or are the benefits too slight to continue this experiment?

If you find some benefit from the new communication styles, select four target situations during the next week where they might be helpful. Make a brief plan for how you'll implement them. For example, "I'll tell Bob exactly why I don't like that cheap linoleum, and I'll work with him to come up with some alternative ways to save money" or "I'm just going to listen to Sarah when she complains about the job. I'll acknowledge how hard it is. I'll ask her questions and show an interest without trying to fix anything."

III

Conflict Skills

10

Assertiveness
Training

Assertiveness training teaches you to express your feelings, thoughts, and wishes, and to stand up for your legitimate rights without violating the rights of others. Assertiveness is a skill you can acquire, not a personality trait that some people are born with and others are not. Like aggression and passivity, assertiveness is a social behavior that can be learned.

Nobody is consistently assertive. You may be assertive with your children in one instance, aggressive with them in another, and passive in still another. You might have no trouble being assertive with your family, yet find it almost impossible to be assertive with strangers. Assertiveness training can expand the number of social situations in which you can respond assertively rather than passively or aggressively.

Learning to be assertive doesn't mean that you must always behave assertively. There are times when it is entirely appropriate to be aggressive, as it is when your life or property is being threatened. There are also times when it's appropriate to be passive, such as when a judge is lecturing you. Learning to be assertive means that you can choose when and where to assert yourself.

Your Legitimate Rights

You learned a set of beliefs early in your life to help guide your social conduct. These beliefs are essentially a set of rules about "good" and "bad" behavior passed on to you by your parents and later role models. While these rules helped you get along with the people you grew up with, they are not cast in bronze and lightning won't strike you down if you decide to act differently.

Read the following list of traditional assumptions. Do any of them remind you of rules you learned as a child? Do you still believe that they apply to you as an adult? Listed beside each traditional assumption is a statement of your legitimate right as an adult. These rights are a reminder that you have a choice about what you believe and that you are no longer an unquestioning child, but rather an adult with alternatives.

Mistaken Traditional Assumptions	Your Legitimate Rights
1. It is selfish to put your needs before others' needs.	You have a right to put yourself first, sometimes.
2. It is shameful to make mistakes. You should have an appropriate response for every occasion.	You have a right to make mistakes.
3. If you can't convince others that your feelings are reasonable, then your feelings must be wrong.	You have a right to be the final judge of your feelings and accept them as legitimate.
4. You should respect the views of others, especially if they are in a position of authority. Keep your differences of opinion to yourself. Listen and learn.	You have a right to have your own opinions and convictions.
5. You should always try to be logical and consistent.	You have a right to change your mind or decide on a different course of action.
6. You should be flexible and adjust. Others have good reasons for their actions and it's not polite to question them.	You have a right to protest any treatment or criticism that feels bad to you.
7. You should never interrupt people. Asking questions reveals your stupidity to others.	You have a right to interrupt in order to ask for clarification.
8. Things could get even worse, don't rock the boat.	You have a right to negotiate for change.

9. You shouldn't take up others' valuable time with your problems.	You have a right to *ask* for help or emotional support.
10. People don't want to hear that you feel bad, so keep it to yourself.	You have a right to feel and express pain.
11. When someone takes the time to give you advice, you should take it very seriously. They are often right.	You have a right to ignore the advice of others.
12. Knowing that you did something well is its own reward. People don't like showoffs. Successful people are secretly disliked and envied. Be modest when complimented.	You have a right to receive recognition for your work and achievements.
13. You should always try to accommodate others. If you don't, they won't be there when you need them.	You have a right to say no.
14. Don't be antisocial. People are going to think you don't like them if you say you'd rather be alone instead of with them.	You have a right to be alone, even if others would prefer your company.
15. You should always have a good reason for what you feel and do.	You have a right not to have to justify yourself to others.
16. When someone is in trouble, you should always help them.	You have a right not to take responsibility for someone else's problem.
17. You should be sensitive to the needs and wishes of others, even when they are unable to tell you what they want.	You have a right not to have to anticipate others' needs and wishes.
18. It's not nice to put people off. If questioned, give an answer.	You have a right to choose not to respond to a situation.

Adapted from *The Relaxation & Stress Reduction Workbook*, 4nd ed., by Davis, Eshelman and McKay.

Identifying the Three Basic Styles of Communication

The first step in assertiveness training is learning to distinguish between assertive, aggressive, and passive behaviors.

Passive Style

When you are communicating passively, you don't directly express your feelings, thoughts, and wishes. You may try to communicate them indirectly by frowning, crying, or whispering something under your breath. Or you may withhold your feelings and wishes entirely.

In the passive style you tend to smile a lot and subordinate your needs to those of others. You also probably do more than your share of listening. If you do speak up directly, you make disclaimers such as "I'm no expert.... I'm really not sure.... I really shouldn't be saying this, but.... " You find it very difficult to make requests. When someone asks you to do something that you don't want to do, you're inclined to do it or make an excuse rather than say no.

A passive speaking style includes a soft, weak, even wavering voice. Pauses and hesitations are common. You are likely to be at a loss for words. You may ramble, be vague, and use the phrases "I mean" and "you know" often. You frequently rely on others to guess what you want to say. Your posture is likely to be slouched, and perhaps you will lean against something for support. Your hands are apt to be cold, sweaty, and fidgety. Eye contact is difficult for you; you tend to look down or away. Because you are often not saying what you mean, you don't look like you mean what you say.

Aggressive Style

In the aggressive style, you are quite capable of stating how you feel, what you think, and what you want, but often at the expense of others' rights and feelings. You tend to humiliate others by using sarcasm or humorous put-downs. You are likely to go on the attack when you don't get your way, and you stir up guilt and resentment in others by pointing a finger of blame. Your sentences often begin with "You ... " followed by an attack or a negative label. You use absolute terms such as "always" and "never" and describe things in a way that implies that you're always right and superior.

When you are behaving aggressively, you tend to move with an air of superiority and strength. Your style may run the gamut from cold and "deadly quiet" to flippant and sarcastic to loud and shrill. Your eyes are narrowed and expressionless. Your posture is that of a solid rock: feet planted apart, hands on hips, jaw clenched and jutting out, gestures rigid, abrupt, and intimidating. Sometimes you point your finger or make a fist. You are so intent on being right that you don't really hear what others are saying, even when you ask them a direct question.

Assertive Style

When you communicate assertively, you make direct statements regarding your feelings, thoughts, and wishes. You stand up for your rights and take into account the rights and feelings of others. You listen attentively, and let other people know that you have heard them. You are open to negotiation and compromise, but not at the expense of your own rights and dignity. You can make direct requests and direct refusals. You can give and receive compliments. You can start and stop a conversation. You can deal effectively with criticism, without becoming hostile or defensive.

When you are behaving assertively, you convey an air of assured strength and empathy. Your voice is relaxed, well-modulated, and firm. While you are comfortable with direct eye contact, you don't stare. Your eyes communicate openness and honesty. Your posture is balanced and erect.

Exercise. A good way to become familiar with the passive and aggressive styles is to role-play them. But unless you're reading this book as part of a class or sharing it with friends, role playing will be difficult. Either role-play or imagine yourself acting the following parts:

1. Passive style: Pretend to be a very dependent spouse. Move one of your feet back and put your weight on it. Extend your arms, palms up. Bend over a bit so you don't get enough air to have a full, rich voice, and so you are slightly off balance. Your voice will be soft as you look up and say, "Whatever you say is all right with me. I'm just here to make you happy. I don't have any power of my own. I depend on you to make the decisions and take care of me. I'd be too vulnerable without you, so whatever you say goes. I'm sorry if I have inconvenienced you in some way. I'd offer an opinion, but it isn't worth much."

   Continue to repeat statements like these in this voice and posture for three minutes. Notice what your voice sounds like. How do you feel? How are you breathing? How are your muscles?

Most people find it exhausting to play this role. They report feeling off balance, tense, sad, vulnerable, resentful, dependent, dishonest, upset, one-down, worthless, and childish.

The major advantage of being passive is that you don't have to take responsibility for your feelings and needs. There is someone else around to make decisions and to protect you. The disadvantages are your loss of independence, your stifled needs, and your stifled feelings. It's hard sometimes to like yourself because you can't seem to change anything or express how you really feel.

People often behave passively in order to avoid conflict. The irony is that passivity creates conflict. The needs and feelings that you hide make you frustrated and angry. You have to manipulate others to get what you want. When others sense your dissatisfaction they feel attacked or pressured by it. They often resent your covert manipulations.

> 2. Aggressive style: Pretend you're an aggressive supervisor bawling out an employee. Stand up and lean forward slightly on one foot. Put one hand on your hip, and point the index finger of the other at the employee. In a loud, accusatory voice say such things as, "You never do anything right. You're always late. . . . You're always doing some stupid thing. . . . What's wrong with you? You're just a lazy s.o.b. We could rent you out as a door stop. I'm the only one around here who does anything. . . . I get sick and tired of having to make all the decisions. . . . You never take any initiative."
>
> Continue for three minutes in this vein, using plenty of "you" messages, negative labels, and sarcasm. What the other person thinks is irrelevant. Never ask a question as though you really expect an answer. Your only interest is in being right and on top. Notice how you feel. How are you breathing? How are your muscles? What do you sound like?

If you are like most people, you enjoy this role more than the passive one. You feel strong and solid. Nothing can touch you. All of your energy is directed outward. You notice that your muscles are very tense, especially in the throat, neck, and shoulders. Your voice tends to become shrill and your breath comes in little gasps as your throat tightens.

The primary objective of being aggressive is to win, to establish your primacy over others. You often achieve your short-term goals, but in the end people resist and resent you. You end up feeling frustrated and alone. You're able to vent your anger, but you always have to stay on guard. You can't express your softer feelings or your uncertainty.

Assertive Goals

Learning assertive skills is one thing. Using them is another. Before you go to the effort of learning assertive skills, ask yourself if it is really worth it to you to change. Consider the following questions carefully:

1. What do you get out of being passive?

2. What would you have to give up if you behaved assertively instead of passively?

3. What do you get from being aggressive?

4. What would you have to give up if you behaved assertively instead of aggressively?

5. What would you gain from being assertive?

Exercise. List at least five assertive goals in terms of social situations in which you would like to be assertive. Write down specifically how you would like to *behave* differently, not how you would like to feel or be. Include the people with whom you would like to behave assertively in each situation. For example, you might write:

1. I want to be able to say "no" to members of my family when they ask me to fix their cars.

2. I want to tell my husband not to change the TV channel when I am watching a program in the den.

3. I want to present my ideas on a new product in a business meeting with my boss and colleagues.

4. I want to tell my mother how I feel when she criticizes me on the phone.

5. I want to take back defective items I have bought in the store and get my money back.

Your assertive goals:

1.

2.

3.

4.

5.

Assertive Expression

If you're like most people, you tend to be fairly indirect about expressing your feelings and needs. Perhaps you were told as a child that it was self-centered to talk a lot about yourself or to overuse the pronoun "I." Or maybe you're afraid how people will react if you are direct.

When you share your thoughts indirectly, you often call on the invisible expert: "They say the economy is getting worse. Of course, some say it's getting better. But you never know who you can trust."

When you state your feelings indirectly you are apt to sound something like this: "They just laid our whole department off. Makes a man feel kind of . . . you know. You work all those years, then it's all gone in a moment. It's frustrating, but what can you do? You just go home and wait."

When you can't express your wants directly, you have to hint: "It looks like a nice day for an outing . . . what do you think?" Or worse: "The newspaper mentioned an airshow this Sunday. . . . " Or even worse: "Gee, it sure is nice out. . . . "

If you're lucky and happen to have a very attentive listener, he or she may understand your feelings and wishes. Assertive expression, however, doesn't leave communication to chance.

An assertive statement has three parts:

1. Your perspective of the situation.

2. Your feelings about the situation.

3. Your wants regarding the situation.

Here are some examples using the three components of an assertive statement:

"When I think about giving a speech I get nervous. I've been feeling butterflies in my stomach since yesterday when I told you I would talk at the next general board meeting. I realize that I don't want to give that talk. Please find someone else."

"I think we have a lot in common. Spending the evening with you has been a lot of fun. I want to get to know you better, and I'd like to go out with you again next Friday night."

"We spend a lot of time talking about your situation at work. I feel irritated and a bit bored when you come home and only discuss office politics. I'd like to have time to tell you about my day. And also to talk about us, how we're feeling about being together."

Notice that assertive statements don't blame and don't use attacking labels. When describing the situation, try to describe it objectively. Don't stack the deck so that the other person sounds like a jerk. State the facts—what happened and what was done—without slipping into negative judgments. In an assertive statement, any feelings—positive or negative—belong to the speaker. "I feel that you're self-centered" is an accusing "you statement," not a feeling, and it would never pass as an assertive expression.

When you state what you want, be specific. The more you hedge, the easier it will be to have your message ignored or misunderstood.

Exercise: For each of the situations described in your assertive goals, write three assertive "I" messages:

1. I think

   I feel

   I want

2. I think

   I feel

   I want

3. I think

   I feel

   I want

4. I think

   I feel

   I want

5. I think

   I feel

   I want

Assertive Listening

When you listen assertively, you concentrate your attention exclusively on the other person, without interrupting, so that you accurately hear feelings, opinions, and wishes. There are three steps in assertive listening:

1. Prepare. Tune into your own feelings and needs to find out if you are ready to listen. Check to be sure that the other person is also ready to speak.

2. Listen. Put your full attention on the other person. Try to hear feelings and what is wanted. If you are uncertain about the other person's feelings or wishes, ask him or her for more expression. For example, "I'm not really sure how you feel about that . . . can you tell me more? What is it that you want?

3. Acknowledge. Let the other person know that you heard his or her feelings and wants. For example, "I hear that you are exhausted from a hard day, and want to spend an hour before dinner taking a nap." You may want to acknowledge the other person's feelings by sharing your feelings about what has been said. For example, "I'm angry to hear that you had to do so much extra work today."

Combining Assertive Expressing and Listening

When you're in conflict with someone and you both have strong feelings, the two of you can take turns using assertive listening and expressing.

Many problems can be solved simply by stating clearly what you each feel, think, and want. Misunderstandings are often cleared up, or solutions to problems quickly appear. Here's an example:

Paul: This house is a mess! It's maddening to come home to chaos after a long day at work.

Mary: I don't understand. . . . What's upsetting you?

Paul: I get really pissed off when I come home to a cluttered, noisy house. I want some peace and quiet when I first get in. I want to be able to walk into my study without tripping over toys and I want to spend some time alone.

Mary: I hear that you're angry because the house is noisy and chaotic when you first get home, and that you need to have some quiet time alone, and that you wish that the place could be picked up.

Paul: Yes, that's right.

Mary: Well, I have my own perspective on the problem. Ever since I took that part-time job, I haven't had time to keep this place spotless. I get exhausted and frustrated trying to work, take care of the kids, keep house, and do all my errands. I want you to help me more with the housework and the errands.

Paul: I wasn't aware you were feeling overworked to the point of exhaustion. What exactly do you want me to do?

Paul and Mary make a deal: he'll do the vacuuming and fold the clothes if she'll have the living room picked up and give him an hour to decompress when he gets home.

Exercise: With a friend or family member practice combining the assertive listening and expressing skills. Begin practicing on a small issue such as what to do next weekend. When you feel comfortable with the skills, try using them with more emotionally laden problems.

Responding to Criticism

One of the major reasons people have difficulty being assertive is that they experience criticism as rejection. This is often a leftover from childhood, when you faced criticism from a one-down position. Each time you erred, your critical parents or teachers would pass judgment on you. You were wrong. And therefore you were bad. In time you learned to feel bad each time you were criticized. You may even have learned to use criticism as a club to beat yourself until you felt guilty and wrong.

Because criticism can be so painful, you may have developed special strategies to minimize the hurts. You may respond to criticism by verbally blowing up. Or you may respond in kind, bringing up old sins to fault your critic. Couples are particularly good at this: "You say *I'm* a spend thrift? Why, you bought yourself a whole new wardrobe last year and then put on 30 pounds so you couldn't wear a stitch of it!" Some partners respond to criticism with sarcasm: "Look at Mr. Perfect who knows so much!"

If you respond to criticism passively, you may become silent, turn red, cry, or try to escape your critic as soon as possible. You might either pretend you didn't hear what was said or in order to avoid conflict quickly agree with everything the critic says. When you respond passively, you hold in your anger and hurt. As a result, you run the risk of developing such physical symptoms as headaches, gastritis, ulcers, and spastic colitis. Sitting on your feelings is also a very good way to get depressed.

Storing resentments and hurts can propel you into the "getting even" syndrome. Either consciously or unconsciously you start "forgetting" important dates, procrastinating, arriving late, going too slow or too fast, being silent, or talking nonstop in an annoying whine . . . whatever will most irritate your critic. The advantage of this tactic is that you don't have to take responsibility for how you feel and what you do. When challenged, you can respond innocently: "Who me? You've got to be kidding. You're too sensitive, " or "I'm sorry, I didn't mean it." The major disadvantage of this tactic is that your feelings and wants often get lost in the process of rationalizing and defending. Your little revenges also tend to alienate your critic and bring on more criticism.

Both the passive and the aggressive strategies for dealing with criticism can seriously disrupt your relations with others. An assertive response to criticism is based on the assumption that you are the final judge regarding your feelings, thoughts, wants, and behavior. You are also responsible for their consequences. Each individual has a different genetic heritage and life history, and therefore different expectations, likes and dislikes, and values. Your set of rules is likely to differ from those of other people, so it's understandable that you will not always agree with them. Ultimately, you are the best person to decide what's best for you.

There are three good strategies for assertively responding to criticism: acknowledgment, clouding, and probing.

Acknowledgment

Constructive criticism can help you improve yourself. When you make a mistake, feedback can assist you in learning how not to repeat the error. Sometimes the criticism you receive is not constructive, yet it is accurate. The other person, for his or her own reasons, is letting you know that you did something wrong.

When you receive criticism with which you agree, whether it is constructive criticism or just an unnecessary reminder, acknowledge that the critic is right. For example, "You're right, Boss, I do misspell a lot of words, and I could use a dictionary at my desk." "Yes, I don't have the report in that was due last week." "Yes, I was half an hour late for work today."

Don't fall into the trap of making excuses or apologizing for your behavior. This is an automatic response left over from childhood when you accidentally spilled milk, soiled your clothes, or came home fifteen minutes late, and your parents asked, "Why did you do that?" They expected a reasonable answer, and you learned to supply an excuse. As an adult, you choose sometimes to give an explanation for your actions, but you don't have to. Stop and ask yourself if you really want to, or if you are just reacting out of an old habit. For example, you might say, "Yes, Jack, I haven't submitted that report that was due last week," and decide not to give Jack any explanation, since he's your peer and not in charge of when you get your work done.

On the other hand, when responding to your boss you wouldn't merely acknowledge that you were "half an hour late this morning." Since you value your job, you hasten to explain: "My car battery was dead and I had to ask a neighbor to jump it."

Clouding

Clouding is a useful technique for dealing with nonconstructive, manipulative criticism with which you disagree. It provides a quick way to dispense with statements that have a grain of truth in them but are intended mostly as put-downs. When you use clouding you find something in the critical comment to agree with while inwardly sticking to your own point of view. This calms critics down and gets them out of the "win/lose" game so that you can either communicate about more important things or end the conversation.

You may think that clouding is manipulative. It is. But it's better than the aggressive or passive alternatives. Although it does not require elaborate rehearsal, it does require that you listen carefully to find something that you can honestly agree with. There are three ways that you can agree with your critic:

Agreeing in part. Find some part of what the critic is saying that you agree with, and acknowledge that they are right about that part. Ignore the rest of the criticism. Modify any words the critic uses that are sheer exaggeration, such as "always" and "never." Rephrase the sentences that you almost agree with, but do not distort the essence of the critic's original meaning.

Critic: You're always working. You think the world would fall apart if you took a day off.

You: Yes, I do work a lot.

Critic: You never have time for your friends anymore. You've become driven and obsessed by work.

You: You're right, I don't have much time for my friends right now.

Agreeing in probability. You agree in probability when there's some chance that your critic is right. Even if the odds are one in a thousand, you can make replies such as "It may be. . . . " or "You could be right. . . . " Using the last example, you could respond to the critic with "It may be that I work too much," or "It could be that I don't have time for my friends anymore."

Agreeing in principle. Sometimes you can agree with the logic of your critic, without agreeing with his premise. You can agree that "If X, then Y" and still not admit that X is true.

Critic: If you don't study more than you do, you're going to
           fail your classes.

You: You're right, if I don't study, I will fail my classes.

Probing

Assertive probing is useful when you can't tell if the criticism is constructive or manipulative, when you don't understand the criticism, or when you think you're not getting the whole story. Criticism is often a way of avoiding important feelings or wishes, so if you're confused by a critical comment, probe for what's underneath it.

To use probing, pick out the part of the criticism that you think the critic feels most strongly about. Generally this will be something that affects his or her self-interest. Ask, "What is it that bothers you about . . . ?" and then restate the part of the criticism you think is most important to the critic. If necessary, ask the critic to provide a specific example. Listen to the critic's response carefully to determine what he or she feels, thinks, and wants. Continue to probe, saying, "What is it that bothers you about . . . ?" until you are satisfied that you understand the critic's intent. Don't use phrases such as "So what's the matter this time?" "What's wrong with what I did?" or "What's bothering you?" These make you sound defensive and will deter the critic from expressing authentic feelings and wants.

Here's an example of effective probing:

Critic: You're just not pulling your weight around here.
           Your work is half-assed.

You: What is it about my work that bothers you?

Critic: Well, everybody else is working like a dog—doing
           overtime. You waltz out of here every night at five
           o'clock.

You: What is it that bothers you about me leaving the
           office on time when other people work overtime?

Critic: I hate working overtime myself. But the work has to
           be done. I'm responsible to see that it is, and I get
           angry when I see you just working by the clock.

You: What is it that bothers you when I work by the clock?

Critic: When you leave, somebody else has to finish your
           work. I want you to stick around until it's done.

You: I see. I appreciate you explaining the situation to me.

In this case, probing got you to a clear understanding of the critic's gripe, and a clear request for you to do something about it. If your critic had continued to put you down in vague terms, you could have turned to clouding.

Exercise: Write assertive responses that exemplify acknowledgment, clouding, and probing for each of the following criticisms:

1. "If you drive like a madman, we're going to have an accident. You're in too much of a hurry."

   Acknowledgment:

   Clouding:

   Probing:

   Possible responses:
   Acknowledgment: "I guess I'm being a little reckless."
   Clouding: "It's true I'm in a hurry."
   Probing: "What about my driving bothers you?"

2. "You spend a lot of time with your Bonsai trees, but very little else gets your attention around here."

   Acknowledgment:

   Clouding:

   Probing:

   Possible responses:
   Acknowledgment: "I've let a lot of things slide to pursue that hobby. Too many. I think you're right."
   Clouding: "It's true that some things don't get attention while I'm working on my trees."
   Probing: "What don't I pay attention to that bothers you?"

3. "You never really get involved. You bail out of a relationship at the first sign of trouble. One harsh word and you're gone."

   Acknowledgment:

   Clouding:

   Probing:

Possible responses:
Acknowledgment: "You're right. I don't seem to get deeply involved with anyone."
Clouding: "It's true that arguing and anger frighten me."
Probing: "What bothers you about my not getting involved?"

Special Assertive Strategies

Broken Record

The broken record is a useful technique to use when you want to say no or otherwise set limits with someone who is having difficulty getting your message. You can use it to say no to your five-year-old, to tell a door-to-door salesperson that you're not interested in buying the product, or to inform your enthusiastic hostess that you really don't want a drink. The broken record can also be an effective way of telling others what you want when their own wishes are blinding them to seeing yours—for instance, when telling your husband that you prefer to go out for French food instead of Mexican, when telling your teen-aged son that you want him home by midnight, or when you want to tell your landlord to fix the leaky plumbing.

The broken record is most handy in situations where an explanation would provide the other person with an opportunity to drag out a pointless argument. It has five steps:

1. Clarify in your own mind exactly what you want or don't want. Be aware of your feelings, your thoughts about the situation, and your rights.

2. Formulate a short, specific, easy-to-understand statement about what you want. Keep it to one sentence if you can. Offer no excuses, no explanations. Avoid saying "I can't. . . . " This is an excuse of the worst kind. The other person will probably return with "Of course you can," and then proceed to tell you how. It's much simpler, more direct, and more honest to say "I don't want to. . . . " Review your statement in your mind. Try to get rid of any loopholes which the other person could use to further his or her own argument.

3. Use body language to support your statement. Stand or sit erect, look the other person in the eye, keep your hands quietly at your sides.

4. Calmly and firmly repeat your statement as many times as necessary for the person to get your message and to realize that you won't change your mind. The other person will probably come up with several excuses for not going along with your wishes. He or she may

simply say no again and again. But most people run out of no's and excuses eventually. Children and salespersons are particularly persistent, but even they will bow to a consistently repeated clear statement. Don't change your broken record unless the other person finds a serious loophole in it.

5. You may choose to briefly acknowledge the other person's ideas, feelings, or wishes before returning to your broken record. "I understand you're upset, but I don't want to work any more overtime." "I hear what you want, but I don't want to do any more overtime." Don't allow yourself to become sidetracked by the other person's statements.

Here's a dialogue that exemplifies the broken record:

Customer: I bought this blouse here a couple of weeks ago and I want to return it and get my money back.

Salesperson: Do you have a receipt?

Customer: Yes. (*She shows it to the salesperson.*)

Salesperson: It says you bought the blouse over a month ago. That's too long. How can you expect us to take back something you bought so long ago?

Customer: I understand I bought it a month ago and I want to return it and get my money back.

Salesperson: This is highly irregular. Our store policy is that all returns must be made within one week.

Customer: I understand that and I want to return this blouse and get my money back.

Salesperson: Given the policy, I would feel uncomfortable authorizing your return.

Customer: I can appreciate your feeling uncomfortable about accepting it, but I want to return this blouse and get my money back.

Salesperson: I could lose my job for doing such a thing.

Customer: I hear your worry about losing your job and I still want to return this blouse and get my money back.

Salesperson: Look, I don't want to take any chances. Why don't you return it tomorrow when the manager is here.

Customer: I hear you would rather have me come back
               tomorrow, but I want to return this blouse and
               get my money back now.

Salesperson: You sound like a broken record. You're unreal.

Customer: I know I sound that way, but I want to return
               this blouse and get my money back now.

Salesperson: Okay, okay, okay. Gimme the blouse.

In this example, there was no compromising. However, if the other
person changes their position somewhat and you think that a workable
compromise can be reached, offer an alternative.

Always prepare your broken record in advance. If you have difficulty saying no to solicitors or to family or friends who ask you for
favors, prepare your broken record now. If you want something but are
afraid to ask, jot it down in a simple sentence: "I want you to clean up
your room right now," or "I want to sit down and discuss the bills with
you tonight after dinner." A good rule of thumb is to try the broken
record at least four times. You will feel awkward practicing this technique at first, especially if people respond by telling you that you sound
like a broken record. But the results you get from this simple but powerful skill will convince you that it's worth the initial discomfort.

Content-to-Process Shift

When you think that the focus of a conversation is drifting away
from the topic you want to talk about, use the content-to-process shift.
You simply shift from the actual subject being discussed (the content)
to what is going on between you and the other person (the process).
For instance, you could say, "We've drifted away from what we agreed
to discuss into talking about old history." "I realize that I'm doing all
the talking on this subject, and you're being very quiet."

A content-to-process shift often involves some self-disclosure
about how you are feeling or thinking in the interaction at that very
moment. "I'm afraid to go on talking about this. You're turning red and
grinding your teeth." "I'm feeling uncomfortable discussing this issue
in a public place, and I notice that we're both whispering." "I feel great
about getting this problem resolved. We're really communicating! I feel
very positive about you right now."

Content-to-process shift is especially helpful when voices are being raised and both people are angry: "I see we're both getting upset.
It's a touchy issue," or "We're talking a lot louder and seem squared
off for combat." The trick is to comment on what's going on between

you in a neutral, dispassionate way, so that your statement won't be experienced as an attack.

Momentary Delay

You may feel compelled to respond immediately to any situation. If asked a question, you feel you have to answer right away. As a result, you may often end up doing or saying something you regret. If you don't take time to check your own feelings and needs, you may be letting others make your decisions for you.

Momentary delays let you (1) make sure that you understand the other person, (2) analyze what has been said, (3) go inside and become aware of what you feel, think, and want in this situation, and (4) consciously influence the situation so that you are more likely to get the outcome you want. Momentary delay is very helpful when you are just learning to use the other assertive techniques presented in this chapter. It gives you time to think and prepare.

Here are some examples:

"Slow down! This is too important to race through."

"That's interesting. Let me think about that for a moment."

"I don't quite understand that. Would you please say it in a different way?"

"This seems important. Would you repeat it?"

"Did I get what you were saying?" *(You repeat what you think you heard while you take time to digest it and reflect.)*

"I must be getting tired. Let's go over this again, only more slowly."

"Wait a minute. I want to give you my honest answer."

"There may be something to what you are saying . . . let me think about it for a little bit."

Time Out

When you know that what you're discussing is important, but the discussion is at an impasse, delay the conversation until another time. Time out is valuable when the interaction is too passive or too aggressive. One of you may be silent, tearful, or frozen into agreeing with everything the other says. Or one of you may be acting hurtful, name calling, and dragging up antique complaints.

Time out can also be used when you just want some room to think. For example, you're having difficulty deciding which car to buy and the car salesperson is pressuring you. Or your girlfriend has just told you that she loves you and wants to know how you feel about her. Or you've just been invited to spend the weekend at your in-laws' beach house.

These are typical examples of time-out situations:

In response to an inflexible, blaming co-worker, you say: "I think what we're talking about is important, and I'd like to discuss it with you tomorrow."

You're about to dissolve into tears or rage, or you're feeling very anxious. Further discussion would be fruitless or just too painful. So you say: "Time out. I'm upset right now. I know that I will be able to deal with this issue much more effectively tomorrow."

You are feeling pressured to do something that you're not sure you want to do. You say: "I want to sleep on it." "I'll get back to you next week." "I want to talk to my spouse (attorney, accountant, friend) about this before I make a decision." "This is important; when's a good time for you next week to discuss it?"

Don't abuse time out by using it repeatedly to avoid a difficult problem. Set up a specific time in the near future to continue your discussion.

Assertive Skills Practice

Using these assertive skills will feel awkward at first. Ideally you will practice these skills with a sympathetic friend or another student before you apply them in your daily life. If you are learning these skills on your own, you will find the "empty chair" technique helpful in rehearsing them:

Imagine that the person with whom you want to be assertive is sitting in a chair facing you. See the person's face in your mind's eye. How are they sitting, how are they dressed? Try to see as clear a picture as you can.

Now make your assertive statement as though the person were really in the chair listening.

When you are finished, move to the empty chair. Pretend you are the other person and respond as you think that person would respond.

Return to your own chair and notice how you feel and what you think of the other person's response. Make an appropriate assertive statement.

Continue this process, moving back and forth between the two chairs until you have finished the interaction.

If you feel too self-conscious using this empty chair technique, try going through its steps in your imagination. Or write out a script with your statements and the responses of the other person set down as in our examples. Many people find it helpful to rehearse their assertive lines in front of a mirror in order to make sure that their body language is consistent with what they're saying. Tape recording an imaginary assertive conversation can also be very useful. All of these techniques give you an opportunity to slowly integrate the assertive skills into your everyday life.

11

Fair Fighting

"Fair fighting" is a term coined by George Bach and Peter Wyden in their 1969 book *The Intimate Enemy*. They described fighting between intimates as an inevitable, natural, and potentially beneficial process for mutual problem solving and prescribed rules for keeping fights fair and effective.

Some of Bach's fair fighting strategies were based on a theory of "constructive aggression," which suggests that the frequent expression of angry feelings acts like a cathartic safety valve to relieve pressure, preserve relationships, and maintain a healthy emotional balance.

This commonly held notion that venting anger is good for you was disproved by Carol Tavris in her 1989 book *Anger—the Misunderstood Emotion*. She reviewed scientific studies that show conclusively that ventilating anger tends to *increase* angry feelings, build pressure, damage relationships, and destroy emotional balance.

This chapter combines Bach's classic fight-for-change technique with some more recent cognitive-behavioral methods of anger management and joint conflict resolution.

Unfair Fighting

Unfair fighting is the loud, bitter, harmful, unproductive, and sometimes violent kind. It usually springs from some combination of these three dangerous assumptions:

1. *Conflict is awful.* We must avoid it as long as possible. We should want the same things. We should agree. We should be nice.

2. *My needs are more valid than yours.* Only what I want is really important. What you want is trivial or stupid. I'm right and you're wrong. I'm good and you're bad.

3. *Only one can win.* If one of us gets what he or she wants, the other can't. A winner implies a loser. Therefore, I'd better attack first, seize the high ground, and make sure the winner is me.

Identifying Unfair Fighting Styles

Read through these descriptions of unfair fighting styles and identify the ones that you have used yourself. In the space provided after each item, jot down examples from your own experience.

1. Bad timing. One person forces his or her agenda on the other, often insisting on discussing something at an inappropriate time—when it's late and you're tired, when you're rushing to get somewhere, when you're busy with something else, when you've been drinking, when there are other people around whom you don't want to hear you fighting, and so on.

For example, Alyssa insisted that her boyfriend Jason make a decision about whether he would spend spring break with her. But Jason was late for a band rehearsal and didn't have time to talk. When she kept pressuring him, he exploded and said, "I don't have time for this shit now." He slammed the door so hard on his way out that he broke the window.

Example from your life: _____

_____

_____

2. Blaming. The dangerous assumption that "I'm right and you're wrong" makes you blame the other person for the whole problem. Blaming can take the form of name calling, accusing, exaggerating, assuming evil intentions, raking up past failures, and so on. "You" statements are common and "I" statements are rare.

For example, Bill said to Harry, "What do you mean you 'forgot' to mail your grad school application? Even you aren't *that* disorganized. Admit it—you chickened out. After you promised me you'd go back for your degree, you betrayed our agreement and just chucked the whole thing without telling me. And you have the nerve to lie to me and say you 'forgot' about the deadline." Bill is blaming Harry for being disorganized, cowardly, untruthful, and untrustworthy.

Example from your life: _____

_____

_____

3. Too many issues. When you're angry, you tend to use any ammunition you can think of, dragging up issue after issue to support how good you are and how bad the other person is.

For example, Jennifer and Rick were fighting about when to go vote on election day. Rick got mad and started recalling Jennifer's idiosyncratic voting history: "Why even bother voting? Everything you vote for loses. Remember the transit tax? School board reform last year? How you fought Proposition 13 and it won by a landslide? You've always been a sucker for impossible causes." He went on to attack her family's politics and, by some weird twist of logic, her reluctance to take the dog to the vet by herself.

Example from your life: _____

_____

_____

4. Covering other feelings with anger. In unfair fights, anger is usually the only emotion expressed. It drowns out any underlying fear, sadness, guilt, envy, disappointment, and so on.

For example, Carl was hurt and jealous when his wife, Claudia, announced that she wanted to spend a weekend Christmas shopping in the big city with her old college roommate and leave him at home with the kids. His feelings were hurt. He felt left out and envious of her friendship. But these feelings were squelched by his angry outburst about Claudia's "selfishness" and "irresponsibility."

Example from your life: _____

_____

_____

5. Impossible demands. Unfair fights often include vague, abstract demands like "be more considerate" or "stop being so picky." These are really impossible demands. They require the other person to read your mind at all times and judge whether what they are about to do is sufficiently "considerate" or overly "picky." Demanding global changes in attitude or feelings never works. People just don't change their personalities quickly or easily.

For example, Jake told his son Brendon to clean up his room. Brendon ignored him. Jake raised his voice. Brendon started to cry.

Jake's wife, Ruth, started a fight with Jake about his lousy parenting style. She wanted him to be more "sensitive" to Brendon's feelings and to "exercise patience." She should have demanded some specific changes in behavior that Jake could more easily remember and perform.

Example from your life: _____

_____

_____

6. Threats and ultimatums. Impossible demands are often backed up with excessive threats and ultimatums: I'll move out. I'll withdraw my support. I'll hit. I'll take the kids. I'll tell on you. I'll destroy something. I won't love you anymore.

For example, Wendy told Peter that if he didn't stop staying up all night in front of his computer, she was going to throw it out the window. At the moment she felt like she meant it, but later she realized it was a dangerous tactic: if she did it, they would be out thousands of dollars, and the fight would escalate. If she didn't do it, she would be seen as making empty threats.

Example from your life: _____

_____

_____

7. Escalation. Unfair fights tend to escalate from quiet disagreements to loud arguments, from arguing to shouting and screaming matches, from shouting to breaking things, from breaking to throwing increasingly dangerous objects, from throwing to hitting, and so on.

Dick and Didi's fights followed a familiar pattern: she would forget to meet him for lunch or pick him up at the gym. Later, his brooding silence would prompt her nervous apologies. He would start to lecture her about "getting her shit together." She would get defensive. He would raise his voice and start pacing around, waving his arms for emphasis. She would tell him to calm down. That would trigger his final outburst—tipping things over, kicking at the cat, or knocking magazines to the floor as he stormed out the door.

Example from your life: _____

_____

_____

Unhappy endings. Unfair fights end in violence, withdrawal, or tears and apologies. They don't end in mutually satisfactory solutions.

In fact, unfair fights don't really end at all—there's just a temporary cease fire until the next round.

Dick would always calm down and come home to apologize, often bearing a flower, a new book, or a can of Didi's favorite cashews. Didi would tearfully forgive him and promise to "be less scattered." Dick would resolve to "be more patient" and "control his temper." Until the next episode.

Example from your life: _____

_____

_____

Fair Fighting

Fair fighting is a frank and open discussion of differences, without shouting or violence. It follows strict rules to keep the exchange fair and peaceful. Ideally, a fair fight ends by reaching a mutually agreeable solution.

Fair fighting springs from three key attitudes:

1. *Conflict is inevitable.* Partners in intimate relationships always want different things. There's no avoiding it, and it's okay. You need to acknowledge that each of you is an individual, with your own needs, desires, opinions, tastes, preferences, fears, and goals.

2. *Our needs are equally valid.* We both want things that are natural, reasonable, and understandable. Just because we want different things doesn't mean that either one's needs are more important or significant that the other's. Your need for rest and privacy is just as important as my need for entertainment and companionship.

3. *We can both win.* Working together, we will come up with compromise solutions to our problems. We can each get a good measure of what we want without depriving or taking advantage of the other.

Fair Fight Rules

1. Set a time. Secure your partner's agreement to have a serious discussion. If your partner doesn't want to fight right now, you should set a time in the very near future. At first you may encounter resistance and may have to be very persistent to set aside a definite time.

After Jason avoided her twice, Allysa had to say, "Look, this is important to me. I've been thinking about it a while, it hasn't gone away, and I can see it won't go away until I can talk it out with you. How about tonight after band practice?"

2. State the problem. Say what your partner does or doesn't do that you don't like. By describing the facts of your partner's behavior, you can avoid blaming.

For example, Bill was very angry at Harry for not keeping his promise to apply to graduate school. But Bill stifled his first impulse to use provocative labels like "coward" or "chickened out" or "broken promises." He clearly stated the facts: "You told me you would apply to grad school this month. The deadline was the tenth. It's now the fourteenth, and you haven't applied."

3. Stick to one issue. You can only solve one problem at a time. When you're arguing, it's very tempting to change the subject or rake up the past. Resist the impulse and confine yourself to a single issue, in the present.

For example, Jennifer reminded her husband, Rick: "Look, it doesn't matter how I vote or whose fault it is that we're often late for things. The issue right now is *when can we find time to vote today*? Let's stick to that."

4. Express the full range of feelings. Use "I" messages to express how you feel about what your partner does or doesn't do that you don't like. Say "I feel mad" rather than "You make me mad." And look beyond irritation and anger to describe your full range of feelings. Expressing feelings is not the same as "dumping" feelings. Dumping is when you raise your voice, blame, or make threats when you're angry. Expressing feelings is describing the feeling without a lot of emotional heat or attacking language.

For example, Carl told Claudia, "When I heard that you and Jane were planning to spend the weekend shopping in the city, I felt angry at being left here alone. I feel like I'll be lonely, with nothing to do and nobody around. I'm also feeling jealous of Jane—of the good time you'll have together. And maybe even a little insecure. What if you have so much fun without me you start thinking, "Why be married at all?"

5. Propose change. State clearly, simply, and directly what you want your partner to do or not do. Be specific. Avoid talking in terms of attitudes, as in "I want you to be more considerate." Instead, state your objective in behavioral terms: "I want you to come right away when I say it's time for dinner and talk to me at the table instead of reading the newspaper."

When Ruth wanted Jake to be more "patient" and "understanding" with their son Brendon, she got nowhere. Nothing changed until she proposed specific behaviors that Jake could perform: "I want you to tell Brendon exactly what you want him to do, give him a deadline for doing it, and say up front what the consequences will be if he doesn't do what you want by the deadline. I want you to say all this in a normal, conversational tone of voice."

6. Describe consequences. Describe any practical, emotional, financial, health, or other benefits of the change you are proposing. For example, Wendy told Peter, "If you turn the computer off and get to bed by eleven, we can snuggle up together, watch the news, and make love like we used to. I'll feel closer to you, and you'll get the sleep you need."

Also include how you'll feel and what you'll do if the change is not made. But beware of making empty threats or predicting dire consequences out of proportion to the problem, as Wendy did when she threatened to throw Peter's computer out the window. There's a fine line between threats and the kind of natural negative consequences that can inspire someone to change. In Wendy's case, she could have described a more reasonable negative consequence by saying, "If you continue to stay up late, you can't count on me to drag you out of bed in the morning and rush around so that you can make it to work on time." In general, your partner will respond more readily to positive rather than negative consequences.

7. Prevent escalation. There are three things you can do to prevent escalation: (1) Watch nonverbal behavior, (2) breathe deeply to slow down the pace of the exchange, and (3) declare a "time out."

First, stay aware of the nonverbal part of every fight. Watch for danger signals: voices getting louder, threatening gestures, a shift from sitting to standing, pointing fingers, clenching fists, a book slammed down or other objects tossed around or broken, fast pacing, shoving, and so on.

Second, as soon as you notice that you are getting excited, stop talking and take a deep breath. Just turn away from your partner, inhale deeply into your abdomen, and release the breath slowly and completely in a big sigh. Suggest that your partner do the same to calm down. You are literally "taking a breather." It calms you down and buys time to think about the rules of fair fighting.

If taking a breather to buy time doesn't work, call a formal "time out." Time out has very specific rules:

a. *Agree in advance on a signal*, such as the T sign that professional sports referees use to call time out during a game.

b. *No last words.* As soon as one person calls time out, you both stop talking immediately.

c. *Leave immediately.* The person who called time out leaves the room or, ideally, the house. If you're in a car or some other place you can't leave, stop talking for a set amount of time. A time out should last about an hour. Stay out of each other's presence the whole time.

d. *Always return* when time's up.

e. *Don't use drugs or alcohol* during time out.

f. *Don't rehearse* what you should have said or are going to say. This will just keep you upset. If possible, get some physical exercise during your time out.

g. *Check in* when you get back. See if this is a good time to resume the discussion. If either of you is still too upset to continue, set a time in the near future to talk again.

For example, Dick and Didi stopped their pattern of escalation when Didi told Dick, "The next time we start arguing and you begin pacing around, getting worked up, I'm not going to keep pushing you. I'm going to give you the time out sign, say nothing, and go for a walk. I'll be back in an hour." That's exactly what she did the next day, when they were arguing about whose fault it was that the sprinkler timer wasn't reset after a power failure. When she returned, they had both calmed down.

8. End in agreement, counter proposal, or postponement. Some fights end in simple agreement: You state your case, propose a change, and your partner says okay.

More often, there is further discussion, and your partner makes a counter proposal for a change that is more acceptable. You talk over the counter proposal and perhaps reach a compromise.

Or perhaps not. Many a successful fight ends with no agreement beyond the promise to fight fairly again. That's all right. There are many issues that cannot be resolved quickly. Postponement is often the only reasonable outcome. The key is to agree on a time and place to take up the issue again.

For example, when Didi returned from her time-out walk, she proposed that she take full responsibility for watering the garden and that Dick take full responsibility for checking the oil in the cars. They went on to agree to split up several other chores that they often squabbled over.

Your Script for Change

This is a good exercise to perform whenever you plan to discuss a problem with your partner. It prepares you to follow the rules of fair fighting.

Pick a minor problem to start with—something that you do have trouble with, but not your biggest conflict. Prepare for fair fighting by composing a script for change:

1. Set a time for the fight: _____

2. State the problem accurately and factually: _____

   _____

   _____

3. Express your full range of feelings: _____

   _____

   _____

4. Propose change: _____

   _____

   _____

5. State the positive consequences of change: _____

   _____

   _____

6. State any negative consequences: _____

   _____

   _____

When you have your script ready, approach your partner and try it out. Remember the remaining rules of fair fighting as you proceed: prevent escalation by watching nonverbal signals and taking time out, be prepared to consider counter proposals, and seek a clear resolution in the form of agreement, compromise, or postponement.

Here's Catherine's script for a fight with her husband over a computer class she wanted to take:

   1. Set a time for the fight: *Tonight after Lacie is in bed.*

2. State the problem accurately and factually: *I want to take a computer class that meets on Tuesday and Thursday nights for eight weeks, starting in February.*

3. Express your full range of feelings: *I feel nervous about asking—I'm afraid you won't want to be home alone with Lacie and Greta. I'm very excited about the class—Marjorie took it last quarter, and it really helped her. She said it was well worth the $150 it costs. I feel guilty about the money, but I still want to go.*

4. Propose change: *I'd like you to take care of the girls from 6:30 to 9:30 Tuesdays and Thursdays for the eight weeks.*

5. State the positive consequences of change: *If I take this course, I'll be able to put all our finances on the computer and do our taxes myself.*

6. State any negative consequences: *If I don't take the class, we'll have to let your nitwit cousin do our taxes again. Two years ago he cost us $300 in penalties.*

Catherine's husband agreed to her taking the computer class. His only counter proposal was that she remind him Tuesday and Thursday mornings for the first couple of weeks, so that he wouldn't plan to work late. And he wanted to take a class himself some time.

12

Negotiation

Everybody negotiates—not just union officials, diplomats, and terrorists. You negotiate when you ask for a raise, apply for a job, dispute a grade with a teacher, buy a car or a house, sue somebody, or ask your landlord to paint your apartment. Any time you want something from someone who may have conflicting interests, you are potentially in a negotiating situation.

Negotiation is a skill that helps you get what you want from others without alienating them. It's for people who are not intimate and therefore wouldn't use fair fighting or expressing skills. Negotiation is a process whereby people with different or even opposing needs can arrive at a fair agreement. Though both sides want to win, their best interests are served by generating a mutually acceptable option.

Even the most complicated negotiations can be broken down into four stages:

Preparation. Before you actually meet the opposing side, you need to figure out what outcome you want most, what would be less satisfactory but still acceptable, and what constitutes the worst deal you'd accept. During time-outs from negotiation, you'll do more preparation by looking up information, planning your strategy, and brainstorming to create optional proposals.

Discussion. You and your opponent describe the facts of the situation, how you feel about it, and what you think about it. You explain to your opponent how the situation looks to you in terms of both sides' interests and needs. Discussion is the major means of resolving deadlocks: you ask for more information about the other side's interests and you elaborate your own point of view.

Proposal/Counter proposal. You make an offer or a request. Your opponent makes a counter offer. This cycle is repeated several times, perhaps interspersed with more discussion or with time-outs to think things over. As new proposals and counter proposals evolve, their terms move ever closer together in the classic ballet of compromise.

Agreement/Disagreement. Disagreement returns the negotiation to the discussion stage, or if a time-out has been called, to the preparation stage. Disagreement is a natural step in negotiation. It's a signal to try again, not a brick wall that stops everything dead. Eventually you'll come to agree on a mutually acceptable option.

Here's how the four stages of negotiation would work in buying a used car:

Preparation. Terry wants to buy a dependable car that's comfortable, gets reasonably good gas mileage, and won't cost him more than $2,500. He researches the want ads, talks to a mechanic, and consults a knowledgeable friend. He decides to look for a five- to ten-year-old mid-size sedan that has had good care. He'll accept an older car if it's in exceptional shape and has low mileage. He wants a radio, but isn't interested in paying extra for fancy stereos or other exotic accessories.

Discussion. Terry calls up Alfred, who has advertised an eight-year-old Ford for $2,800. Terry tells him that he is looking for a dependable car in good shape. He gathers information: Mileage? 79,000 miles. Engine? Recent valve job. Tires? Fair. Body? One small dent in right fender. Paint? Faded. Based on this discussion, Terry sets up an appointment to test drive the car. He does not mention money at this stage, since he doesn't really have enough information to make a definite offer. Although the car is priced over his limit, he suspects that Alfred will probably come down.

Proposal/Counter proposal. Terry drives the car and finds it satisfactory. At the end of the test drive, he says to Alfred, "Well, you're right, it's a nice car. I like everything about it, but the price is just a little more than I want to pay. How about $2,200?"

Terry arrived at this amount by figuring that if the car was priced at $300 *more* than he wanted to pay, he'd better offer about $300 *less* than he wanted to pay, so he'd have some room to negotiate.

Disagreement. Alfred isn't pleased with the offer and declines. He says that he has to get at least $2,600 for the car. Terry knows that Alfred's disagreement is actually an invitation to return to discussion.

Discussion. Terry asks for more information: $2,600 seems like quite a bit for an eight-year-old car. Is there something special that sets it apart?"

Alfred points out the car's expensive tape deck, AM/FM radio, and mag wheels. He shows the receipt for a rebuilt transmission. He says that the car has always had regular maintenance and only two owners.

Proposal/Counter proposal. Terry agrees that these considerations are important, although he isn't interested in fancy extras like tape decks and mag wheels. He offers $2,450. Alfred comes down to $2,550 and says it's as low as he can go.

Terry says, "Look, it seems like we're stuck because you want an extra $100 for a stereo system that I don't even care about. How about taking the stereo out? You can keep it."

Agreement. Alfred laughs. "Forget it," he says, "it's too much trouble. Let's split the difference. You can have it for $2,500." Terry drives home in his new car, stereo blasting.

Conflict

Your attitude toward conflict will determine your success at negotiation. Conflict is inevitable no matter how you try to avoid it. The smart way to think about conflict is to see it as a positive opportunity for change. By skillful negotiating you can make the change a favorable one for you.

Dealing with conflict often seems to boil down to a no-win decision: Should you be softhearted and make friends, or should you be hardheaded and make enemies?

In the softhearted approach the goal is agreement at all costs. You make concessions, you trust everybody, you yield to pressure, you disclose your bottom line early in the game, and you end up paying too much for a car you don't really like.

In the hardheaded approach the goal is winning at all costs. You demand concessions, you distrust everybody, you apply pressure, and you lie about your bottom line. You end up with either a cheap car and an enemy for life or no car and an enemy for life.

You can steer between these two extremes by taking the principled approach. In the principled approach the goal is a fair, mutually agreeable outcome. Personalities and trust don't enter into it, so you can stay friends or stay strangers and still benefit from the outcome. You avoid talking in terms of a firm bottom line or digging into a position. You reason with your opponents and are open to reason. You yield to principle, but never to pressure. Proposals and counter proposals are judged according to objective criteria rather than seen as contests of will. You end up paying a fair price for the car you want.

Rules of Principled Negotiation

Separate the People From the Problem

Conflict doesn't have to mean hostility. A situation can be considered separately from the personalities involved. Conflict becomes hostile when both sides choose positions. You settle on your position in the matter and dig into it. You identify with that position so strongly that an attack on your position becomes an attack on your self-worth.

The way out of this trap is to keep the people separate from the problem at hand. Don't enter negotiations with a single rock-solid position. Instead, enter with the attitude that many options are open to you. You and your opponent are decent, reasonable people who want to reach a fair solution to a problem in which you both have some legitimate interests.

For example, suppose you and three other tenants are meeting with the owner of your apartment building to discuss maintenance of common areas. You want the halls cleaned more often, you want burnt-out bulbs on landings replaced promptly, and you want the back fence repaired. The wrong way to approach this meeting is to show up with a typed list of nonnegotiable demands, throw it in your landlord's face, and say, "You've got one week to shape up, Slumlord, or it's rent strike time."

This approach will get you nothing but a crash course in local eviction law. The right approach is to quietly say, "We've come to discuss how we might improve the common areas of the building. When you hear our requests, we think you'll agree that they're reasonable, and probably you'll want to make some suggestions of your own."

Understand the People

Empathy, active listening, and honest self-expression are as important in negotiation as in everyday communication with intimates. Put yourself in your opponent's shoes. Imagine what he feels, what he thinks about the situation, and what he needs to get out of it. But don't mind-read his intentions as a projection of your own fears. Just because you're afraid the boss has picked someone else for a promotion, you shouldn't automatically assume that he has.

Use your active listening skills to elicit your opponent's feelings, thoughts, and needs: "The way I understand it, you're *afraid* a younger person in that job might not be effective. You *think* experience is important in the department. You *need* a capable, hard-working employee who can start making changes right away." Feeding back information makes an opponent feel that he or she has been heard and shows that you take the opposing side seriously. You sound intelligent, considerate, and fair.

Honestly share your own feelings, thoughts, and needs. Let your opponent understand you, just as you are trying to understand your opponent: "I *feel* frustrated by the old paradox: you need experience to get good jobs but only good jobs give the right kind of experience. I *think* I have what it takes in terms of judgment, energy, and dedication. All I *need* is a chance to show what I can do. How about a three-month trial assignment?"

State the Problem in Terms of Interests

Behind conflicting positions lie shared and compatible interests as well as opposing ones. The shared interests are the reasons people keep negotiating. You'll never hear a TV news announcer say, "Talks between U.S. Steel and the United Steel Workers broke off forever today. U.S. Steel quit and decided to go into the franchise food business, and the Steelworkers quit and took up gardening." You'll never hear it because shared interests will drive both sides back to the bargaining table again and again until a new agreement is forged.

When an opponent states a position or demand, uncover the interest behind it by asking: "Exactly why do you want _____? Why don't you want _____?"

For example, ask the owner of the house you want to rent, "Exactly why do you want a $500 cleaning deposit?" You may find out that the last tenant stabled a horse in the back bedroom, or that $500 is exactly what it costs to clean the house the last time it was vacant, or that the landlord is $500 behind in the mortgage payments. By uncovering the landlord's interests in the matter, you may uncover a way to compromise: a written no-pets clause in the lease, three months in which to pay the deposit, or a deposit that's partially refundable in six months upon inspection of the premises.

In looking for the interests behind positions, be sensitive to basic human needs for security, trust, intimacy, and self-esteem. They can be more important to you and your opponent than dollars and cents. For example, many Japanese companies are organized to show a consistent concern for their employees' emotional needs. These companies enjoy high productivity and profits, low staff turnover, excellent worker morale, and virtually none of the labor problems that plague American corporations.

Often your opponent will stick to a position not because he or she needs the additional $300, but because giving in on the $300 means losing self-esteem. You can help your opponent save face by reframing the compromise as generosity rather than giving in. Labeling the act of compromise as a positive virtue is often very helpful.

It takes time to explore interests. You should hold off from blurting out your preconceived solution until both sides have had a chance to air their concerns. You may discover some flaws in your pet solution or find ways to improve it as the discussion continues.

Stating problems in terms of interests makes you focus on the future, since that's almost always where your interests lie. Focusing on future desires is helpful because it discourages old, familiar foes from raking up past complaints. For example, suppose you want to have a room added onto your house. You have $10,000 to do the job, but the lowest bid you've received is for $11,500. You state your interests to the low-bidding contractor like this: "We want another bedroom because my sister is coming to live with us next January. We have exactly $10,000 saved up to do the work. I think the specifications I gave you are as simple and economical as possible. I don't want to settle for a smaller room or cheaper materials that won't match the rest of the house. Is there any way you can see to get this job done for $10,000?"

The contractor reveals his interests in this manner: "I've done a careful estimate on materials and labor, and there's just not that much slack. At $10,000 I'd be losing money. This is my busy season and there's plenty of work around at top rates, so it doesn't make sense for me to squeeze in a job like this now, at less than a full profit."

You're quick to sense where his interests lie, so you ask, "What about your slow season? You could do the foundation, framing, roof, and walls now, at full rate. Then, next fall, when you have more time and need the work, you could come back and finish up the interior at a reduced rate. I'll pay part now and put the rest of the $10,000 in the bank at interest. When we settle up, I'll throw in the interest so the total will be more than $10,000. You'll have some work in the slow season and I'll have my $10,000 room by January."

By exploring your mutual interests, you have uncovered one of the classic tradeoffs: time for money. You're on your way to getting what you want at a fair price without alienating the contractor.

List Options

Preparation. Before you start looking for options, work on your attitude. Adopt the attitude that there are probably several possible solutions that will be acceptable to both sides. Get rid of the notions that there is only one best way to divide up the pie, that the pie is only so big, and that you absolutely must get the biggest piece. These are all self-defeating ideas. There are actually several good ways to cut up a pie. You may even find a way to make the pie bigger. And ending up with the biggest piece isn't always ideal, especially if you antagonize people and end up getting your pie in the face.

Do your homework so that you really know what's fair. Find out what's common practice, how much others are earning, what similar items are selling for, the rent on comparable houses in town, the medical benefits supplied by other companies, other respected teachers' grading practices, other departments' sales figures or absentee rates, and so on. Precedents and benchmarks help you generate reasonable proposals.

Brainstorming. To generate opinions, try brainstorming with your constituents or other interested parties. Gather together five to eight people in a place somewhere other than your usual surroundings. Pick one person to keep the meeting on track, enforce the groundrules, and encourage participation. Seat the people side-by-side or in a circle: the feeling of formality that comes from being squared off across a table may inhibit creativity. Have the leader explain these ground rules: criticism is absolutely forbidden, the session is off the record, and ideas won't be attributed to the individuals who suggest them.

Come up with a long list of ideas, the more and the wilder the better. Approach the problem from all angles. Record all the ideas on a blackboard or large sheet of paper so that everyone can see them. When no new ideas are forthcoming, declare the freewheeling part of the session over.

Now you can be critical. Underline the most promising ideas. Try to combine and alter the best ones to make them better. You should end up with a list of good ideas, any of which could become an acceptable proposal in the next negotiation session.

If you're on your own and don't have any brainstorming partners handy, try looking at the problem through the eyes of many imaginary experts. How would the problem be solved by a judge, a cop, your mother, your father, an engineer, a lawyer, a psychologist, a priest or minister or rabbi, a salesperson, a politician, or any other kind of expert? Looking at the problem this way can momentarily free you from your personal set of blinders.

To increase the number of your options, consider some of the time-tested methods of compromise. Even very young children understand the obvious fairness of "You cut the pie and I'll choose my piece first." A classic way of fairly dividing disputed property or goods is splitting it down the middle. The buying-and-selling equivalent is splitting the difference.

If you think the options you've come up with are too hardheaded for your opponent to accept, consider the many ways in which agreements can be softened. Fundamental changes in policy can be made into merely procedural changes. Permanent alterations can become only temporary. Comprehensive plans can be applied partially. Final agreements can be changed to agreements in principle. Unconditional demands can be made contingent. Binding decisions can be made non-binding.

An example of generating options is the case of Thelma's raise. Thelma worked for an advertising firm that had come on hard times. She was up for her annual salary review and she wanted a twenty percent raise. However, her co-workers had been getting annual raises of five percent, so her chances didn't look good. She decided that despite the unpromising precedents, she would adopt the attitude that there were probably several ways for her to get the raise she wanted from the company.

Thelma brainstormed her options with her family, friends, and a colleague from another department. Putting several people's imaginations to work gave her many different ways to look at her problem. Some of the suggestions had to be tossed out. Threatening to quit was impractical, and embezzlement and blackmail were illegal. However, one suggestion made Thelma realize that more fringe benefits might be just as good as a raise in pay. She could ask for a company car to drive, a nicer office, better equipment, secretarial help, time off, or a flexible schedule. The company might be willing to give her some of those goodies in addition to the five percent raise that everybody else got.

Thelma also realized that she had been thinking in terms of getting paid more for the job she was doing. Brainstorming made it clear that a promotion or transfer could mean more money automatically, without the company having to leap the psychological hurdle of a larger-than-average raise.

Thelma then tried looking at the situation through the eyes of raise experts—her boss and the head of the personnel department. This simple exercise made it clear that the only compelling reasons for giving raises were increased cost of living, increased productivity, increased profit, or increased responsibility. Her personal financial needs would carry little weight with management.

Thelma faced the fact that she might have to compromise or soften her requests. She decided that she would be willing to split the difference between the twenty percent she wanted and the five percent she was likely to be offered, especially if the pot was sweetened in some other way. She was also prepared to spread her raise over time or to make it contingent on increased productivity.

She found that her original option—demanding a big raise because she needed it—had now expanded to a long list of strategies and options:

Point out increased cost of living and increased productivity in present position.

Show that productivity could be increased by secretarial help and use of a company car.

Ask for more responsibility, such as taking over the quality control reports when Jones retires.

Volunteer to head up the market research project that everybody says should be done. Offer to work some free overtime to get it started.

Ask for twenty percent, secretarial help, company car, and flexible hours.

Compromise on fifteen percent now and twenty percent in six months if productivity increases as predicted.

Thelma was now ready to go into her boss's office and negotiate effectively.

Turning options into proposals. You've established a good working relationship with your opponents. You've stated and discussed the problem in terms of your mutual and conflicting interests. You've privately prepared your list of acceptable options, and now you're ready to make a proposal.

Approach the proposal slowly. Describe the option you like best in detail. Then move on to the next best one. Ask your opponents which option they prefer. By offering choice and inviting discussion, you avoid confronting them with an ultimatum that will lock them into a defensive position. Sometimes the opposition will even start brainstorming with you in a genuine attempt at joint problem solving.

If at any point in describing your options you find your opponents in an agreeable frame of mind, hit them with a "yesable" proposal. A yesable proposal is one of your acceptable options stated as a direct question to which "yes" is an easy answer. For example, if you want a twenty percent raise, you should ask, "If I can straighten out the production bottleneck and increase productivity, would you be willing to give me a twenty percent raise?" This proposal is much better than "I really need a twenty percent raise. Why can't I have it?" The first proposal is conditional on something the boss wants, and can't be denied without implying that increased productivity is undesirable or that excellence shouldn't be rewarded. The second proposal is poor because it's based only on your needs and invites the boss to make a list of reasons why not. The following is a list of deniable proposals restated as yesable proposals:

Deniable	*Yesable*
I want this apartment painted and I want it painted by the time I get back from vacation.	Would you rather paint our apartment right now, or next month when we'll be out of town?

Give me the preliminary report on the 15th and the final figures no later than the 30th.	If I give you until the end of the month to get the final figures, can you provide a preliminary report by the 15th?
No matter what you say, I'm not paying more than $150,000 for this house. How about it?	Assuming we can agree on all the other terms and contingencies, I'm prepared to offer up to $150,000 for this house. Does that seem like a reasonable offer?

Note: If you are having trouble getting a "yes" from an otherwise agreeable opponent, make sure that the person you're dealing with is actually empowered to make the decision. If not, you'll need to go over his or her head and negotiate with the person who does have the power to say "yes."

When the Going Gets Tough

Opponents Who Have All the Power

When you are faced with an opponent who has all the power, you have to be realistic. The odds are that you'll lose. Before going into the negotiation, you should figure out your best alternative to a negotiated decision. What are you going to do if you get turned down flat? Knowing this before you go in gives you some certainty.

If your best alternative is a strong one, you can let your opponent know about it in the form of a threat: "If you don't give me this promotion, I plan to quit and go into the dry cleaning business with my brother-in-law." Be sure that your threat is believable. If you're not really prepared to go through with it, it's not believable. It's an empty bluff and a bad tactic.

When your best alternative to a negotiated agreement is a weak one, you should conceal it. For example, you should keep quiet if you have no brother-in-law in the dry cleaning business to fall back on. If your alternative to getting the promotion is to continue meekly in the same dead-end job, you're in no position to make threats.

Whatever your alternative, make sure you've done your homework. Have all your facts and figures complete and accurate. Come down very hard on objective criteria. Appeal to your opponent's sense of fairness and hope for the best.

If many other people share your one-down position in relation to a powerful opponent, you can adopt the tactics of minority power politics. This means pulling power out of thin air. You go around drumming up support among like-minded people. You form a committee or a party. You hold meetings and rallies and press conferences. You become an expert on the problem. You focus the harsh light of publicity on your opponent's unfairness.

Hardliners Who Won't Cooperate

Sometimes an opponent will dig into a position and refuse to budge. When this happens, resist the impulse to launch an all-out attack on the position. Instead, look behind the position for the underlying interests. If management absolutely refuses to even consider a dental plan, make a list of all the reasons they might have: funding a plan will be too expensive, new employees will run up huge bills for long-standing dental problems, people will get expensive cosmetic work done, it's too hard to administer, available plans conflict with the existing medical plan, and so on.

When you think you understand your opponent's interests, ask a question: "Why do you refuse to consider a dental plan?" Then set back and wait for an answer. Let the silence drag on and on. If you get a non-answer like "It's against company policy," counter with "Why is it against company policy?" Then try more specific questions such as, "Is it too expensive . . . ? How expensive is it . . . ? What would it cost to administer . . . ? Are you afraid employees will take advantage of your generosity . . . ?" Don't forget the long silence after each polite question. Your goal is to get the hardliner talking about the problem.

Other times an opponent talks too much, and the entire response is an attack on your position. When this happens, resist the impulse to dig in and defend your position. Rather, adopt the judo tactic of diverting your enemy's force. You divert attacks on your position by welcoming criticism: "That's very interesting. What other ideas do you have about my plan? How could we improve it?" You involve your opponent in helping you create additional options.

Sometimes a hardliner will attack you personally. The way to divert personal attacks is to redefine them as attacks on the problem. For example, when the management spokesperson accuses you of "irresponsibly stirring people up with this ridiculous dental plan fantasy," you must stifle your impulse to call the spokesperson a hypocritical stooge of a reactionary management. Instead, you should reframe the attack like this: "You're right, people are very stirred up about the dental plan, and I appreciate the fact that you feel strongly about it too. It's a serious problem that deserves the attention of all the responsible leaders in the company." Reframing personal attacks is a highly subtle use of flattery and flimflam. It defuses hostility and gives hardliners a graceful way to start cooperating.

Then there are the times when both sides of a dispute have so much at stake that neither is willing to relax from a hardline position.

In these situations the best solution is to use the "one-text" procedure. That's how the Camp David agreement between Egypt and Israel was reached. The United States prepared the text of a possible agreement and presented it to both sides. Each turned it down, giving specific reasons. Then the U.S. came up with a second draft and submitted it. Thirteen days and twenty-one drafts later, the agreement was signed. The success of this method depends on each side simply saying yes or no to successive texts, without direct confrontation or argument.

Opponents Who Play Dirty

There are many kinds of dirty negotiating tactics: lies, deceptions, psychological warfare, bribery, blackmail, and so on. Some books are full of tips on what to do if they seat you with the sun in your eyes or how to deal with a bribe. They make entertaining reading, but actually you need only one tactic to handle dirty tricks: call process and negotiate for fair play.

"Calling process" means that you stop talking about the subject of the session and talk about the process that's going on: "Before we get into the discussion of rate hikes, I'd like to point out that this chair is too low and the sun is in my eyes. Surely we're not going to play one-upmanship games in a serious negotiation like this?"

Expose the dirty trick for what it is. Then negotiate for an agreement to proceed according to the rules of principled negotiation. Explain that you understand the temptation to take every possible advantage, and that you don't take it personally. But point out that everyone's interests will be better served if you approach the problem as honest people who are amenable to reason. Explain that you're here to find some options that will serve your shared interests and reconcile your opposed interests. Invite your opponents to help you look for options that will benefit everyone. Suggest some objective criteria by which these options can be judged. Conclude with, "If we're agreed that we should proceed in a civilized manner, then let's find me another chair and get on with it."

Most of the time, this approach will work. If it doesn't, it may be time to call in a neutral mediator.

You may encounter a conflict that can't be negotiated. This happens when your opponents want the conflict more than they want resolution. For example, the union may want to keep tempers and uncertainty high until the contract deadline is closer. Management may want to prolong negotiations until the union's strike fund is exhausted. Student demonstrators may want publicity more than they want grading reform or job placement programs. Until you uncover and deal with such hidden agendas, negotiation is impossible.

IV

SOCIAL SKILLS

13

Prejudgment

Prejudgment is the process by which you take in and interpret information about other people. Since your first impressions of others take place automatically, the prejudgment process goes on largely unnoticed by your conscious mind. Your past experience, your needs and wishes, and your assumptions about the context in which you encounter a new person all greatly influence what information you attend to and how you interpret it.

Prejudgment is an immensely useful skill which helps you categorize the many strangers that you meet. Sometimes it is very accurate. But often your first impression of a new person may be more illusion than you care to imagine. Based on little information, you infer a great deal and make an instant evaluation. The evaluation then influences how you listen and how you respond.

For example, a young man at a party sees a tall, slender woman standing awkwardly by herself and frowning. He infers that she is a boring wallflower and heads in the other direction. Later he almost spills his drink when the boring wallflower introduces herself. Somehow she has learned his profession and asks about his job. The young man feels trapped and avoids eye contact. He answers her "boring" questions with curt replies. Eventually he mumbles an excuse and retires to the bar. There he meets his best friend who tells him that the very woman he is trying to avoid is a beautiful, fascinating creature. The first young man, of course, thinks his friend has taken leave of his senses and says, "She's a total dud . . . she reminds me of my old Aunt Sally."

Inaccurate first impressions often go uncorrected. Research indicates that roughly two-thirds of your first impression of another person will remain unchanged after months of regular interaction. In short, you are likely to freeze your first impression of a person with only minor modifications. The young man in the example above ends up working in the same department with the woman he labeled a "dud." He concedes to his friend months later that she is indeed very attractive, but he cannot fathom how she can be so popular with the other people in the office. He continues to find her as boring as old Aunt Sally.

Since first impressions are so important, it's equally important to become aware of some of the most typical traps of prejudgment.

The Limits of Perception

You never get complete information because the perception process simplifies and eliminates some of the data. Your eyes, ears, and skin are constantly bombarded with stimuli that are not intense enough to excite the nervous system receptors. Once messages enter the nervous system, they are further simplified by the process of inhibition, which eliminates messages inconsistent with the dominant messages received. For example, if your friend nods his head, smiles, and says yes, you are unlikely to notice that the knuckles on his fingers are white from clutching his arms. The latter nonverbal cue is inconsistent with the dominant message and is therefore inhibited.

Generalization of Expectations

In a new or unfamiliar situation, your brain jumps to conclusions to fill in any missing pieces, basing its conclusions largely on past experience. You tend to perceive what you are in the habit of perceiving. Before reading on, do the following exercise. Connect all nine dots with only four straight lines without lifting your pencil from the paper or retracing a line. Spend at least ten minutes on this puzzle. There is a solution.

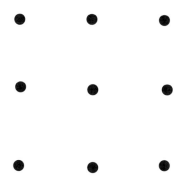

If you solved the problem within ten minutes on your own, you are indeed the rare person. Most people add an extra assumption, true in most puzzles, that isn't part of this puzzle. They assume that they can't draw the four straight lines beyond the square formed by the eight outside dots. This assumption makes the problem insolvable. If you made this erroneous assumption, try to solve the puzzle again, allowing the lines to extend beyond the square.

This exercise points out the importance of checking out the assumptions underlying your perceptions. When you make unverified assumptions about new people and new situations, you run the risk of communication breakdown. For example, you assume that a party means inviting everyone you know, and your new live-in boyfriend assumes that a party means inviting close friends only. If you don't check out each other's assumptions, you are likely to be in for a bitter awakening at the first party in your new home. (See page 178 for the solution.)

Perceptual Accentuation

When you need something, even a poor version of it will do. If you are lonely, even a boring date is better than no date at all. Suddenly your job seems more valuable when six of your co-workers have been laid off due to an economic slump. Perceptual accentuation causes you to see what you expect and want to see. Research has demonstrated that when poor and rich children are shown pictures of coins and are asked to estimate their size, the poor children guess that the coins are much larger than the rich children do. Studies have also demonstrated that you are likely to assess people whom you like as more attractive and more intelligent than people whom you don't like.

As an exercise, ask yourself which of the following activities you would most like to do right now. Rate the activity you most want to do as 8. Repeat this exercise at a later date at a different time of day. Compare your ratings.

___ smell a freshly cooked steak

___ smell a rose

___ smell peppermint

___ smell nature after a rain

___ smell a fire in a fireplace

___ smell freshly baked bread

___ smell your favorite perfume or after-shave lotion

___ smell a pie baking

Depending on your current needs, different items will seem more attractive to you at different times.

Stereotypes

Read the following sentences and fill in the blanks as fast as you can. Do not ponder your responses.

1. Italian men make excellent _____ .

2. Politicians are often _____ .

3. Most basketball players are _____ .

4. Women with big _____ are very _____ .

5. Fat people are _____ .

6. Hard-working, energetic people usually _____ .

7. Sunday school teachers are usually _____ .

8. People born to wealth are _____ .

Without much difficulty, you are able to generalize from almost no information to form expectations about people based simply on their membership group. Stereotyping is a shortcut to forming impressions of others. Based on as little as one trait or behavior, you classify an individual as belonging to a group of people who you infer share other qualities in common. For example, research indicates that if you classify a person as being attractive, you are more likely to think that he or she is friendlier, has a better character, is more exciting on a date, has a higher occupational status, and would be a better marital partner than a person you classify as unattractive.

On the positive side, stereotyping helps you avoid cognitive over-load by allowing you to package stimuli into manageable numbers of categories. Although many stereotypes are inaccurate, many others have at least some truth to them. For instance, women are dispropor-tionately represented in secretarial positions, blacks in athletics, and Jews in academia.

Stereotyping becomes dangerous when traits ascribed to a group are assumed to be biologically or ethnocentrically negative or inferior. Racism, sexism, and ageism are all negative products of stereotyping. Stereotyping is most dangerous when there is no accommodation of beliefs to new information. The stereotyper dogmatically holds on to his opinion no matter how much contradictory data is presented to him.

Another danger of stereotyping is the self-fulfilling prophecy. The best known example of the self-fulfilling prophecy is the "Pygmalion effect." As part of a study, teachers were told that certain students would be expected to do exceptionally well because they were "late bloomers." The names of these students were selected at random by the researchers. The results were spectacular: the students whose names were given to the teachers actually did perform at a higher level than the other students. The selected students even made greater improvements on IQ tests than the others did.

Self-fulfilling prophecies are an important part of first impressions and ongoing relationships. If you expect others to act in a certain way, you are likely to communicate your expectations to them with subtle cues, increasing the likelihood that they will act as you anticipate. If you expect people to reject you, you are likely to avoid eye contact, frown, speak in curt sentences, and have a rigid, closed body posture. Seeing your behavior, they in turn fulfill your expectations, which makes you more confident of the accuracy of your predictions. In the future your expectations are apt to be still more definite and rigid when you encounter a similar situation.

Self-fulfilling prophecies can be used in very positive ways. For example, you may expect that your mate is going to be very loving and generous with you. If you behave in a manner that conveys your expectation, your mate is likely to act accordingly. By what he says and does, a successful salesman conveys to his customers his confidence that he is going to make the sale. A positive self-fulfilling prophecy can be created in just a few words. For example, a speaker introduced to her audience as an expert in her field is much more persuasive than a person who is given no introduction.

Exercise: In a social setting where at least several strangers are present, comment to yourself about each of the people in the following manner:

Say to yourself, "I notice _____ ." Fill in the blank with a statement of something you perceive about them with one of your five senses. Then add, "I imagine _____ ." Fill in the blank with a statement of something you infer about them but cannot perceive with your five senses.

Examples: "I notice that man is very fat. I imagine that he does not exercise, has no will power, and that he is lazy." "I notice that woman is very neatly dressed. I imagine that she is very organized, a perfectionistic, and demanding." "I notice that black man is very tall. I imagine that he is a basketball player."

As this exercise illustrates, many of your impressions about people are based on inferences drawn from minimal perceptual cues. It is from such minimal cues that you stereotype others.

Approval and Disapproval in Prejudgment

On first meeting people, you tend to make judgments about them in terms such as intelligent or stupid, strong or weak, warm or cold, and active or passive. These critical pairs of opposite traits form a core from which many other traits are inferred. They help you arrive at an overall evaluation of the "goodness" or "badness" of people you meet.

Exercise: Rate a person you like and a person you don't like in terms of the following pairs of opposite traits. Put a checkmark on one of the blanks between each pair indicating your evaluation of this person. The middle blank indicates no feelings or opinion at all and the blanks at each end represent extreme evaluations. The other blanks represent moderate evaluations.

hard-working	___	___	___	___	___	*lazy*
warm	___	___	___	___	___	*cold*
active	___	___	___	___	___	*passive*
trustworthy	___	___	___	___	___	*untrustworthy*
knowledgeable	___	___	___	___	___	*uninformed*
strong	___	___	___	___	___	*weak*
intelligent	___	___	___	___	___	*stupid*
friendly	___	___	___	___	___	*aloof*
attractive	___	___	___	___	___	*ugly*

To make these scales complete, add any other trait pairs that you frequently use in making judgments. When you finish the scales for each person, make an overall evaluation of:

good	___	___	___	___	___	*bad*

Repeat this scale for four additional pairs of people.

These scales reflect the kind of judgments you make daily. Although they are highly intuitive, such evaluations largely determine how you interpret the messages that come from others.

In the above exercise, did you find that certain traits went together? For instance, did you rate a person as good, warm, and friendly? Or bad, passive, and weak? Research suggests that warmth and friendliness are traits that are perceived as being closely allied with goodness. In our culture, activeness and strength are also associated with goodness. Do you think that the clustering of certain traits is truly reflective of the people you evaluated? Or is this clustering more a function of your expectation that these traits occur together?

Exercise: To further explore this question, make a new list of five people you like and five people you don't like. You can include public or fictional characters as well as acquaintances and family. For each individual, list his or her traits. Examine the traits of the people you like. Are certain traits repeated two or more times? Examine the traits of the people you don't like. Do certain traits appear two or more times? Do you find yourself using the same scales of opposite trait pairs for people you like and don't like? For example, do you often rate people on the warm/cold or knowledgeable/uninformed scales?

You may discover that you use certain trait scales repeatedly in evaluating people. If you compare your lists of traits with lists filled out by other individuals, you are very likely to find some evaluative traits that would not normally occur to you. Remember that how you evaluate others will be largely determined by the specific trait scales you habitually use.

The famous personality theorist, Harry Stack Sullivan, provided a possible explanation for why certain traits reoccur again and again in your evaluation of others while other traits are never used. He suggested that from a very young age the individual becomes attuned to those things he or she does that either result in approval and satisfaction or result in disapproval and dissatisfaction. The child focuses *only* on those behaviors that are cause for approval or disapproval. Much like looking through a microscope, this narrow focus interferes with noticing the rest of the world. What the child is aware of through this very narrow field, he or she identifies with and calls "self" or "I."

The self doesn't notice parts of the personality except those that are approved or disapproved of by significant others. And one can find in others only what is in the self. A favorite saying of Sullivan's was, "As you judge yourself, so shall you judge others." Many times when you respond strongly to something in another person, it has more to do with you than with them. Your microscope is focused on traits that you habitually find significant. To explore this point, do the following exercise.

Exercise: Fill in the blanks for ten people. "When I think of _____ (name of person), I become aware of the part of me that notices _____ _____ (behavior or trait)."

Example: "When I think of ___*Madeline*___ , I become aware of the part of me that notices ___*physical fitness*___ .

Note for each person that the behavior or trait you notice is only one of many ways that he or she could be described. Your awareness of each particular trait is based on how strongly significant it is to you.

Madeline may be in great physical condition, but it is something in you that causes you to pick this particular trait of hers to focus on.

Parataxic Distortions

Have you ever had the experience of walking into a room full of strangers and almost immediately being drawn to a particular person? You instantly like them and may have a sense that you've known them a long time. Perhaps they remind you of someone out of your past. You may be able to recall who that someone is, or you may just have a vague sense of something familiar that you can't quite put your finger on. Usually the association between the person in front of you and the person out of your past is small and superficial: the same hair style, the same name, the same profession, or a similar accent.

When you do have a strong positive or negative reaction to someone you are meeting for the first time, consider the possibility of Parataxic Distortion—that the person in front of you is reminding you of someone else. Proceed with caution, because you may superimpose on the new person a set of inferences and assumptions that really belong with the person out of your past. The result can be confusion and misunderstanding.

Parataxic Distortion is sometimes easier to spot when someone else is relating to you as though you were someone else. You notice that they are either strongly positive or negative in their attitudes about you from the beginning of your contact with them. The way they treat you is inconsistent with objective reality. You may find yourself thinking that they have little idea of what you are really like. A good example of Parataxic Distortion is presented in the introduction of this chapter: the young man who associated a woman he met at a party with his old Aunt Sally.

You might think that once you have uncovered your association between the person in front of you and the person out of your past that the influence from the past association would be done with. Not so. Research suggests that if you feel that the person in your history is similar to the person with you in the present, no amount of reality testing with current contradictory information is likely to change your feelings and attitudes for the present person. For instance, you might meet a young woman at the party with a "special smile." You realize as you talk with her that she reminds you of your old girlfriend, whom you still care for. Later your best friend tells you that this new woman is really the two-timing, deceitful bitch who's broken the heart of two other mutual friends. You shake your head in disbelief and say that may be so . . . but that smile is so sweet that deep down you know she is good and you decide to ask her for a date.

Parataxic Distortion doesn't always function as an instant like or dislike. Sometimes it only influences specific interactions. One man kept interpreting his new lover's depressed feelings as a complaint and a demand that he change. Every time she talked about feeling sad and lost, he inferred that she was really trying to badger him into marriage. He responded with anger instead of support. And his lover, hurt and bewildered, became more depressed. Unconsciously, the man had confused his mother with his girlfriend. It was the mother who used her unhappiness like a club, whose sadness was always a veiled complaint. Because of Parataxic Distortion, the two women became one.

Unless the association between the person in your past and the person in your present can be separated in your mind, you will continue to react to the traits of the person from your past and relate to the new person accordingly. For example, you see a new person at a meeting at work and instantly distrust him. You think that it must be something about his eyes and mouth, and then realize that he bears a slight resemblance to Richard Nixon. You decide to talk to him after the meeting. He has an easy, direct manner which causes you to set aside the association to the former president. You feel comfortable with him as sales manager of the company.

Whenever you have a strong, immediate attraction to or revulsion for someone, whenever you find yourself making assumptions, think about associations between the person in front of you and people out of your past. Compare the person in front of you with the person out of your past by: (1) contrasting how each responds to the same situation, and (2) checking out what the current person actually wants or feels rather than assuming you know what these wants and feelings are.

If you suspect that someone is superimposing a Parataxic Distortion on you, try the following. Ask him or her: "Do I remind you of anyone else in your life? Perhaps someone in your past?" If the other person says yes, then explore the similarities and differences between you and the remembered person. If the other person denies that you remind him or her of someone else, but you have an idea of who it might be, very cautiously suggest the specific person. "Perhaps I remind you of some young girl out of your past . . . maybe your little sister. You sometimes treat me as though I was an eight-year-old playmate." Sometimes the origin of a Parataxic Distortion escapes conscious awareness, and no amount of exploration will cause it to surface. That can spell trouble for any ongoing relationship.

Perpetuating Illusions

Prejudgment is interactional. More often than not, when you first meet someone you are both on good behavior. However, if you try to maintain an unrealistically good image in order to win the approval or affection of the other person, you create an uncomfortable relationship that is likely to break down eventually. You can't delude other people forever. Sooner or later they are likely to notice that you are not living up to your idealized image, and they will probably feel disappointed, if not cheated. Consider the following dialogue:

Alice: You don't want to go to the party tonight? In the six months since we've been married, you've gone to only two parties with me. When we were single, we went to a party almost every weekend.

Jacob: I'm not really all that much of a party-goer. I can't stand all the noise.

Alice: I met you at a party and you were the life of it! You said you loved to be center stage.

Jacob: Oh yeah. I guess what I meant was that I like to be center stage with you.

Alice: That's nice to hear, but I miss our friends and parties.

Jacob: Why don't we have our own little party.

Alice: It's just not the same. You're not the same. You seem different now. I want your old self back.

In this example, Jacob clearly led Alice to believe that he was a much more extroverted person than he really was. He was only able to maintain the facade for a little while before it became too unnatural to continue. As a result, Alice's initial expectation that they would be a party-going couple is being disappointed. She holds on to her first impression and feels cheated by Jacob for denying her his more sociable side. An acknowledgment that she was mistaken in her initial assessment of Jacob would be a threat to her self-confidence. She would have to admit that her ability to evaluate people, in particular potential mates, is not foolproof.

Clarifying first impressions. Misleading first impressions can lead to later disillusionment. According to George Bach in his book *Pairing,* it is much easier to replace illusions with reality by checking out and sharing first impressions as soon as possible. You don't have to be potential best friends or lovers to make clear where you stand with a person. If you want or have to continue relating to a person after your initial meeting, the following steps should clear up most illusions you have about each other. Before the initial meeting is over:

1. Let the other person know that you are interested in getting to know him or her better, or at least let them know how you feel about them.

2. State what happened during the meeting from your point of view.

3. State what you expect and hope of the other person.

4. Give the other person an opportunity to object to or correct any false perceptions.

Returning to our conflicted couple, note that Jacob might have avoided misleading Alice had he followed these four steps when they first met:

Jacob: I really had a great time with you tonight and I want to see you again soon so that we can get better acquainted.

Alice: I really enjoyed you. You had us all in stitches 'til my ribs ached. How about going to a party next week?

Jacob: I guess I was a little rowdy tonight. I get that way when I've had too much to drink and I'm trying to impress a pretty woman. That's not my usual style. Basically, I'm a homebody.

Alice: Boy, you could have fooled me. You looked as though you were really in your element tonight.

Jacob: Not really. I wouldn't want you to get the wrong impression about me. Actually, I'd like to spend some quiet time with just you.

Alice: That's fine with me.

These four steps should reduce considerably the illusions of first impressions. As a relationship develops, it is essential to continue to check out each other's assumptions in order to keep communication lines clear. Never assume that you know what the other person is thinking or feeling until you have checked it out with him or her in plain language. Once you treat an assumption as a fact, it's very hard to change your opinion and acknowledge that you have misread someone. To avoid this trap, maintain a healthy skepticism about your assumptions and continue to test their reality by considering information contradicting as well as supporting your perspective.

Here is the solution to the puzzle on page 168.

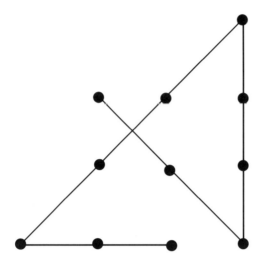

14

Making Contact

The world is full of interesting strangers. Every day potential friends and lovers pass you in the hallway and the parking lot. They eat next to you. They wait on you in the store. Your glances meet and shyly slide away. It's frightening to step out of your anonymous role and make contact. What would they think? What would you do if you were rejected?

This chapter is about breaking ice and making conversation with the people who attract you. It's the art of beginnings. By following a few simple rules and suggestions you can vastly reduce your shyness with strangers. You can learn to talk with virtually anyone, anywhere.

The Fear of Strangers

The fear of strangers comes from two sources: outmoded nineteenth century social restrictions and your own self-depreciating internal monologue. Nineteenth century rules mandated that strangers must be introduced by a third party before initiating conversation. It was off-limits for unacquainted people to approach each other for anything more intimate than asking directions. People out in public were isolated from those around them. These rules contributed to the modern day phenomenon of loneliness in the midst of crowds—people bustling everywhere but forbidden to make the slightest contact.

Your fear of strangers has also been influenced by habitual negative thoughts. You say things to yourself such as: "They don't want to talk to me." "He or she probably wouldn't like me." "It's hopeless." "I'm too awkward, too ugly, too short, too stupid."

In each case you view yourself as someone inferior, unworthy, and unattractive. In the tradition of comic-strip character Charlie Brown, you imagine that other people are always heroes while you are always the goat. The belief that you are not worthy inevitably leads to awkward self-consciousness and the painful conclusion that people you could enjoy won't enjoy you.

Here are five ways to cope with your fear of strangers.

1. Analyze what you say to yourself. Imagine that you are in a doctor's waiting room and have just started a conversation with an attractive person of the opposite sex. The person listens for a moment, makes a few perfunctory responses, and returns to reading a magazine. Now notice your internal monologue. Are you blaming yourself for the rejection? What fault have you found with yourself for the other person's disinterest? Are you using global labels such as "lame," "stupid," "ridiculous," and so on?

Negative judgments and labels should be changed. Make a list of your negative labels and devaluing statements. Next to each of the statements write the same thing in a purely descriptive manner. For "stupid" you might write "My mind periodically goes blank when trying to think of conversation." Instead of "flat chested," put your actual bra size. Instead of "dumpy," you might put your actual height and weight. Make a commitment to yourself to use the descriptive rather than the negative labels in your internal monologue.

The hard part, of course, is sticking with your nonjudgmental descriptions when trying to approach someone or after being rejected. These are the times when all your old habitual put-downs come on strong. You're so used to hearing them from yourself that you hardly notice. The solution is to make a list of your significant positive and negative qualities, five or six of each. The negative qualities are nonjudgmental descriptions. The positive qualities are things you realistically like or take pride in. Every time you find yourself tempted to approach someone, go over the memorized list. Give yourself a shot of reality rather than the old distorted labels and judgments.

2. Reframe your approach behavior. The fear of rejection is largely a product of how you conceptualize, or frame, your meeting with an interesting stranger. Here are some negative frames that will inhibit you when meeting people:

"They'll think I want something from them."

"He probably wouldn't be turned on to me."

"They're nice, but wouldn't want a relationship with me."

"She's gorgeous, what would she see in me?"

Notice that all these statements leave you one down, the supplicant hoping for something undeserved. It's time to reframe the meeting experience so that the stakes aren't so high. Meetings with interesting strangers shouldn't be a test to see if they want to sleep with you, want to be your friend or mate, or even particularly like you. It's merely an opportunity to begin getting to know someone who interests you. You're *curious* about what will happen, but not worried about it. You don't want anything from the other person, you are merely offering your time and interest. A refusal of your interest is a lost opportunity, nothing more or less.

3. Reframe rejection. When you approach a stranger, you are offering a gift—the gift of interaction. If he or she declines the offer, you can frame the rejection in a variety of ways. You can see yourself as inadequate and unworthy, you can focus on your physical and character flaws, or you can beat yourself up as socially incompetent. The trouble with these frames is that they assume facts not in evidence. You are mind reading.

There could be literally hundreds of reasons for any particular refusal or rejection. Let's suppose you invited someone at the office to lunch. The person smiles and says, "Not today, but please ask me again." You will be crushed if you conclude that your big nose has again turned someone off. But that's just one of many explanations. The person might be on a diet, might have just eaten, might be meeting someone else, might be too busy to eat, might be in some emotional turmoil, and so on.

Right now, as an exercise, list at least 25 reasons why you might turn down a relative stranger for a lunch date. Now examine the list. How many items would you consider rejections of the core person, of some basic emotional or physical characteristic? The fact is that you don't know strangers well enough to reject *them*. If you don't want to go on the lunch date, it probably has more to do with you—your schedule, your willingness to meet someone new, your mood.

Mind reading will almost always get you in trouble by leading you to the most negative possible interpretation for any refusal. The best thing to do if you are rejected is to assume there are personal reasons for the refusal which have little to do with you. If you want more information, ask for clarification. For example, if someone refuses to let you buy her a drink, you might check out whether that means an actual disinclination to talk to you or whether the person simply wants to buy her own.

4. Deal with the emotional blow when rejected. Even a minor rejection can take your breath away. The first thing to do is literally to take a few deep breaths and tune into how your body is doing. Feel your feet against the floor, the chair against your buttocks, notice the sensations in your stomach. Concentrating on your body can turn off for a few minutes the negative internal monologue that may follow rejection. Your deep breathing and body awareness can act as a sort of thought stopper and keep you from psychologically kicking yourself.

5. Plan to get rejected. You should expect to get soundly rejected at least three times a week. This means that you've found yourself interested in someone who, for one of hundreds of possible reasons, wasn't receptive to your interest. Try initiating conversations for the express purpose of experiencing and learning to deal with rejection. As an exercise, pick someone out whom you would like but who might not like you. Before initiating anything, think through the answers to these questions:

"What wouldn't he or she like about me?"

"How would he or she probably act?"

"What would I do to salvage the situation if I were rebuffed?"

When you've answered the questions, go ahead and approach the person. As you interact, observe what's going on between you. Also keep track of what you're thinking and feeling. Later, when you're in a quiet place, think back and notice how many of your assumptions were right or wrong. Did you enjoy yourself at all? Did you experience any sense of accomplishment in meeting a challenge?

Making Contact

There are only two basic rules for successfully making contact. First, you have to give what you would like to receive. Which means that the attention, interest, respect, and liking that you want must also be something you offer to others. Second, you have to have an outward rather than an inward focus. You listen to the other person instead of rehearsing your next remark or worrying about your hair or your awkwardness.

Giving what you would like to receive and staying other-focused are easier said than done. The fear of strangers often has the effect of making you awkward and self-conscious. No matter how much you want to reach out, your attention is riveted on your own appearance and behavior. The following sections will show you how to make contact so that others will feel your genuine interest.

Body Language

One of the biggest ways you can turn people off is through body language. Shy people characteristically avoid eye contact, keep blank expressionless faces, and physically retreat from others. The message sent is "Don't bother me." Here's the body language you need for making contact:

1. **Move toward the other person.** This means getting into the circle or group rather than watching from the outside. It also means that you don't converse from ten feet away. You must find a distance at which you can talk and interact comfortably.

2. **Lean forward.** Leaning back against the seat communicates fatigue or disinterest, while leaning forward indicates that you are engaged and ready for contact.

3. **Uncross your arms and legs.** Crossed arms and legs indicate a defensive, protective position, while an open posture indicates a willingness to listen.

4. **Make eye contact.** Most people have trouble looking someone in the eye and trying to think of what to say at the same time. Eye contact can be anxiety-provoking and make you lose your train of thought. The solution is to focus your eyes somewhere else on the face. For example, you can keep your eyes glued to the person's nose, mouth, or left ear. As long as your focus is within eight inches of the nose, the other person won't be able to tell that you aren't looking him or her in the eye.

5. **Smile.** A smile is the most universally understood statement that you are open and interested in making contact.

6. **Let your responses show.** Nod, frown, raise your eyebrows in surprise.

7. **Touch the other person.** Briefly touching on the shoulder, arm, hand, or knee says far better than any words your feelings of warmth and liking.

Here's how to practice your body language skills. Sit in front of a TV talk show and imagine that the guest is speaking directly to you. Except for touching, you can practice every aspect of body language. Keep a checklist of the skills nearby and refer to it while you practice your responses to the talk-show guest.

Icebreakers

The only way to begin a conversation is to start talking. It's safe to assume that other people want and enjoy contact just as you do. They need that excitement which can only come when two people express genuine interest in each other. And just as you want the same things, you are probably afraid of the same things too: embarrassment, rejection, or being forced to do something you don't want to do.

It doesn't matter a great deal what you say to get a conversation started. What's important is that you say enough to invite some response. When you need an icebreaker, stop for a moment of meditation. Not the transcendental kind. But focus for a brief period on your immediate experience. Meditation means that you relax, open yourself to what you see and feel, and wait for an awareness you can share. What's unusual, what can you deduce from his or her appearance or behavior? Notice the environment you're sharing. How would you describe it to a friend? Check your feelings. What's it like to be you right now? How does it feel poised on the edge of making contact?

At the end of your meditation, choose which awareness you will share. One woman, who was seated next to an attractive man on a train, was racking her brain for a conversational opener. Finally she paused to meditate on her experience. The train was taking her to a new job and a new town. She thought how hard it had always been to meet people. And that gave her the icebreaker. "You know, I'm moving to a place where I don't know a soul. I've been thinking that I better get in practice for meeting people. Hi, my name is Jill." A university student, observing a young woman in his class, smiled and said, "You haven't taken a note either. Are you as bored as I am?"

If a few moments of meditation fails to suggest an icebreaker, try one of the following standard openers:

1. Ask for information. "Can you tell me where Filbert Street is?" "Is there a gift shop in the lobby?" "How do I get to the nearest bar?"

2. Give a compliment. "Your purse has some of the most intricate tooled leather work I've ever seen."

3. A little humor. "Do you mind talking to a man who's lost?" "You could get old waiting for a table in this restaurant." "I was looking for the porter but I'd rather talk to you."

4. Use current events. "This city's full of muggers. Look at that guy. Right now he's doing an appraisal on my watch." "I'm starting to like the idea of a moratorium on high rises. This street is a wind tunnel."

A tried and true icebreaker is the *ritual question.* "Hi, what's your name?" "How are you?" "How's it going?" "Do you live around here?" "Do you work in this building?" "Is this your son?" "How did you like the play?" Ritual questions don't require a lot of work to think up and they don't require a lot of work to answer. Therein lies their strength and their shortcoming. It's easy to get a brief remark. But then, almost immediately, the ball is back in your court and you have to follow up with specific questions and comments to generate a real conversation.

One of the most challenging and rewarding of conversational ice-breakers is the direct approach. This involves telling the other person exactly what you feel and what you want. "I feel attracted to you and I want to spend a few minutes talking and getting to know you." "It's a little scary walking up to a stranger but you seem like an interesting person to me." "I see you're reading Steinbeck. I've always loved those *Cannery Row* characters and I was curious about what you thought of them."

When searching for an icebreaker, two things to watch for are similarities and differences. Anything you have in common is a good way to start a conversation. Noticing that you both like the same book, admire the same view, are both slumped in your chairs, or are both wearing band-aids will generate good ice-breaking remarks. Noticing contrasts is a provocative way of encouraging self disclosure. "I'd never have the courage to come here alone." "I was always more drawn to the impressionists, but I see that you like the Hopper prints."

The Art of Conversation

Once you can break the ice, the question is how to make satisfying contact with another person. You only have to know how to do three things to make good conversation: ask questions, listen actively, and disclose a little about yourself.

Questions

There are basically two kinds of questions. The ritual questions, already discussed, focus on learning a person's name, where he's from, and what he does. Ritual questions are most often used as the opening gambits of a conversation, but soon give way to *informational questions*. These are more specific, and are designed to elicit important facts about the other person's experience, beliefs, and feelings. While a ritual "How are you doing?" might reap a "Fine, how are you?" an informational question such as "What's it like to work with children?" will promote more intimate contact.

Whenever you pose an informational question, you will probably find out a little more than you asked for. This is called *free information*. If you ask somebody whether she lives in town, and she replies yes, you receive no free information. But in most cases you will get a response such as "I just moved up to Twin Peaks because I really love the view." You've gotten two free pieces of information: the location and the preference for a view. Through a series of questions you might get such free information as marital status, number of children, taste in art, and the story of a past vacation.

Informational questions allow you to begin sketching a picture of who the other person is. The secret to exciting conversation is to follow your curiosity and ask questions that you really want the answer to. You may want to know how a person could survive on a wind-swept hill like Twin Peaks. Go ahead and ask. You may want to know how much she pays in rent. You may want to know if she lives alone. The most basic rule of conversation is to *pry*. People are their own favorite topics of conversation. They're flattered by your attention and interest. Be outrageous, because each question continues the excitement and pleasure of a growing intimacy.

In this country there are well-established social rules about minding your own business. You can get around those rules by tempering really direct questions with techniques of active listening and self disclosure. The next sections will show you how.

Active Listening

The second hallmark of a good conversationalist is the ability to listen in such a way that others feel heard. An active listener feeds back what's been said in his own words. He does this for three reasons: (1) to make sure that he understood and got it right, (2) to give the speaker the reassurance that he or she was listened to, and (3) to promote more disclosure on the part of the speaker. For example, if a mountain-climbing friend was explaining the details of a difficult ascent, you might listen actively by putting a little amazement in your voice: "And you were able to sleep in a hammock suspended by only two pitons!" Your friend might say, "No, I had three, but that was only for safety." Then, encouraged by your attention, he might go on to describe how he feels sleeping with nothing but a piece of nylon keeping him from a 2,000-foot drop.

It should be clear that listening is more than merely keeping your mouth shut. You carefully attend to what is said, you remember it, and you feed it back. The inability to listen is the most common cause of conversational disaster. Some people can't listen because they are pre-occupied with their fears of embarrassment, others are perennially preparing their next remark, and still others fail to listen because they are too busy advising or winning an argument. If you aren't able to listen, you are not able to give the interest, attention, and respect that you yourself would want to receive. People grow bored with you and slide away. For more information on the blocks to listening and how to overcome them, read the listening chapter.

Self-Disclosure

Disclosure makes intimacy possible. Trying to achieve closeness without revealing something about yourself is like trying to hit home runs with a toothpick. You haven't got what it takes.

If you have difficulty talking about yourself, try this exercise. Write a four- or five-page autobiography. Think back to important incidents in your life that helped make you who you are. Focus on information that will enable others to understand you better. Include:

- Important or formative events in your childhood

- What school was like for you

- Your favorite teacher

- A few of your more interesting jobs

- The people you've loved and cared for

- Your biggest loss

- Your most wonderful moment

- Your greatest achievement

- Your hobbies

- Your best vacation

- The funniest thing that ever happened to you

Now add anything else that you think is important or appropriate. You can read over your autobiography whenever you expect to be in a social situation. It will give you a wealth of information for stories and anecdotes.

Self disclosure doesn't mean that you have to reveal your deepest needs and secrets. There are three levels of self disclosure. The first level is purely informational: describing your job, your last vacation, a funny experience. This level persists during the first few minutes of a conversation when you aren't yet ready to reveal your feelings.

To deepen the contact, you can move to the second level of self-disclosure. This level of intimacy involves thoughts, feelings, needs—but only about the past or future. Typical statements at this level might include:

- A belief or opinion that you've felt committed to

- A story that makes you seem foolish

- An emotional event from your childhood

- A fear you once had or a concern for the future

- Some of your hopes for the future

- General preferences and tastes

- Problems in old relationships

Each thing that you reveal about yourself adds spice to your relationships. The other person feels flattered to be let into your world and you both enjoy the excitement of deepening contact. When you talk about your hopes and fears, preferences and beliefs, you become a unique individual rather than a cardboard character. You are making an impact.

Some people are afraid to express their tastes and feelings because they feel that disclosure might destroy an illusion of similarity with the other person. They worry that revealing differences will undermine potential closeness. The fact is that contrasts are exciting, and differences in taste and viewpoint can enliven a relationship. You may feel a little less anxious if you withhold your feelings, but inauthenticity will ultimately suffocate your relationship.

Many people never get past the second level of self-disclosure. The feelings and events they talk about are safely in the past. They don't express feelings about a here-and-now relationship. The third level of self-disclosure involves revealing your feelings about the person you're speaking to. This means doing any one of the following:

- Saying what attracts you to the person

- Saying how you are affected by the other person's behavior at this moment

- Telling about your reservations and some of the things you don't like about the other person

- Saying what you hope for from the encounter

- Saying what you feel about how the other person responds to what you say

The key to this deepest level of intimacy is to say what you feel right now. It's risky and you may get a little anxious. But you will also feel undeniable excitement. As you take risks, particularly by revealing your negative feelings, you are creating strong bonds. Just as soldiers in combat feel a special intimacy, people who risk sharing their hidden feelings can very quickly become close.

To get practice at this level of intimacy, try an exercise for sharing your reservations. Seek out a friend you feel close to. Tell him or her this: "I'd like you to share your reservations about me. I won't defend myself, but I'd also like to share mine with you at the end." Explain that you're trying to get practice hearing and saying negative things.

Putting It All Together

Conversation is the art of combining questions, active listening, and self disclosure in such a way that people keep talking and enjoy it. Remember, the basic rule of conversation is to pry. But your probing questions must be tempered with self disclosure so people feel they're getting to know you while you're getting to know them. Two examples: "I have a hard time saying no to my daughter. How do you manage to keep good discipline?" "I've always wanted to ski. Do you go up to Squaw Valley often?"

Another way to avoid being obnoxious is to combine informational questions with active listening. "So you've had a series of relationships that seem to end when you finally stand up for yourself. Did you tend to wait till you just couldn't bear it anymore to stand up for your rights?" "You toured Europe for five months all alone at the age of seventeen. Incredible. Was it your father's death that brought you home?"

Prying is fun. It helps you satisfy your curiosity and also get more information so you can keep the conversation going. When you are no longer curious enough to pry, it's probably a good sign that the conversation has run its course and you should look for a graceful close.

Here's how a conversation might go if you used questions, active listening, and self disclosure to the best advantage.

Warren: That was a tremendous analysis of the Populist Movement. I think Professor Sims loved it. ICEBREAKER

Beth: Thanks. You're Warren, aren't you? RITUAL QUESTION

Warren: Right. You can always tell when Sims likes something. He gets all excited and starts wiping his glasses. Are you enjoying the seminar? RITUAL QUESTION

Beth: Not much. In fact, I haven't a single class I really like this quarter. I'm a little depressed about it. Are you worried about finding the primary sources Sims wants, the old newspapers and all that? SELF-DISCLOSURE/INFORMATIONAL QUESTION

Warren: No, they're all on microfilm, and frankly I sometimes just make it up. SELF-DISCLOSURE

Beth: (Laughs) Are you going home this Christmas? INFORMATIONAL QUESTION

Warren: I'm going to stick around here. I had a horrible time last year when my stepmother got drunk and fell into the tree. She's a lot younger than my father, unfulfilled and bitter. I'd just as soon stay clear of it. SELF-DISCLOSURE

Beth: There's no family feeling, a lot of hassling? ACTIVE LISTENING

Warren: Yeah. I think they're ready to split. Is Christmas any better at your house? SELF-DISCLOSURE/ INFORMATIONAL QUESTION

Beth: We don't stay home. We all go to the mountains for cross-country skiing. Every year there's this cabin we rent for the holidays. I have three sisters. There's a real close-knit feeling. SELF-DISCLOSURE

Warren: I'd give a lot to have a family like that. Especially this time of year. Sometimes I wonder if there's any hope for a decent marriage. I mean, it's scary. I think even if I find someone who's wonderful now, five years later it might be a nightmare, just like my parents had. SELF-DISCLOSURE

Beth: It's like you can't make a commitment for fear the whole thing will turn into some terrible trap. I worry about that; time changes people incredibly. My sister was really in love with this guy and she hates his guts now. I worry about my own affection changing suddenly as much as I do about the other person's. ACTIVE LISTENING/SELF-DISCLOSURE

Warren: Yeah, you worry about something breaking the spell, suddenly you're not in love anymore. ACTIVE LISTENING

Beth: That's it. It's fun talking, do you want to go out on the grass? By the way, how did you get Sims to let you do a paper on Dashiell Hammett? Now there's something that would be fun doing. SELF-DISCLOSURE/INFORMATIONAL QUESTION

Warren: I love detective novels. As long as they have lots of cigar-smoking cops and Sam Spade-type gumshoes. I'm addicted to them. I've even been to that place in San Francisco where Miles Archer was supposedly killed in *The Maltese Falcon*. Do you like Hammett

too? SELF-DISCLOSURE/INFORMATIONAL
QUESTION

Beth: Not as much as Raymond Chandler. I've read every
          word Chandler ever wrote. In fact, I've written some
          short stories imitating his style. SELF-DISCLOSURE

Warren: You write? How do you find time?
          INFORMATIONAL QUESTION

Beth: Well, I guess between writing and studying there
          isn't time for much else. SELF-DISCLOSURE

Warren: I hope you won't be offended, but I have always
          thought you were kind of asocial, just preoccupied
          with books and not very interested in people. I was
          kind of attracted to you and always wanted to talk to
          you but you seemed so . . . reserved.
          SELF-DISCLOSURE

Beth: I think that's true to some extent. But I'm enjoying
          talking right now. The only trouble is that I'm five
          minutes late for class.

Warren: I'm a little scared to ask you, but I'd love to take you
          to a movie tonight. *The Thin Man* is playing.
          SELF-DISCLOSURE

Fortunately for Warren, Beth suspends her prejudice toward
Dashiell Hammett and accompanies him to *The Thin Man*. The conversation moves easily from point to point. It gets off the ground with
icebreakers and ritual questions. Informational questions are the lubri-
cant that keeps it going, while active listening and self disclosure
deepen the contact. Neither is afraid to abruptly change the subject to
follow a new line of interest. Beth has learned a lot about Warren in a
few minutes. She's reassured him that she was listening by feeding back
what he said in her own words. She's offered him information about
herself so her questions come in the context of her own disclosures.
Warren has allowed Beth to see into his painful family situation. He's
exposed some of his fears, and even offered a reservation about her.
Each of these disclosures increased the opportunity for bonding and
made it more likely that Beth would say yes to a date with *The Thin
Man*.

V

Family Skills

15

Sexual Communication

It is an amazing paradox that the most fascinating subject known to humankind is often the most difficult topic for a couple to discuss with each other. In spite of the importance sexual relationships have, many couples spend more time talking about what color they are going to repaint the kitchen. Largely because of poor communication, couples develop sexual problems such as the following:

Tracy feels ambivalent regarding her new boyfriend Alex. She likes his companionship, but finds that he touches her too roughly. To keep from feeling overwhelmed by him, she tries to avoid physical contact on their dates. Alex, who interprets her "arm's-length" policy as rejection, seeks reassurance by pressing for physical contact. Tracy redoubles her defenses.

A woman yawns and stretches and heads for bed at 8:30 p.m., saying to her husband, "Coming to bed, Dear?" Her husband glances up from the TV and mumbles, "Going to bed so early?" "Yes, I'm really tired. Aren't you?" "No, I'll be up after the news. Sleep well." "Oh, alright then." This undemonstrative conversation actually contained a sexual invitation to a husband who complains about the low frequency of sex in his marriage.

Bill complains bitterly to his wife, Cynthia, that their sex life is in a rut: "There's more to sex than the Missionary Position!" Cynthia, who comes from a strict religious background, feels safe with her sex life the way it is. She

resents being pressured by her husband, and tries to
change the subject whenever he brings it up. Bill tries a
positive tack: "I would be really happy if we were to try
sex front to back just once to see what it's like." Cynthia
starts crying and says, "Don't you love me anymore?"
Stymied once again, Bill tries to comfort his wife. Secretly
Cynthia fears that if she gives in to this one request it will
be followed by many others . . . give an inch and he'll take
a mile. And what happens if she does these things for him
and he's still not satisfied . . . then they would be in real
trouble.

These examples are typical of the problems that can develop in sexual
relationships when people do not communicate their thoughts, feelings,
and wishes fully and directly. Nonverbal cues are missed entirely or are
misinterpreted. Couples become locked into win-lose battles. The way
one partner seeks reassurance always seems to threaten the other, leading to a perpetual vicious circle. Honest efforts to communicate directly
often meet with resistance which is perceived as rejection.

Myths of Sexual Communication

This chapter will explore three myths that help to limit communication
between partners regarding their sexual relations. Guidelines for effective sexual communication based on a free exchange of feelings,
thoughts, and wishes will be suggested in their place. The three myths
are:

1. You shouldn't have to talk about sex with your partner because
   sex will naturally take care of itself.

2. Your partner should be sensitive and considerate enough to
   know how to sexually satisfy you.

3. You should avoid conflict at all costs.

**1. You shouldn't have to talk about sex with your partner be-
cause sex will naturally take care of itself.** Since sex is a natural biological process, many people think that it should occur spontaneously.
Some people go a step further and equate "naturally occurring good
sex" with love and romance. If you are one of these people, sex is a bit
of a mystery to you. When it is going well, it's great; but when you
have difficulties, you are at a loss about what to do. The following are
examples of statements and decisions based on this belief.

Emmy Lou, who had been dating Walt for three months and cared
for him very much, was surprised when she suddenly lost sexual inter-

est in him. Rather than talk about the situation, she simply said, "Well, I guess it was not meant to be," and abruptly ended the relationship, much to Walt's dismay.

When Joe approached his wife to discuss the low frequency of their sexual relations her response was, "Talking about sex takes the romance out of it! It will work itself out . . . just let it be."

This belief in spontaneous sexuality gets much of its support from the early part of a relationship when two people are first getting to know one another. This is when you and your partner tend to focus only on what is positive. Your heightened need to approve and be approved and your desire to please makes this a time when sexual needs tend to get gratified easily . . . almost magically.

Inevitably, individual differences in sexual preference are noticed. If sexual difficulties develop, there is a tendency to think, "This just isn't right." Rather than consider the possibility that there is a communication problem, many couples throw in the towel. Others simply say "The honeymoon is over" and resign themselves to a mediocre sex life.

As a complex human being, your sex life is much more than a natural biological process. It is keenly sensitive to such psychological and interpersonal factors as beliefs and roles learned in childhood, past sexual experiences, and such current stresses as job or financial worries, health problems, relationship conflicts, or losses. Preoccupation regarding an upcoming deadline or resentment regarding unspoken, unmet needs does not mix well with sexual enjoyment. Such unexpressed thoughts, feelings, and wishes will likely interfere with your sexual desire or performance.

At such times, it's important to tune in to what you are thinking, feeling, and wanting. Then express it to your partner so that you can develop an ally who truly appreciates your position. The more open you are, the more likely you are to get support and cooperation.

One note of caution: you can over-talk a sexual problem. This is particularly true if it is an isolated incident or a problem due to a temporary external stress. If you feel turned off one night, or fail to maintain an erection or have an orgasm, it's best to accept it as an inevitable disappointing event that happens to everyone sooner or later. Dwelling on it in your mind or repeatedly discussing it with your partner is only likely to stir up anticipatory anxiety, which can itself cause the difficulty to reoccur.

2. Your partner should be sensitive and considerate enough to know how to sexually satisfy you. This belief contains two of the worst traps that a couple can fall into. First, it assumes that your partner is capable of knowing what would sexually satisfy you without your having to tell him or her. Unless your partner is a very good mind reader, it is highly unlikely that he or she is going to have a clear picture of what turns you on or off at any given moment. You are a far better judge than your partner is of your needs and wishes.

The second trap is the assumption that if your partner does not satisfy your sexual needs and wishes, it's a sign of his or her lack of consideration for you. Many people so firmly believe this that they balk at asking for what they want sexually. For example, one woman reported: "It just wouldn't be the same if I told him what I wanted. If he doesn't do it of his own accord, how will I know if he really cares?" The result of this reasoning is that her husband is left in the dark regarding her sexual preferences. He is also condemned as uncaring for not figuring out and meeting her unspoken needs. Inability to mind-read is recast, in this case, as insensitivity and inconsiderateness.

In addition to these two traps, you may hesitate to express your wishes, because asking for what you want involves risk. By stating your sexual preferences to your partner, you make yourself vulnerable to direct rejection. Maybe your partner will think that you are perverted, self-centered, or asking for too much. Yet failing to state your needs greatly increases the chances of sexual unhappiness. Whether you choose to be silent or to confide your needs, some risk is inevitable.

At the other extreme, you may fear that if you ask for what you want directly, your partner will not feel free to say no. He or she might go through the motions of pleasing you, all the time resenting being asked. Preserving your own and your partner's right to say no allows each of you to take responsibility for setting your own respective limits.

3. You should avoid conflict at all costs. If you express negative feelings or wishes and thoughts that differ from those of your partner, you may fear turning off your partner and making matters worse. Although some of your feelings and wishes may create conflict, the real problem is chickening out and not pushing through to a resolution. Here are some typical examples of chickening out at the first sign of conflict.

> When I mentioned to Sam that I was having fantasies of having sex with other men when we made love, he went into a sulk and didn't speak to me for two days. I love my husband, but I keep imagining sleeping with other men. I'll certainly never talk about it again.

> I used to tell John that I didn't have an orgasm during intercourse and ask him to masturbate me. He just kept doing the same old thing. I've stopped nagging him about it, but I must admit I really resent his selfishness.

> I know Margie doesn't like oral sex, so I have never brought it up to her. But it's something I really enjoy and

I'm thinking of breaking up so that I can have oral sex
with someone who likes it as much as I do.

These examples reflect the ongoing unresolved sexual problems
that partners often do not fully express to one another. Perhaps you
have tried to talk with your partner about something that bothers you
sexually and immediately received such a negative reaction that you
never even finished explaining what it was you had in mind. Maybe
you have repeatedly asked for something and your partner has been
unreceptive. Perhaps you have said nothing out of fear of turning your
partner off or creating an unpleasant, awkward situation in which he
or she tries half-heartedly to comply.

A major reason for not insisting on what you want is guilt. You
feel unentitled to what you are feeling and wishing for. After all, what
right do you have to want your partner to do something that he or she
finds distasteful or frightening? How dare you have such strong negative feelings about individual differences in sexual preferences?

Guilt distorts your communications. When you feel unentitled to
your own sexual preferences, you often express them in indirect ways
that are likely to be rejected by your partner. You may express them in
an exaggerated form through accusations or in a passive manner
through pouting, withholding, or nagging. When you feel entitled to
your thoughts, feelings, and wishes, no matter how bizarre they may
be, you are more likely to express them directly and fully. You are then
free to deal with your partner's response. Even if the response is a direct
refusal, it's better than continuing to repeat the same old frustrating
patterns.

When Your Partner Refuses

When you meet with refusal or rejection of your sexual requests, you
would be wise to fully explore your partner's position on the issue, in
particular his or her fears. Your partner may have a series of cata-
strophic "what if" fantasies that are not clearly defined.

Examples:

What if I agree to your having an affair? You'll learn there
are much better lovers out there and you'll leave me. I
couldn't live without you.

What if I agree to give you oral sex? I'll choke to death.

You need to address each of your partner's very real fears and then ask
if there are any others.

It is also important to ferret out and fully explore any hidden resentments or unexpressed wishes that may be contributing to your partner's resistance. For example, "Why should I have sex as frequently as you want it when you just rush through it?" or "You want me to touch you more? You never touch me except when you want sex. I just want to be held sometimes," or "You just roll over and go to sleep after sex and I lie there awake . . . I feel used!"

While it may be hard for you to listen to these criticisms and indirect demands, it will be worth it in the long run. Your partner is much more likely to feel close to you and want to satisfy your needs if he or she feels that his or her thoughts, feelings, and wishes are also being listened to and acknowledged. While you and your partner will not reach accord on every sexual issue, you will significantly reduce that sense of isolation, deprivation, and desperation that develops when you lack a way of talking about how you feel about a particular sexual issue.

Example: Hal and Justine have been married ten years and have two children. Justine wants to make love more often, but when she brings up the subject Hal doesn't want to talk about it and puts her down. She finally decides to press through the conflict and explore Hal's fears and reservations.

Justine: Would you agree with me that you do tend to avoid sex more often than you used to?

Hal: Of course.

Justine: What is it that you are avoiding?

Hal: I don't know . . . I'm pretty tired with that new job . . . most nights I'm not into it.

Justine: Weekends too?

Hal: I feel like you're always pestering me . . . I feel pressured to have sex when I don't feel like it.

Justine: I agree I have been pestering you lately, but that's because we haven't had sex in so long. Is there anything else that's bothering you?

Hal: I don't want to get into it.

Justine: If we don't get into it, we're going to stay the way we are or get worse.

Hal: Well . . . you're not going to like this . . . I don't seem turned on to you any more . . . the feeling just isn't there.

Justine: This is going to be hard for both of us, but would you please tell me specifically what turns you off?

Hal: Well, as you recall, I used to initiate sex most of the time. You were so passive . . . it was like making love to a mannequin. Even recently when you started trying to seduce me, as soon as you saw an erection you would become passive. I would prefer masturbating to having to do all the work. I'm really tired of lifeless sex.

Justine: You sound angry.

Hal: You're damn right! And sad . . . it used to be pretty good between us . . . now we've lost it.

Justine: How would you like to see our sex life different? Be specific.

(Note that Justine does not entirely agree with Hal's observations, but rather than argue with him, she asks about his unexpressed wish.)

Hal: You could let me know that you're enjoying yourself by saying so or moaning. You could move your hips around more, kiss me, caress me, occasionally just take charge and make love to me passionately.

Justine: Anything else?

Hal: Stop wearing cotton nighties . . . I prefer silk or something slinky.

Justine: Have you any other feelings about our sex life that you want to tell me about? Any fears?

Hal: Well, I mentioned before I feel real pressured when you ask for sex and I'm tired or otherwise not interested. I feel like I have to perform. I guess I'm like most men . . . I dread not being able to get it up and keep it up. I think that I've been avoiding sex because of that fear . . . it's really caused my sexual feelings to die down. I think about that, and then think about all I would lose . . . you and the kids, the life we have built together . . . if we were to split up. I get so down about that that I can't enjoy sex. I've felt pretty cut off from you . . . like I couldn't talk to you about anything that really mattered because this was hanging over me. This conversation is a kind of relief. I feel a little closer to you now.

Justine: You sound like you have been going through hell. I
thought it was just me. I've felt so alone . . . I've
thought of having an affair just to get some intimacy.
I was feeling really bitter and shut out . . . now that I
understand what this is about, I feel that I want to
do everything I can to make sex feel good to you
again.

Evaluating Your Sex Life

Before you talk with your partner about your sex life, you will find it
useful to reflect on what you enjoy and don't enjoy.

1. What beliefs and fears make you hesitate to talk with your partner
   about your sex life?

2. What about your sexual relationship brings you the most pleasure?

3. List external stressors (for example, finances, in-laws, children, ill
   health, relationship conflicts other than sexual ones) affecting your
   sex life.

_____

_____

_____

_____

_____

4. Was there a time in your relationship when your sex life with your
   partner was more satisfying? If yes, how was it different from now?

5. If you answered yes to question 4, what do you think has contributed to the change? In particular, what have you done or not done
   that influenced the change?

6. Recall in detail a time recently when you and your partner had sexual relations that were fairly typical of your sex life.

   • How did it begin?

   • How did it unfold?

   • How did it end?

   • What did you like about it?

   • What did you dislike about it?

- What could you or your partner have done differently that would have made it a better experience for you? Be as specific as possible.

- How could the circumstances (time, place, sounds, temperature, and so on) have been improved?

7. Stepping outside the realm of ordinary reality for a moment, take a few minutes to recall some of your wildest sexual daydreams. What are the recurring themes? (For example: surprise, romance, slow undressing, dominance/submission, oral sex, group sex, sex in public places.) While these fantasies might not be something that you would want to actually carry out with your partner, they may give you an idea of how you might add excitement to your sex life if they were in a modified form.

Guidelines for Effective Communication

Once you have become more clear about how you perceive your sex life with your partner and how you would like it to be different, you are almost ready to talk with him or her about it. The second step is to review the expressing and listening rules and skills presented elsewhere in the book. Here is a synopsis.

1. **Prepare yourself.** Be clear about what you think, feel, and want regarding your sexual relationship.

2. **Check to see if your partner is in the mood to communicate with you on this topic.** If not, reschedule for another time that is convenient for both of you.

3. **Be positive.** Point out to your partner what you like about your sex life and your relationship in general. Try to phrase what you don't like in positive terms. For example, instead of saying, "Don't rub me so hard," say "I'd enjoy it much more if you rubbed me more gently."

4. **Use "I messages."** Take responsibility for your ideas, feelings, and wishes. You can reduce confusion greatly by clearly stating your position on an issue. Asking your partner "What do you think about such and such?" before you have stated your position is a cop-out.

5. **Avoid "you messages."** Accusing your partner of not meeting your sexual needs or calling him or her names only creates defensiveness and is more likely to lead to a "win-lose" argument than to honest communication.

6. **Be specific.** You are more likely to get the response you want from your partner if you let him or her know exactly what you think, feel, and want. For example, rather than saying "I wish you would be more affectionate with me," say "I would really enjoy you greeting me at the door when I come home at night with a hug and kiss. I'd also like a hug and kiss before we go to sleep."

7. **Use active listening.** Make sure that your partner has understood what you have said to him or her. Don't rely on nonverbal signs or the statement, "Yes, I understand." Ask for a paraphrase of what your partner thinks he or she heard you say. If the paraphrase is wrong, correct your partner's misinterpretation. Also use active listening when you listen to your partner.

8. **Stay focused.** Keep your goal in mind and when you find that the conversation is wandering to other topics, bring it back to what you originally started talking about.

9. **Agree on an experiment.** Once you have stated your position on a sexual problem, and you have heard your partner's position on it, come up with a tentative solution that is acceptable to both of you. Agree to try it out for a specified period of time before you talk about it again and review how satisfactory it was for both of you. If it wasn't satisfactory, negotiate a new tentative solution and test it out.

10. **Thank your partner for communicating with you about your sexual relationship.** Remember that positively reinforcing your partner for cooperating with you will make him or her more likely to cooperate with you in the future.

The following is an example of how not to talk about your sexual relationship. Sharon's and Jim's efforts to discuss their sexual problems inevitably went like this:

Jim: You never initiate sex any more. *(you message)*

Sharon: You never give me a chance . . . you're always on me. *(you message)*

Jim: *(becoming defensive)* What am I supposed to do? I'm a normal, redblooded American horny toad. Is there something about me that repulses you?

Sharon: Look, we've been over this a hundred times. I'm tired. You never help me around the house. *(you message)* By the way, did you take out the garbage yet? *(loss of focus)*

Jim: You're always nagging me to do something. I'm just
            a chore boy to you. *(you message)* If you loved me,
            you'd give me a little more T.L.C.

At this point Sharon storms out of the room.

Jim and Sharon both end up losing in this argument. Each becomes defensive and makes accusations, and neither really listens to the
other's statements. The results are feelings of being discounted, resentment, and alienation. Using the guidelines for effective communication
listed above, their conversation could have a more satisfactory conclusion.

Jim: Sharon, I want to talk to you about something that is
            bothering me about our sex life. Are you willing?

Sharon: Okay.

Jim: I really enjoy our sex together. When we go long
            periods of time without having sex, I really miss the
            intimacy. I start feeling irritable with you about little
            things that normally wouldn't bother me. I know I
            would be much happier if we were to have sex at
            least twice a week. Before you give me an answer,
            would you be willing to tell me what you heard me
            just say, so I can be sure you understood me.

Sharon: Wow! You're sure coming on different today.

Jim: I know, we didn't seem to be getting anywhere with
            my old complaining. But that's beside the point.
            What did you hear me say before?

Sharon: That when we don't have sex for a while you get
            grouchy about little things and that you'd like more
            sex.

Jim: That's part of what I said. I also said that I really
            enjoy our sex together and that I would be much
            happier and less grouchy if we were to have sex at
            least twice a week. Now what did you hear me say?

Sharon: This is a little corny. You said that you enjoy our sex
            together and that you would be happier and less
            grouchy if we were to have sex at least twice a week.

Jim: Perfect! Now, what do you think of that?

Sharon: I think it's great in theory, but you know how tired I
            always am when I have to do all the housework on

top of my job. To feel less tired, I'd need you to help me with it. Now, what did you just hear me say?

Jim: You agree in theory, but that in order not to feel so tired you want me to help you with the housework. What specifically would you like me to do?

Sharon: Hmm . . . split dinner and dishes, vacuum and dust once a week, and take out the garbage. You already do a nice job on the yard, which I really appreciate.

Jim: So you want me to continue doing the yard. You also want me to take out the garbage, and vacuum and dust once a week. And you want me to wash the dishes when you cook dinner.

Sharon: Right, except I'd really like you to make dinner sometimes and let me wash the dishes.

Jim: You know I can't cook! I'd be willing to take you out for dinner once a week though.

Sharon: Sounds okay with me. Does that mean that you agree to my other requests?

Jim: I think so, yes.

Sharon: One other thing: I don't want to have to remind you to do these things. How are you going to remember to do them?

Jim: I'll take responsibility to remember, and I'll make a list to remind myself. Are you willing to give my request a try?

Sharon: Sure.

Jim: Let's try our agreements for a month. Then we can discuss whether they are working or if we need to try something else.

Sharon: Sounds okay to me.

In this conversation, both partners end up winning. This is possible when there isn't a great deal of pent-up ill feeling and when the individuals can clearly articulate their positions and offer alternatives that they can both agree to try.

Using the guidelines for effective communication, try the following exercise: Negotiate with your partner for one small thing that you want him or her to do differently.

If you are reading this chapter together, this exercise will be much easier than if you are reading it on your own. Assuming that you are both familiar with the guidelines, you can coach each other to follow them. Tape-recording your discussion and listening to it later will also help you learn where you tend to get off the track.

If you are doing this exercise without your partner having read this chapter, you may feel self-conscious about initiating the conversation. If so, you will probably find it helpful to tell your partner how you feel. For example: "I want to talk to you about something that has been on my mind about our sexual relationship. I feel really awkward bringing this up and I'm shaking inside because I don't know how you will respond."

Enhancing Your Sexual Communication

Sexual Vocabulary

How is yours? Some people admit that part of their hesitancy to discuss sex is that they lack an adequate sexual vocabulary. Your vocabulary may be outdated. Your names for various anatomical parts when you were 16 years old in the locker room might be a turnoff to your partner now.

To extend your sexual vocabulary, make a list of sexual anatomical parts and sexual behaviors, using medical terms. Alongside of each medical term, list your favorite synonyms. Have your partner do the same. Discuss your results with each other. Let each other know what terms are acceptable or turn-ons to you and which are distasteful. Are there certain words or phrases that you would like your partner to say to you while you are making love? Are they the words you would like your partner to use when you are discussing sex outside of bed?

Anatomy Lessons

Learning more about your own and your partner's body will make you a better lover. The following exercises suggest ways of enhancing your knowledge of one another.

Real anatomy. Using as a guide a book with diagrams of male and female exterior sexual organs, explore your own and your partner's body. Learn to identify by sight and touch the various sexual parts of yourself and your partner.

Sensate focus. In a room at a comfortable temperature, have your partner lie naked on his or her stomach on the bed. For fifteen minutes, give your partner a very gentle massage. Just use your fingertips to explore his or her body. Do not speak to each other. Rely on subtle nonverbal cues from your partner to determine what is pleasurable for him or her and what is not. At the end of fifteen minutes, discuss the experience. Were you correctly reading your partner's nonverbal signs? Reverse roles and repeat the process.

Teacher/student. Tell your partner exactly what you want him or her to do to give you pleasure, step by step. This can be kept at the level of a massage or extended to include sexual activities. Let your partner know exactly how you want things done: how hard, how fast, how long, and so on. Demonstrate for your partner or guide his or her hand if necessary.

Instant replay. After a sexual experience, talk about it. Tell your partner what you liked about it, and what you would have preferred to have done differently. Instant replay gives you an opportunity to validate the pleasurable aspects of your sexual relationship and it provides your partner with immediate feedback.

Turn-ons/Turn-offs. Tell your partner what you find most pleasurable. Be sure to give your partner validation when he or she does something that really turns you on. Tell your partner what you don't find pleasurable. Remember to state turn-offs in positive terms. Example: Instead of saying, "Hey, not so fast!" say "I'd really enjoy it if we went more slowly."

Nonverbal signals. Guess what your partner's nonverbal signals are for (1) "I like that!" (2) "I don't like that." (3) "I want sex." (4) "I want physical contact but no sex." (5) "I don't want sex right now." (6) "Maybe I want sex but I'm not sure." Ask your partner to confirm if your guesses are accurate. If not, find out from your partner what the correct signals are. If your partner doesn't have a signal for one of these six messages, or if it is difficult for you to accurately read it, perhaps the two of you will want to come up with a signal that you can both agree on.

This section has provided guidelines for you and your partner to give your relationship a kind of sexual "tune-up," along with suggestions for how to keep communication lines open regarding day-to-day changes in your sexual ideas, feelings, and wishes. It assumes that you own the manual detailing the switches that turn you on and off and that it is your right and responsibility to tell your partner what's in your manual in a straightforward, nonaccusatory manner. Once your partner realizes that it is in both of your interests to cooperate, he or she will be open to hearing you out and experimenting with you.

While this approach works for many people, it requires a level of nondefensiveness that is often not present in relationships in which sexual problems have existed for some time. In such relationships, there are built-up resentments, hurts, and fears that have never been fully expressed or acknowledged. In order to communicate under these circumstances, you must be willing and able to work through conflict. This often requires the assistance of sex or couples therapist.

16

Communicating
With Children

To be an effective parent is to realize two things: that you are a human being with problems and that your children are human beings with problems.

As a human being, you have basic needs for food, clothing, shelter, warmth, affection, love, security, relaxation, and so on. You go about getting these needs met in ways that are more or less effective. Sometimes you succeed and sometimes you make mistakes and fail. Sometimes other people thwart your attempts to get your needs met, and then you have a problem.

As a human being, a child has the same needs, tries to get them met, makes mistakes, and has problems when needs are thwarted.

How well you and your child communicate will determine how well you solve your problems. There are three critical communication skills required for effective parenting: listening, expressing, and joint problem solving.

Listening

Reread the chapter on listening, realizing this time that it applies to communication with children as well as adults. If you're like most people, you don't listen to children the same way you listen to adults. You fall into "adult chauvinism."

When you're being an adult chauvinist, you tend not to listen to kids because they are smaller, younger, weaker, uninformed, inexperienced—what of value could they possibly have to say to you? You automatically assume that you know how they feel because, after all, you were a kid yourself and you know all about it.

When you talk to your children, you are likely to engage in many of the common blocks to listening outlined in the chapter on listening, especially these:

Judging	"That's where you're wrong." "You're too emotional."
Advising	"Try asking Jack over here to play." "Why don't you do your math first, when you're fresh?"
Placating	"Right, right, you'll feel better tomorrow." "Uh huh, these things happen."
Derailing	"Haven't I heard this story before?" "Just blow their stupid clubhouse up, then." "Can't we talk about something pleasant at dinner for a change?"
Mind Reading	"He's just jealous of his sister." "You're doing this to spite me."

You are also prone to special listening blocks that you'd seldom fall into with your adult friends, but that arise out of power struggles between children and adults:

Ordering	"Go to your room and clean it up now." "Don't you ever use that tone of voice with me."
Threatening	"You'll be sorry." "If you don't behave tonight, there'll be no allowance for you for a month."
Moralizing	"Nice girls don't talk like that." "You should always respect adults."
Lecturing	"Let's analyze this rationally. . . . " "College years are the best time of your life."
Ineffective Praising	"Well, I think you look just fine." "But you did real well for your age."
Pitying	"Poor baby." "I'm sorry you're in such a mess."
Shaming	"You're disgusting." "What a rotten, dirty thing to do."

Interrogating	"So how do your friends spend their money? On what? How much?"
	"Exactly what will you do if you drop out of school now?"
Denying	"You don't miss that ugly old neighborhood."
	"You don't hate Grandma."

Your child needs to express important feelings and desires. They can't be denied, shamed, interrogated, or threatened away. Nor can they be ignored. If you fail to listen, the feelings may go underground or turn into confusion or rage. The feelings won't simply disappear.

In actively listening to children, the most important ability a parent needs is empathy. Children have intense feelings and little experience in effectively communicating them. You need to accurately decode your child's feelings, separate them from the content of what's said, and give them a name.

For example, here's a father responding to the *content* of a question:

Son: Are there big kids in nursery school?

Father: No, they're all about the same age as you.

Son: Oh.

The father thinks nothing more about this interchange, and his son throws a tantrum the first day of nursery school and refuses to get out of the car. Here's the same question, with a response to the *feeling:*

Son: Are there big kids in nursery school?

Father: You're *nervous* about nursery school.

Son: Big kids might hit me.

Father: You're *afraid* of being hit.

Son: Yeah, and they don't play with you.

Father: You'd *feel left out* if they wouldn't play with you.

The father doesn't have to reassure his son by making up lies about the complete fairness and safety of nursery school, or shame him for being a sissy. Responding to the feelings by naming and feeding them back is enough. The son gets to work through some of his vague fears before they mount to panic in the car on the way to school.

Another effective strategy this father is using is that of making his responses in the form of statements rather than questions. This may seem artificial and contrived at first, but it can be very helpful. All too often, questions asked of children take on a badgering, cross-examining tone. Making simple statements instead of asking questions is a way of avoiding the temptation to cross-examine your child. Also, since questions require answers, they have a way of leading the conversation. When you make simple statements that can be confirmed, denied, or ignored, you allow your child to retain more control of the conversation.

Exercise: To get practice in recognizing feelings, read these typical messages children send. Listen carefully for feelings. In the second column, write the feelings you heard. Discard the content and write in only the feelings in two or three words. Some of the statements may contain several different feelings.

	Child Says	*Child Is Feeling*
Example:	I don't know what is wrong. I can't figure it out. Maybe I should just quit trying.	Stumped. Discouraged. Tempted to give up.
1.	Oh boy, only ten more days until school's out.	_____
2.	Look, Daddy, I made an airplane with my new tools!	_____
3.	Will you hold my hand when we go into the nursery school?	_____
4.	Gee, I'm not having any fun. I can't think of anything to do.	_____
5.	I'll never be good like Jim. I practice and practice and he's still better than me.	_____
6.	My new teacher gives us too much homework. I can never get it all done. What'll I do?	_____
7.	All the other kids went to the beach. I don't have anyone to play with.	_____
8.	Jim's parents let him ride his bike to school, but I'm a better rider than Jim.	_____
9.	I shouldn't have been so mean to little Jimmy. I guess I was bad.	_____

10. I want to wear my hair long—it's _____
    my hair, isn't it?

Possible Answers: 1. Glad, happy, relieved. 2. Proud, confident, pleased. 3. Afraid, fearful, nervous, apprehensive. 4. Bored, restless, stumped. 5. Inadequate, discouraged, envious. 6. Defeated, discouraged, overwhelmed. 7. Left behind, abandoned, lonely, jealous. 8. Discriminated against, competent, confident. 9. Guilty, regretful, sorry, repentant. 10. Resentful, defiant, threatened.

Active listening alone will often clear up your child's problem without any further input from you. For example, this mother's eight-year-old son has had a run-in with his teacher:

Son: Why did that old bag make me stay after school anyway? I wasn't the only one who was talking. I hate her.

Mother: You're really *angry* at that teacher.

Son: Yeah. But I don't hate her for making me stay after. It's the other guys who got away with it.

Mother: You *feel persecuted.* She singled you out.

Son: She just picks on one kid to punish so that everybody else will shut up.

Mother: You don't like that.

Son: Aw, I can take it. I guess I was just unlucky she saw me first. Next time I'll be more careful and she can pick on someone else.

Mother: You'll play it cool.

Son: Yeah.

When active listening alone doesn't clear up a problem, you'll have to move on to joint problem solving. But you'll be surprised how listening can "solve" apparently impossible problems by reducing your child's anxiety to the point where it can be endured or ignored.

Expressing

Reread the chapter on self-expression, noticing that you need to make yourself clear to your children just as carefully as you do with adults. As with listening, adult chauvinism can be a trap: Why take care when a mere child is bugging you?

There are six basic principles for effectively expressing yourself to your child.

Specificity

What you want and feel should be communicated as specifically as possible. Children want and need clean limits—boundaries within which you can operate freely and securely, and outside of which they can expect natural consequences. Here are some examples of clearly stated expectations:

> I expect that you will take your bath before doing your homework.

> I want you in tonight by five o'clock.

> Please clean the counters, the stovetop, and the sink when you're working in the kitchen today.

The following are examples of nonspecific expectations:

> Don't go to school stinky again.

> I want you in early.

> I want you to clean up the whole kitchen.

Praise should also be specific. Telling your child "Great . . . fantastic . . . beautiful" isn't always believable and doesn't help the child learn to praise himself. Specific praise tells exactly what you like and why you like it. Here are some examples:

> You did the dishes without my asking.

> You were warm and friendly to your cousin, and included her in everything right away.

> The homework was really carefully printed and showed a lot of effort.

When your child hears specific praise that describes exactly what she is doing right, she can begin to say the same things to herself:

> I do chores without being asked.

> I'm a warm and friendly person.

> I do much neater work now.

Feelings can also be expressed specifically. "I messages" that describe what you feel and what provoked the feeling give your child important information about what goes on inside you. "I feel hurt and unappreciated when you forget to thank me for driving you to Becky's house."

Your child learns much more from this "I message" than if you angrily accuse her of ingratitude.

Immediacy

Say what bothers you *when* it bothers you. Reward good behavior right away. Studies show that children learn best when they are rewarded or punished immediately following what they do. The longer you wait to express your reactions, the less impact you'll have on your child's behavior.

When you establish a consequence for misbehavior, it should be immediate. For example, suppose your daughter doesn't stop jumping up and down on the couch when you tell her to stop. Putting her in time out for five minutes, right away, would be an immediate consequence that would adequately reinforce your rule about standing on the furniture. The delayed consequence of "no TV tomorrow" would be harsher, but would actually be less effective because it would occur long after the misbehavior.

Some parents always try to "be nice." They gunnysack their negative feelings until some minor infraction triggers a massive explosion. The child gets the message that he or she is bad and worthy of rejection. And the behavior doesn't improve because there's no way of linking your anger to the specific things the child has done.

Nonjudgment

All your communication to a child should include the implication that he or she is basically a lovable, capable person. Blaming, name calling, and sarcasm communicate that the child, and not just his or her behavior, is not okay.

Let's say that your son, who's habitually messy, can't find a vital homework assignment in his room. You have a choice. You can vent your feelings by labeling him inept and stupid. Or you can take the position that this is a problem that needs attention. The room needs to be cleaner, and homework needs to be kept in a special place.

When things go really wrong you can still express strong disapproval without attacking character. "Stop that right now. There will be no playing with your food at the table" is a stern but nonassaultive message. The child can still feel basically loved. "Why do you have to act like a slob? You're always making a mess" communicates a basic contempt for the child. The message is "You're not an okay person."

There are three good ways to avoid blaming and name calling: (1) Omit the word "you" when describing a situation or problem. "I see a little boy with dirty hands and dirty face at the dinner table." "I see a bedroom with toys on the floor and dirty and clean clothes mixed up in the drawers." (2) Give information: "Dirty dishes belong in the sink." "Milk gets sour if it's left out of the refrigerator." "Toys rust when they're left outside." (3) Say the message in one word: "Bedtime," instead of "What are you doing up past bedtime?" "Teeth," instead of "You always forget to brush your teeth."

The development of good self-esteem in your child very much depends on the messages you communicate. Consistent "you're bad" messages eventually create an "I'm bad" self-concept. A commitment to non-judgment is a major step toward raising a healthy child.

Consistency

Children are confused by inconsistent messages. If you tell your son that he has to be in by five, but you only enforce the rule once in a while, you'll find that your son habitually ignores the five o'clock deadline. The rule ceases to affect his behavior, but it can afford a perfect opportunity for you to vent some anger when you've had a bad day. If homework is supposed to be done before your daughter gets on the phone, but most days you're too tired to remind her, the rule will soon be forgotten. You can always resurrect the rule, however, when you feel annoyed about something else.

Allow children to consistently experience the consequences of misbehavior. Letting them off teaches a lesson you don't want them to learn: that irresponsibility pays. If you and your child have agreed that failure to clean the bedroom on Sunday will result in grounding on Monday after school, keep your word. You'll be a believable person and your child will learn that misbehavior does have consequences.

It's easier to be consistent if your consequences are natural—if they follow logically from the infraction. For example, the natural consequence of forgetting your coat is to be cold until you retrieve the coat from where you left it. The natural consequence of not doing your chores is no allowance this week. The natural consequence of not sharing a toy is to have the toy taken away for a while. The natural consequence of rowdiness at a birthday party is sitting quietly in a corner or leaving the party early. The natural consequence of not making your lunch before the school bus arrives is going to school without lunch. Sometimes these consequences seem extreme, but they work much better than nagging, lecturing, or applying unrelated punishments inconsistently.

Praise should also be consistent. Children need to hear when they've done well. They need approval the first time and every time until they've mastered a particular developmental skill. Each Saturday when your son keeps his promise to vacuum he needs to hear how nice the carpet looks.

Disclosure

In most families disclosure is a one-way street. Parents know everything about their kids, but kids know almost nothing about their parents' inner lives. Letting your child in on some of the things you feel and want makes you a real person. You cease to be an authority figure who hands down rules and punishments. The limits you set make more sense to your child when presented in the context of your feelings and needs. "Turn down the stereo" is just another irritating command unless it goes with a little self disclosure. "They were doing some construction in the office next to mine and my nerves are shot—would you please turn the stereo down?" "I feel lonely with your dad out of town and need you around tonight" makes a lot more sense to a child than "I told you, no overnights."

The key to effective disclosure is the use of "I" messages in place of "you" messages. Notice how "I" messages are more self-expressive, include more feelings, are more specific, and are less likely to provoke resistance:

> *"You" message:* "How dare you waltz in here at one in the morning? You're getting damn irresponsible."

> *"I" message:* "*I* was very worried when twelve thirty came and you weren't home yet. *I* imagined something terrible had happened. *I'm* relieved that you're all right, and *I* feel really angry about having stayed up worrying."

The rules for composing effective "I" statements are very simple:

Use appropriate force. Don't undershoot. If you feel strongly, let your child know it. And don't overshoot with a Vesuvius-like eruption over a relatively minor irritation.

Include all feelings. If you feel relieved, frightened, concerned, or loving in addition to feeling angry or disappointed, be sure to mention these other emotions too.

Avoid "you" messages in disguise. "I feel that you are a stupid, lazy bum" is not a legitimate "I" message. It's a name calling "you" message with "I feel" pasted on the front like a clown mask on a battering ram.

Persist if ignored. Sometimes children ignore "I" messages, especially if they have been receiving a heavy barrage of "you" messages. You might say, "I feel very sad and upset when I see my flowers pulled up," and little George will just grin as he goes by on his tricycle, plowing up more of the flowerbed. Persist. Restate with more force: "Hey, George, I really mean it! I'm real sad and mad about these flowers."

Switch to active listening if you get an "I" message back. Let's say you complain about the dishes not being done and your daughter says, "Yeah, but why do I have to slave in the kitchen while Bill has it easy in the yard?" You should then switch to active listening ("You resent how chores are divided") until you hear out your daughter's problem. This may lead to a full scale joint problem-solving session, or it may result in a brief interchange, after which you can return to your original "I" message.

Joint Problem Solving

The most difficult time to be an effective parent is when there is a genuine conflict of needs. You have a legitimate need that interferes with your child's legitimate need, or vice versa. Common areas for this kind of conflict are chores, neatness of shared rooms like the kitchen, TV programs, loud music, the family car, where to go on vacation, and so on. Everyone has a stake in these situations, and it's easy to see them as win/lose propositions. There are three possible approaches to resolving these conflicts.

The first is the traditional *authoritarian* approach. You are the boss. You make the rules and enforce them. This solution sounds easy in theory, but unfortunately it doesn't always work. If you are over-authoritarian, your children may resist and resent your solutions to their problems. And because their behavior is externally controlled by your strict rules, they may also fail to develop self-discipline. As adolescents they can become rebellious, withdrawn, or both. You'll then find that you spend an inordinate amount of time nagging, yelling, and punishing. A vicious cycle starts: the more they resist, the more you punish, the more they resist.

Authoritarian orders do have their place in emergency situations when you genuinely do know best and there's no time to discuss matters. You don't let your three-year-old topple into a roaring fireplace or allow your intoxicated daughter to stay overnight at a party.

The second traditional approach is *permissiveness*. It's less common, but many parents try it. You give your child whatever he or she wants. In every conflict, the child gets his or her way.

The trouble with excessive use of this approach is threefold. First, you will inevitably feel resentful about continually giving up your own needs. No matter how you try to project loving acceptance, your kids will pick up the resentment underneath. These two opposed feelings can make them feel very insecure about your love. Second, because you don't take the trouble to provide a structure for your kids, they may get the message that you just don't care about them.

The final problem with over-permissiveness is that the rest of the world isn't so indulgent. School, work, and most peer groups have rules and expectations. Spoiled, demanding kids have a hard time surviving in a world that doesn't bend to their wishes.

The time to be permissive is when you genuinely don't have a strong opinion in the matter, when your child can be trusted to make an acceptable decision, or when a poor decision won't hurt you or your child.

The third and most consistently effective approach to resolving conflict with your children is the *cooperative* approach. It avoids the drawbacks inherent in being either over-authoritarian or over-permissive.

The root of the "evil" in authoritarian or permissive systems is power—your power over your child or your child's power over you. Power at its most effective can only *compel* or *prevent* behavior. It can't *change* behavior in the sense of making someone else *want* to do what you want them to do. A child obeys an authoritarian parent in order to avoid punishment or gain a reward. Thus your son can be classically conditioned to pick up his room, but the conditioning won't teach him to value neatness or feel a sense of responsibility for taking care of his environment.

You automatically have a considerable power over your children simply because you are physically and psychologically bigger than they are. In the cooperative approach to resolving conflicts, you have to be willing to set that power aside. You must be willing to meet your kids as a reasonable adult meeting younger people who are also reasonable and capable of making decisions.

The goal is to jointly use systematic problem-solving techniques to discover a solution to each conflict that is acceptable to everyone. You have to sincerely want this, and convince your kids that you are sincere. At first they may be resistant and suspicious. Try a frank approach: "I'm learning about a way to be a better parent, and I want you to try it out with me."

There are six steps to joint problem solving. Sometimes a mutually acceptable solution will pop up before you have progressed through all these steps, but generally you should go through all of them in order.

1. Identify and Define the Conflict

1. If this is your first attempt at joint problem solving, pick a problem that is long-standing, but not one that will make tempers hot.

2. Pick a time when the kids aren't busy, distracted, or about to leave.

3. State clearly, concisely, and firmly that there is a problem that must be solved.

4. Use "I" messages to convey your feelings as strongly as you feel them.

5. Avoid "you" messages that put down or blame the child.

6. Use active listening to elicit your kids' view of the problem. This is a way of getting down to the real problem, which may be different from the apparent problem you started with.

7. Explain that you want to find a mutually acceptable solution.

2. Generate Possible Solutions

1. Get the children's solutions first. Younger kids may not come up with anything at first, but keep asking them. It helps develop their thinking ability and shows that you want their contribution.

2. At this point, only variety and quantity count. Brainstorm freely. Keep pressing everyone for one more suggestion, no matter how far out, until all the ideas are squeezed out.

3. Accept all solutions without judgment. Evaluation comes later. No one should say "That won't work" or "I can't accept that."

4. Encourage contributions from everyone: both parents, all children. Treating kids as valuable sources of solutions is a good idea for two reasons: it improves their self-esteem and produces a lot of good ideas.

5. Write all the solutions down so you can remember them.

3. Evaluate Solutions

Now is the time for judgments. Narrow down your written list by crossing off the solutions that are unacceptable to anyone in the group, for whatever reason. Eliminate the crazy, dangerous, and too expensive solutions.

4. Pick the Best Solution

1. The best solution is the one that is most acceptable to both you and your kids. The key is the acceptability of solutions, not arriving at the "correct" solution. The same problem will have different best solutions in different families.

2. Keep testing the remaining solutions against your kids' feelings. Make sure no one is being railroaded into acceptance.

3. Point out that the chosen solution may not be the final word. The objective is to try it for a while and see if it works.

4. Make sure everyone understands that by accepting the solution they are taking responsibility for carrying it out and making it work. This will motivate the kids and make any agreement easier to enforce.

5. Be sure to identify contingencies. What happens if someone breaks the agreement? Is there a penalty? Extra work? Loss of privileges? Another problem-solving session? Discuss the penalties as matter-of-fact consequences that will happen if the kids choose not to carry out the agreed-on solution. This lets them know the cost of breaking an agreement, and they can weigh it in an adult manner.

5. Implement the Decision

1. Agree on who is to do what, when and where, how and under what conditions. What are the standards to measure success? Is there a time limit to the agreement? A way to call an end to a trial period?

2. Go do it.

6. Evaluate Results

Not all solutions will work well. Check from time to time that you and your kids are happy with how the solution is working. Circumstances may change. If your solution needs to be scrapped or modified, return to the brainstorming step.

Example: Doug and Diane want to try joint problem solving with their twelve-year-old, Mark, and their ten-year-old, Susan. Susan is supposed to sweep the kitchen floor and put the clean dishes in the cupboard after the dinner dishes are done. Mark is supposed to empty all the wastebaskets whenever they're full and wheel the trash can out to the curb on Wednesday nights for pickup Thursday morning.

1. Identify and define conflict.

Dad: I want to talk about chores. I really think evening chores are a problem. I get angry and depressed when I come into the kitchen at ten o'clock and the dishes are still sitting on the sink and the trash is overflowing onto the floor. I'd like to solve this problem together.

Mom: I'm tired of nagging two or three times before the work gets done. I feel like I have to crack the whip, and I don't want to. Does this chore stuff bother you?

Mark: But I almost always do the trash before she does the dishes.

Susan: I can't sweep the floor until you're through making your trash mess.

Mark: It's not in your way.

Dad: Sounds like you guys do have some problems with chores. Do you want to find a way to get chores done so everybody's satisfied?

Mark: Sure.

Susan: Yes.

Mom: Let's make sure we know what the real problem is. We want the chores done each evening. And you want not to get in each other's way. Right?

Susan: And sometimes we just can't do it, like when there's company and you don't even wash the dishes till the middle of the night.

Mark: And I can't stand the nagging.

Mom: So you feel sometimes it's impossible to do the chores, and you don't want to be nagged.

Mark: Right.

Dad: Okay, we want chores done by a reasonable time—say eight thirty. And you want to not interfere with each other, get out of chores when they're unreasonable, and not get nagged?

Susan &
Mark: Yeah.

2. **Generate possible solutions.** They went on to list these solutions:

Susan: Use paper plates
Do trash first, floor, then dishes

Mark: Everybody takes turns doing all chores
Do dishes and floor first, then trash
No blaming the other guy for not doing your job
Put up reminder signs

Mom: No dessert until chores are done
No nagging
If chores aren't done by eight thirty, no dessert at all
Post a calendar in the kitchen for keeping records

Dad: Buy a dishwasher and get a maid
Susan and Mark do each other's chores for variety
Allowance cut if chores aren't done
One day a week off

3. Evaluate solutions. They went down the written list and crossed off what was too silly (paper plates), too expensive (dishwasher and maid), unacceptable to kids (doing each other's chores, no dessert), and unacceptable to parents (parents having to take turns doing kids' chores).

4. Pick the best solution. They combined the remaining solutions and came up with:

Kids have until eight thirty to do chores

No blaming the other guy for preventing you from doing your job

Mark has Thursday nights off for baseball practice

Susan has Friday nights off because that's when company usually comes and there are many dishes that aren't ready to put away by eight thirty

Mom and Dad won't remind or nag

For every night kids don't do their chores, they lose fifty cents allowance

We'll try it for a month and see how it works.

5. Implement the decision. Everyone was clear about what they had to do. Mom agreed to buy and post a calendar in the kitchen for keeping records. Mark made himself several signs reminding him that Thursday was trash day.

6. Evaluate results. After a month, chores were getting done consistently and everyone was satisfied. They agreed to continue the contract indefinitely. Later, Susan was allowed to choose Friday or Saturday for her night off, depending on her parents' plans for entertaining.

When To Let Go

Sometimes chronic conflicts between parents and child can be alleviated by recognizing that some decisions and problems belong completely to your child. How he does his hair, who he picks for friends, how she dresses and keeps her room, or how she spends her allowance may best be left up to the child.

To be sure, you undoubtedly have strong feelings and opinions about these things. That's only natural. And there is an almost overwhelming impulse to cast your opinions into a set of rules which must be strictly enforced. But if you try to involve yourself in these decisions, you're likely to get caught in a protracted conflict. If no basic harm is being done, you may be better off letting your child deal with these problems him or herself.

When You Have To Say No

When you say no, you run the risk of generating tears and resistance. A good strategy for saying no is to say it indirectly. Here are five ways to set limits without using the dreaded word.

1. *Give a choice.* Instead of saying "No TV, you've got to finish your homework," you can say "Do you want to finish your homework now or in fifteen minutes?" "Do you want to brush your teeth before or after the story?"

2. *Substitute yes for no.* "Can we play baseball?" "Yes, after lunch." "Yes, you can go over to Tommy's as soon as you finish your room."

3. *Give information.* "We're leaving in ten minutes," instead of saying "No, you can't go outside." Instead of saying, "No football," say "You could get really hurt, how about touch football?"

4. *Accept feelings.* "I know you really want to stay overnight, it must be hard to come home in the middle of all the fun." "It's an awful disappointment to have gotten this cold and not be able to go skiing."

5. *Explain the problem.* "I know you wanted to go to the movies tonight, but it turns out your sister will be alone in the house— she needs to have you around."

The Point Is . . .

Effective parenting is based on respect for your child. Your message must be that your child is lovable and good. You can object to specific behaviors without rejecting the essential value of this little person.

Saying "Your artwork is fine, but I'm upset about the crayons on the sofa" is typical of messages that promote self-acceptance. The child is still a good person, even though he or she makes mistakes. Naturally there will be times when you forget and attack your child. But a commitment to separate the child's person from his or her behavior will help the child grow toward a basic feeling of self-worth.

Some parents get discouraged when they look back and see a pattern of blame and attack. "Why do I keep calling her stupid all the time? It just seems to pop out of my mouth." The truth is that it takes a long time for a child to grow up. You have time to change old patterns and correct mistakes. Children are amazingly forgiving and will respond to your efforts. It's never too late.

17

Family Communications

There is one major difference between communication within a family setting and communication with the world at large. The stakes are a lot higher with your family. You can escape from conflicts with a neighbor down the street, the union rep, or your auto mechanic, but you can't get away from your family; you still have to go home every night. A family with chronic, poor communications becomes a pressure cooker. Each member is vulnerable to emotional devastation. The children, especially, are susceptible to a range of physical and psychological symptoms.

Families get into trouble when members are prohibited from expressing certain feelings, needs, or awarenesses. Rules for what can't be asked for, talked about, or noticed are learned from your parents. They become unconscious inhibitors that prevent you from sharing important parts of your experience. Here are some examples of unhealthy rules that distort family communication. **It's wrong to:**

- Ask for help

- Talk about your hopes and dreams

- Express anger at your parents

- Seek acknowledgment or recognition for work

- Ask for emotional support

- Show that you've been hurt

- Show your emotional pain

- Talk about your sexual needs or feelings

- Notice or comment on mistakes and problems

- Voice disagreement or bring conflicts into the open

- Directly express your anger (unless you can prove that the other person is horrible and disgusting)

- Express fear

- Express ambivalence, reservations, uncertainty

- Show affection

- Ask for attention

In addition to the general rules, families may have very specific regulations limiting perception. They govern what can and can't be seen and talked about. These rules are particularly stringent for the children, who have not yet been socialized into blocking their awarenesses. The following are typical for this category of family rules.

- Don't notice that Daddy is drunk and disfunctional

- Don't notice hostility at the dinner table

- Don't mourn or talk about Grandmother's death

- Don't express your fears of a Martian invasion

- Don't ask for hugs or reassurance

- Don't notice Mom's affair

To survive in a family, you have to follow the rules. The rules are created and continually reinforced by the fear of rejection. If your father reacted angrily when you were anxious as a child, you quickly learned that anxiety should not be expressed. You were conditioned to expect being hurt if you talked about your fears. Eventually the rule dropped out of your awareness and became a hidden influence. As an adult, you remain uncomfortable with fear and may become irritated with your children for expressing it. Your spouse may also accept your rule because it has reciprocal benefits: "I won't show my fear, if I don't have to deal with yours."

For most people, the powerful rules that limit their expression are completely unconscious. In the family therapist's office, when finally asked to communicate their hurt or fear or need for support, they feel strangely paralyzed. It all seems very dangerous, but they don't know why. That sense of danger, of course, derives from conditioning long ago, when their parents rejected them for saying what they felt, needed, or observed.

Family Communication Disorders

The rules limiting expression within families result in four major communication disorders. Restricted from direct expression, you must either deny, delete, substitute, or incongruently communicate aspects of your experience.

Denial

People tend to deny what they are afraid to express. Your needs and feelings can be denied overtly or covertly. Overt denial involves statements such as "I don't care," "No problem," "Whatever you want," "I'm fine," "Who's angry?" "Who's upset?" "I don't need you to do anything." Covert denial is harder to spot, but often involves shrugging, speaking in a monotone, slouching, or withdrawing contact. The message is "It doesn't matter, I don't feel anything."

Deletion

Deletion involves leaving parts of a message out, particularly the parts that directly express your needs and awarenesses. Instead of saying "I'd like to go to a movie," you may catch yourself saying "It's sure a lousy TV night, isn't it?" With deletions you have to say everything roundabout. Statements don't specify who, what, where, or when. The following are some typical examples:

- "It's been a little lonely." (*Meaning:* "I've missed you the three nights a week you've been in class, and I hope you take fewer night classes next quarter.")

- "There's a new French restaurant down the street." (*Meaning:* "Let's eat out tonight.")

- "Damn, the threads are stripped, I'll never get this running." (*Meaning:* "Give me a little sympathy and bring me a cup of coffee.")

- "Now what do you want me to do?" (*Meaning:* "Leave me alone right now, this is the first time I've relaxed all day.")

- "I guess you're a little tired." (*Meaning:* "How come you're so angry all of a sudden?")

Deletions are usually constructed in one of three ways:

1. *Statements in the form of a question.* "Are you still here?" (*Meaning:* "I would like to be alone for a few hours.")

2. *Requests in the form of neutral observations.* "It's a gorgeous day." (*Meaning:* "Let's take a drive to the country.")

3. *Deleted references.* The message is vague and doesn't say who feels what about whom. "There's been some anger lately." (*Meaning:* "I have been angry at *you* because of all the extra work since you fired the housekeeper.") "There hasn't been much contact." (*Meaning:* "I've felt out of contact with my *husband* and oldest *daughter*.")

Substitution

Feelings have to come out sometime, and substitution allows them to be expressed in a safer way or with a safer person. Substitution lets you express your feelings indirectly. If you have a rule against showing hurt, you might channel the hurt feelings into anger. If it's forbidden for you to express anger toward your wife, you might attack your son about his chores. The following are some typical examples of substitution.

1. Your boss criticizes your work. You're angry, you attack your wife for mismanaging the food money.

2. You're frightened when you see your boy run into the street. You angrily attack him as "stupid and crazy."

3. You feel hurt and a little lonely when your daughter spends three hours a night on the phone. You attack her for leaving the milk out of the refrigerator.

4. You're hurt and angry when your spouse announces the desire to take a vacation without you. Your rule against expressing anger forces you to convert the feeling to depression.

5. You are unable to express your secret happiness that the children will spend the summer with your ex-spouse. You express the feeling as anxiety about their health and safety.

Incongruent Messages

Incongruent communications occur when the messages carried by your posture, facial expression, tone of voice, and tempo of speech don't match the content of what you are saying. A woman says to her daughter, "I'm not upset that you were out late." But her voice has a strident, harsh quality, she talks quickly, and she's pointing her finger, while her other hand is on her hip. The words simply don't match what the body and voice are saying. "I'm very sad that we can't pull this family together," a man announces at the dinner table. His eyes bore into those of his son, his jaws are clenched, one hand forms a fist around the napkin. He says he's sad, but he's also communicating something else. It may be anger, or it may be a kind of agitated despair.

When messages don't match, family members are forced to decide which message is the true one. They have to mind-read and try to guess what the speaker is really saying. The following examples of incongruent communication are divided into four parts: (1) words, (2) voice and body language, (3) listener's interpretation, and (4) real message.

1. *Words:* "I'm terrifically glad to see you home."
2. *Voice and body language:* Flat monotone, eyes looking at the floor, a half-smile, body turned slightly sideways.
3. *Listener's interpretation:* Chooses to respond to voice and body language. Assumes that the speaker is uncomfortable and disappointed. Listener feels hurt.
4. *Real message:* "I'm glad you're home. Unfortunately I couldn't finish the work I wanted to do, and I'm afraid I won't complete it now that you're back." The speaker has a rule against expressing anything but joy at a reunion. The result is incongruent communication.

1. *Words:* "I don't mind not going, there are lots of things to do around the house."
2. *Voice and body language:* A bright smile that fades unnaturally fast, stooped shoulders, neck bowed, a high, placating voice.
3. *Listener's interpretation:* Choses to respond to the reassuring words, but feels anxiety and discomfort because the body language shows extreme disappointment.
4. *Real message:* "I'm extremely disappointed that we couldn't go to the movies tonight."

1. *Words:* "I just want some more support, the feeling that you care about me."
2. *Voice and body language:* Voice high and loud, almost whining, mouth drawn out in a flat line, shoulders and arms shrugging, looking over the top of glasses.
3. *Listener's interpretation:* Chooses to respond to the voice and body language. "He sometimes shrugs like that and stares over his glasses when he's angry. He must be angry." The listener experiences the message as a demand.
4. *Real message:* A request for help and a feeling of hopelessness that any will be forthcoming. The speaker's body language for expressing hopelessness is apparently similar to that used for anger. The listener, confused by incongruent messages, assumes that the speaker is hiding irritation.

1. *Words:* "I worry terribly about you when you're late like this."
2. *Voice and body language:* Arms crossed, weight on one leg,

mouth drawn in a thin line, voice harsh and loud.

3. *Listener's interpretation:* Chooses to respond to the words. Feels vaguely uneasy that the words don't match the body language.

4. *Real message:* "I waited for you and worried about you. I'm angry that you didn't have the courtesy to call."

1. *Words:* "Why don't you get the kid a couple more toys?"

2. *Voice and body language:* Voice slightly high and singsong, torso leaning forward, head shaking from side to side, finger pointing.

3. *Listener's interpretation:* Chooses to respond to the voice and body language. The voice and finger pointing are interpreted as critical, taunting.

4. *Real message:* "It worries me that she has nothing to play with at your house. I'm afraid she'll stop wanting to be with you because she's bored there." Because the speaker has used finger pointing and a singsong voice in the past to express annoyance, the listener mind reads annoyance and responds by getting angry.

Incongruent messages form the basis of much family pathology. People usually assume that the voice and body language communications are the true ones. But these messages are easily misinterpreted because of *overgeneralization.* This is the tendency to believe that a particular posture or intonation *always* means the same thing. "When Harry shrugs, that always means he's upset with me." "When Jane frowns and points her finger, that always means she's making a demand." "When Natasha has a high, strident voice, that always means she's anxious." Overgeneralization cancels out any other meanings the gesture could have. It increases the opportunity for misinterpretation.

Family Pathology

Mind Reading

Because family members have rules about what can and cannot be expressed, they are forced to communicate covertly. Through deletions, substitutions, and incongruent messages family members say what they need to say. But often no one understands them. When you try to interpret covert messages you are forced to mind-read. You have to make a guess as to what the covert request or feeling really is. Take the example of the man who remarks that the house is infested with fleas. Since he has deleted his feelings and needs about the matter, his wife must try to divine if his hatred for the cat has surfaced again, he wants her to have the house flea-bombed, or wants her to acknowledge and commiserate about the problem. If he has a history of substitutions, she may be worried that he brought up the flea business because he's angry about her purchasing new drapes. The matter is further complicated if there are incongruent messages. If he stands with his hands on his hips and talks very rapidly, the wife may conclude by virtue of overgeneralization that her husband is violently angry.

All this guesswork results in just one thing: mistakes. If you are mind-reading, you are going to be wrong a certain percentage of the time. You will respond to what you think is going on, rather than the real message. Your inappropriate response then creates a chain reaction like the proverbial falling dominoes. Consider the following interaction: Margaret, whose husband demands peace and quiet when he arrives home, hastily ends a fight with her son as she hears his keys in the front door. She's anxious when she greets him. Her voice is high and clipped. She avoids eye contact. By virtue of overgeneralization, Al assumes that the clipped, high-pitched voice means that his wife is angry. He mind-reads that she is irritated with him for being late. He makes himself angry by telling himself that she doesn't care about the long, hard hours he works. Al can't express the anger, and instead substitutes by complaining about the toys left on the floor. Margaret feels hurt, but substitutes by complaining that he's late again. The ensuing melee is entirely a result of mind reading.

There are two ways to break out of the mind-reading trap.

1. As a speaker, you have to ask yourself these questions: "What feeling, request, or awareness have I left out of my message? Do my tone of voice and body language match the content of my message?" If you find that you are simultaneously communicating more than one message, break it down into two separate communications. Suppose, for example, that you have a rule against expressing anger. You're telling your child to clean up his room, but you notice a lot of anger in your voice and that you are pointing your finger. You might separate and express the messages in this way: "I want you to clean up your room by an hour from now. I asked you to do it this morning and now I find myself a little frustrated and angry that it's still not done."

2. As a listener, you can combat mind reading by checking out all ambiguous messages. If you notice that the content doesn't match the voice or body language, describe in a nonjudgmental way what you observe. Ask if there is more that needs to be said. "I notice your shoulders were kind of hunched and you were staring at the floor while we talked about the kitchen remodeling. Is there something more that you feel about that?" You need to catch yourself when you make assumptions about the needs and feelings of others. A red flag

has to go up inside when you mind-read. As you catch yourself, you'll notice that certain assumptions typically come up over and over again. You may be prone to imagining that people are angry, disappointed, or making covert demands on you. These typical assumptions derive from overgeneralization, in which you invariably read certain gestures or tones of voice as anger, disappointment, or demands.

Alliances

Family alliances are formed to help you express forbidden feelings and needs. If Dad gets angry when his son discusses problems in school, maybe Mom will listen. And perhaps Mom will also share some of her negative feelings about Dad. As the mother-son alliance develops, Dad becomes more and more isolated. He doesn't hear the anger and the hurt, and he is also cut off from any warmth or support. Dad, as he feels increasingly peripheral, may seek an alliance with his daughter. They may complain to each other about how cold Mom is, and secretly collude to support each other in family conflicts.

Sibling alliances are a good way to deal with a punitive parent who focuses more on rules than on the particular needs of his children. Parent-child alliances are helpful when a parent has been dying on the vine emotionally and feels trapped in a dead marriage. In general, alliances are very useful short-term strategies for getting support and acknowledgment. But they are death on family happiness. The feuding camps continue to attack and hurt each other, often until the children leave home or the parents separate.

A family contract for directness is the antidote for the alliance. Feelings and wants are expressed to the person who needs to hear them. Secrets (an implied alliance) are not allowed. For example, a mother-son alliance that would keep Dad from knowing about the boy's poor grades is prevented by a contract for openness. A dad-mom alliance, in which Dad bitterly gripes about his daughter's laziness, is likewise prevented. The contract for directness says that gripes are expressed to the offending person. With such a contract, the whole family enters an alliance. They agree to support each other in expressing and hearing important messages. They agree that feelings and needs that two of them share should be shared by all.

Covert Manipulation Strategies

All communication has an implied request built into it. You're always trying to influence people in some way, even if it's only to listen and give your attention. The problem is that many people have rules against asking for things. If you have such rules, you can't openly request support, help, or acknowledgment. Nobody knows what you want. As a consequence, you are forced to use covert manipulative strategies to get the things you need. The following eight manipulative strategies are widely used in pathological families.

1. **Blaming and judging.** The blamer attacks other family members for not meeting his needs. They should be more supportive, more loving, more helpful around the house. If they really cared, they would get home earlier, do more things with the kids. A blamer's weapon is the pejorative attack. He aims at people's vulnerable self-esteem in the way a Doberman goes for the jugular. Certain blamers have refined their strategy to an art. Some attack with a needling sarcasm that ostensibly seems funny, but cuts deeply. Others make unreasonable demands, then explode with "justifiable" rage after they are turned down. Through judicious fault-finding, the blamer can push family members to give him some of what he wants. He can get grudging attention and help. The problem is that the strategy only works for a while. Though it is initially successful, and people are quite responsive to the fear of being hurt, the blamer's knives grow dull. Family members can become thick-skinned and oblivious to assaults. The blamer's once effective strategy for getting his way loses power. He is left with a simmering, impotent rage.

2. **Pulling for guilt.** This strategy banks on everyone's need to feel like a good person. Good people care for others, giving time and energy. They sacrifice themselves. Pulling for guilt involves subtly, sadly, letting family members know that you're in pain. If they cared, they would do something about it. If they were good people, they would stay home with you instead of going to the movies; if they really loved you, they would keep the lawn mowed. The best way to pull for guilt is to sigh a lot, refer bleakly to past sins and mistakes, tell everyone you're fine while looking miserable. Pulling for guilt is very effective. People secretly resent you, but they will often do what you want.

3. **Pulling for pity.** This strategy is designed to arouse sympathy rather than guilt. The demeanor is helpless and pathetic. There are sad stories, hopeless shrugs, all filling in the portrait of a victim. Pulling for pity has a period of maximum effectiveness. After a while exhaustion sets in, and family members begin to lose patience with the seemingly endless stream of problems.

4. **Blackmail.** Blackmailing involves threats to withhold something other family members need. Overtly or covertly the suggestion gets made that there will be no more sex, dinner won't be cooked, forget that birthday party. Some blackmailers play for high stakes by con-

tinually threatening to leave the family. As every parent who has threatened to take away a child's allowance knows, blackmail quickly becomes ineffective if you don't make good on the threats. This puts the blackmailer in a difficult bind. He's either making empty threats (which are soon ignored) or he must follow through on his spiteful and destructive schemes. If he follows through, and family members are damaged, he is courting the possibility of real hatred.

5. **Bribery.** This strategy involves insincere use of flattery, favors, or affection to induce other family members to change. Sex is turned on and off like a spigot. Attention and support are forthcoming only when the briber is in need. Like most of the covert manipulative strategies, bribery has short-term benefits. In the long run, however, family members cease to trust the integrity and authenticity of the briber. Resentment sets in.

6. **Placating.** Placators are nice. They fear conflict and avoid it at all costs. They try to please, to ingratiate, to garner approval. They are always quick to apologize. The placator gets his way by making people like him and owe him things. He's so agreeable, he's done so much for everyone, how could family members deny him the things he needs? Surely they will be as nice and as sacrificing as he has been. The problem for the placator is that people take him for granted. In the end he becomes a martyr with a long list of hidden resentments. He thought he had made a deal: "I'll be nice if you'll be nice." But other family members don't keep their end of the unspoken bargain.

7. **Turning cold.** This strategy turns on the eloquent silence, the clenched jaw, the back turned in bed. The message is "You're getting nothing from me." It's a powerful strategy because it frightens people. Children in particular, who depend for their very survival on a parent's love, are enormously vulnerable to sudden coldness. But the withdrawal of love is more than a way of influencing behavior: it is a weapon that makes scars. Both children and spouse become distrusting. And a secret rage develops that anyone would take away the most precious and necessary of human resources: emotional energy.

8. **Developing symptoms.** When all else fails, and people have no other way of getting what they want, they develop symptoms. They get headaches, they begin to drink, they have dark bouts of depression or impulsive spending sprees, they become unfaithful. Children get into fights at school, try to run away, develop asthma, attack their siblings. The symptoms are a covert attempt to get certain needs

met. Headaches may get Dad some time off work. Vaginismus may help a woman get time off from a sexually aggressive mate. A child may get important attention needs met with asthma. Symptoms are extremely useful, but they can also mutilate the family member who suffers them. A depressed woman finally gets her husband to take her on a vacation. But she's paid for that vacation with months of pain.

Covert manipulative strategies are only necessary when people have rules against the expression of needs, feelings, or awarenesses. If two or more family members have rules limiting what they can say, the resulting covert strategies are called a family system. Here are two examples of family systems at work.

The Martyr. The martyr in this case is Joyce, a woman who has rules against asking for support and acknowledgment of her hard work. She also has rules against expressing anger unless she can prove the other person worthy of execution. Joyce works seven days a week cooking, cleaning, picking up after her family, and runs a little mail order business out of her bedroom. The money earned pays for her sons' private school. She needs help around the house, she needs recognition for what she gives, and she needs to express her anger about being taken for granted. Joyce *deletes* the expression of her needs. Instead she *blames*. She accuses her sons of "taking all my time," calls her husband lazy, and says he's turned her into the maid.

The children have also been taught not to express anger. They covertly show their feelings by messing their rooms, being late, and embarrassing their mother in front of friends. Joyce's husband, Sean, uses *incongruent messages* to express what he feels. He says, "Yes, yes, you work very hard, of course we all know that." He speaks loudly and quickly, his hands are in his pockets, and he's leaning against the wall. Joyce interprets Sean's body language as meaning he doesn't care. She assumes that her children don't care. The result is further attempts at meeting her needs through blaming. But the children continue to destroy their rooms. Sean *turns cold* and repeats his incongruent "Yes, yes, we know you're working."

The problem in this family is that no one can talk straight. The children can't express anger, and Joyce interprets their passive-aggressive behavior as "not caring." Sean can't express his anger either. He talks loudly and quickly and makes an elaborate show of casualness. His message is also interpreted as "not caring."

This family system would be defused if Joyce could do three things: (1) Ask for the help and acknowledgment she needs, using nonjudgmental words. (2) Express anger instead of blame. This means describing what *she* feels, not punishing and attacking the self-esteem of others. Anger says "I'm in pain and I don't like it." Blame says "I'm in pain and bad people did it to me." (3) Check out rather than mind-read Sean's real message.

The Newlyweds. Jack is 32 and Henrietta is 35. They get married with a lot of hoopla, have a weekend honeymoon in Carmel, and return to the apartment they have been sharing for the past year and a half. Jack works in a restaurant until ten p.m. He often stays around for another hour or two having a few drinks and hanging out with the bartender. A month after the marriage Jack is coming in later and staying out more frequently. Henrietta becomes alarmed and discovers in herself an enormous insecurity. She's afraid of losing Jack. She fantasizes for hours about his involvement with various waitresses. Henrietta has a rule against expressing her insecurity and fear of loss. She *deletes* her feelings and tries *pulling for guilt*. She tells Jack she's losing sleep and can't function on her job when he stays out past eleven. Jack continues to stay out, so Henrietta changes her strategy to *blackmail*. She tells Jack not to bother being amorous when he comes in late. As the problem continues, she becomes increasingly desperate and tells Jack she'll move in with a girlfriend unless he gets in by eleven.

Jack, too, has feelings he can't express. Following the wedding he feels a strange deadness and apathy. He suddenly becomes afraid that he has signed up for a joyless commitment. He also feels guilt when he yearns for the excitement of his old single days. Jack has a rule against sharing any negative feelings. Instead, he *substitutes* anger for the fears and guilt he's experiencing and then attacks Henrietta for being overcontrolling. At other times Jack uses the strategy of *turning cold*. He talks reasonably, but his voice and body language indicate withdrawal.

Faced with these incongruent messages, Henrietta mind-reads that Jack is trying to get out of the marriage. Her threat to move in with a girlfriend was an empty one. And now, in a last effort to influence Jack, she begins to *develop symptoms.* Henrietta starts to drink when Jack stays out late. Jack is disgusted by the drinking, and his unexpressed fears and misgivings only increase.

This system could be resolved if Henrietta and Jack communicated directly. Both are afraid. Both have rules against expressing the feelings that torment them. Jack needs to know what happens inside of Henrietta while she waits. She needs to know the fear that keeps Jack lingering at work. These feelings won't suddenly disappear, but the covert strategies may be less necessary. With everything in the open, Henrietta can begin focusing on getting her safety needs met (for example, having Jack call if he'll be out past eleven). Jack can directly examine his needs for autonomy (deciding, for example, to schedule visiting time with friends).

How To Keep Family Communications Healthy

The best way to keep a family healthy is to allow each member the freedom to say what he feels, what he sees, and what he wants. Here are two exercises to help you reach those goals.

1. **Checking out.** Each time a family member says something that disturbs or confuses you, write down the following:

    a. *Words:* The actual content of the message.

    b. *Voice and body language:* Write down your memory of the pitch and tone of voice, the posture and facial expression. What gestures were used?

    c. *Your interpretation:* Notice whether the words match the voice and body language. If they seem to be saying different things, which do you believe? What do you assume to be the true message?

    d. *Real message:* Ask the family member for further clarification. Describe in a nonjudgmental way any discrepancies you see between the words and the nonverbal message. Ask if some feeling or need might have been left out. Now compare what you've learned with the previous assumptions you made.

This exercise helps you to combat mind reading by soliciting the information you need to accurately hear a message. Do this exercise at least once a day for two weeks. At the end of that time you'll get an idea of how much or how little you are distorting what family members say to you.

Remember that the tendency to mind-read is a natural one. Because important feelings or needs are often deleted, or show up only in body language, you may have developed a habit of guessing at the "real" message. The problem is that your guesses will not always be accurate. Just as Henrietta tortured herself by assuming that Jack was trying to escape their marriage, your mind reading may be adding fuel to a painful family system.

2. **Hearing yourself.** This exercise is designed to help you uncover your own deletions, substitutions, and incongruent messages. Whenever you take part in a painful or problematic bit of communication, write down the following:

    a. *Words:* Write down the first four or five sentences you said.

 b. *Voice and body language:* As you remember, how did your voice sound, what was your posture, what were your hands doing? What were you saying with your voice, your posture, your hands?

 c. What *feeling* did you leave out of your communication?

 d. What *implied request* was hidden in your communication?

 e. *Review the covert manipulation strategies:* Notice if there is anything in your message that indicates the use of one of those strategies.

 f. *Rewrite your message:* Include the original content of your message (if it was accurate), plus what your body and voice were saying. Include any feelings or needs that you are now aware that you deleted.

VI

Public Skills

18

Influencing Others

Much of your communication is about trying to get what you want: attempting to influence others to change and behave in ways that you'd prefer. The problem is that most people don't know how to do this. After a while they end up feeling frustrated and bitter, while their friends, family, and co-workers feel defensive and pushed around. Their strategies for influencing others work about as well as Sonja's:

Sonja: Why don't you want to go over to Bill and Meg's house? They're a lot of fun.

Larry: I'm tired.

Sonja: You're always tired. You're a walking dead man. I can't go out for a simple evening with friends because you're chained to the couch and that damned detective novel. Can't you just say yes once in a while? Yes to a little fun?

Larry: What can I say, Sonja? I'm *really* tired.

Sonja: (*loudly*) Maybe it just doesn't work. Maybe it just doesn't work between us. You know? Maybe I've got to do some thinking about that.

Larry: This is a nice life, isn't it?

Sonja wants Larry to be different, but her strategies aren't working. Blaming and criticizing only seem to make Larry more obstinate. When that doesn't work, Sonja tries threats. But in response, Larry withdraws into sarcasm.

Influencing others is an art that requires an understanding of the principles of change. The first thing you need to know is what *doesn't* work for influencing change.

Ineffective Strategies for Influencing Change

Blaming, criticizing, or complaining. Your basic message to the other person is that he or she is bad or wrong. In your mind, there are basic rules of decency, fairness, and caring that are being violated. When someone breaks these rules, it feels like you have every right to let them have it.

Threats. Here the message is: *Do what I want, or else.* Or else I'll hurt you back, take something away that feels good to you, to just plain scare you with my anger.

Belittling. You communicate that the other person is unworthy if he or she doesn't do what you want. He or she is flawed, stupid, or contemptible.

Pouting or withdrawing. The message here is: *You won't have me if you won't do what I want.* This strategy runs the continuum from a brief shutdown all the way to threatening to abandon the other person.

The strategies that don't work all act the same way: they are aversive, and they hurt people. There are two reasons why so many people rely on them. First, these strategies for change are modeled in dysfunctional families. If you grew up in a family in which people hurt each other as a strategy of influence, you'll sometimes find yourself doing the same thing. It's what you witnessed, and what you learned how to do. The second reason these strategies are so popular is that they are initially effective. In the early stages of a relationship, when someone still wants to please you, blaming, threats, belittling, and withdrawing can be powerful motivators. But over time, they lose their power as people stop caring about what you think. Over months and years, these strategies make others defensive and resistant to you. They stop listening. They stop caring. They build a thick emotional armor that makes them impervious to even the most stinging rebuke.

Threats are a particularly disappointing strategy. A person's initial response to your threat may be quite reinforcing. He or she may try noticeably harder to please you, but the changes you observe are created and maintained by fear; they will last only as long as the fear lasts.

As soon as the threat diminishes or is forgotten, the old behavior patterns are likely to reassert themselves.

Many people use ineffective strategies for influence because they're angry. And they justify their anger with this thought: "X sees how much pain and unhappiness he's causing me, he ought to...." There's a strong feeling that the other person should change to mitigate your unhappiness and help you fell better. But people will only change in response to your unhappiness if two conditions are simultaneously met. First, the person whom you want to change must have a strong empathic bond with you. Your unhappiness makes them unhappy. Second, their own needs, fears and limitations must not strongly reinforce the status quo. In other words, their needs can't be stacked up on the side of staying the same. Because these two conditions are very rarely met at any given time or with any given issue, your pain typically has very little impact on the behavior of others.

Effective Strategies for Influencing Others

The most important principle to remember is that people change only when they want to, not when you want them to. People behave the way they do because of powerful reinforcers—mostly fears and needs—that drive them to cope and respond in predictable patterns. Because these reinforcers are so strong, change is hard to make. It's often not enough to *ask* someone to change. Their fears and needs may overwhelmingly shout you down.

Consider the case of John and his girlfriend, Simone. He's asked her to be more open, to tell him more about her past and how she feels at various times when they're together. But Simone grew up in a family in which teasing and ridicule were common occurrences and information was often used to hurt people. Her sisters read her diaries and repeated passages at very embarrassing moments. Simone has enormous fears of being laughed at, along with a parallel need to feel safe, even invulnerable. John's request, no matter how appropriate or well-meaning, simply can't compete with the reinforcers created by Simone's traumatic past.

If people behave the way they do because of strong and complex patterns of reinforcement, it follows that changing their behavior must often involve changing those reinforcers. In other words, if John wants Simone to be more open, he'll have to find a way to make her feel more safe, less fearful of ridicule.

Effective strategies for influencing others fall into two categories: positive reinforcement and negative consequences.

Positive Reinforcement

There are four types of positive reinforcement that you can use to influence behavior.

1. Praise. You can praise past behavior that is similar to the changes you now want to reinforce. Praising past similar behavior is a powerful reinforcer because it sends the message "I see your goodness and worth when you act like that." Everyone is hungry for esteem and appreciation. Praise is a way of giving a valued gift while at the same time pulling for behavior that you'd prefer.

2. Trading. The basic message is: "I'll give you X if you'll give me Y." Life is full of little deals, and is often made much easier by them. "If you could get those big trees trimmed, I'd help you relax with a neck massage." "If these reports get in on time, I think we can give you some more interesting assignments next week." "If you could walk me to my car in the evenings, I'd be glad to give you a lift home." "Would you mind going with me to visit my grandmother this weekend? I could make it worth your while with a dinner down at Salerno's." While trades can often sound like low-key bribery, there's nothing wrong with this. They are effective because they acknowledge the other person's needs and promise to provide something real as compensation for the desired behavior.

3. Building in rewards. Studies show that positive reinforcement is the most effective way of influencing behavior. Building in rewards is much like trading, but the reinforcement in this case is woven into the desired behavior. "Come shopping with me. There's a huge bookstore in the mall. You can browse around and see what new biographies they have." "If you help me with Jennifer's birthday party, we can at least be together and talk and hang out while we're keeping things organized." "Look, I want to see Colorado, and you love trains. Let's take the Durango and Silverton, and then later we can head up the Million Dollar Highway to Ouray and points north." When you build in rewards, each person gets something from the experience; each person's needs are assumed to be important and worth planning for.

4. Verbal and nonverbal appreciation. Verbal thank-yous are important. But a hug, a pat on the shoulder, a warm smile, even a nod and a look of contentment can also be powerful reinforcers when someone has done what you want. Appreciation conveys the message that you are grateful, you are pleased, and you value what the person has done. It greatly increases the chance that the behavior will be repeated and you will continue to get what you want.

Negative Consequences

Negative consequences should be used as a last resort when positive reinforcement isn't working. They tend to create a backlash of anger and resentment, thereby diminishing the desire to cooperate and please you. However, when negative consequences have a real impact on the other person, they can be strong motivators for change.

There are three types of negative consequences that you can use as strategies for influence.

1. Stop rewarding the person for behavior you don't want. If you want someone to be punctual, don't wait for them while they diddle with endless last-minute preparations. Leave on time *without* them. If you want someone to stop drinking alcohol when you're around them, leave when they pop open their first beer. Staying has the effect of *rewarding* drinking behavior with your presence. If you want a roommate to wash the dishes, don't wash them for him when he skips his turn. Influencing others is bound to be frustrating when you consistently reward them for staying the same.

2. Design self-care strategies to meet your needs when the other person is unable or unwilling to make desired changes. If you've asked your partner to help with household chores and he resists doing so, your self-care strategies would focus on cutting down your workload. The consequences for his unwillingness to help might include no longer doing his laundry or no longer cooking or shopping for him. If a friend keeps borrowing things without returning them, a self-care strategy might be to insist that only one thing can be borrowed at a time. If you've unsuccessfully requested that your partner get home earlier in the evenings, your self-care strategies might include going out to the movies and visiting friends when he is not home by a certain hour. Self-care strategies should not be framed as punishment or described in an angry tone that implies wrongdoing by the other person. They are merely efforts to meet your own needs *without the other person's help.*

3. Identify natural consequences. If someone is always late for your lunch dates, stop eating with them in restaurants. If someone has a pattern of being rude to you when you attend social events together, stop going with them. If you've driven with a friend to a party and he refuses to leave when you become tired, the natural consequence would be leaving and allowing him to find his own way home. The secret of natural consequences is that they aren't contrived. They are normal, natural outcomes of certain behavior. If your children haven't gotten fully dressed when it's time to leave for school, natural consequences would dictate leaving anyway, with whatever they have on, and having them finish dressing in the car.

Your Plan for Influencing Change

It's time for you to develop a plan that will help you reinforce desired changes in others. Your plan should have six parts.

1. Direct request. Start by identifying the person whose behavior you'd like to influence. Select a single issue or problem. (If you try to deal with more than one issue at a time, your plan will falter for lack of focus.) Write out in advance a request that is *specific* and *behavioral*. This means that you're not asking the person to change his or her feelings, attitudes, or awareness. Few people are willing or able to change on that level. You're merely asking him or her to do more or less of a particular behavior. "Could you please get home by 6:30 and call me if you're going to be late?" "Could we please schedule time on Saturday afternoons for hikes and shared time together?" "When we're walking, could we stay together instead of you getting so far ahead?" "Could you listen to me when I'm talking instead of starting to read or looking around the room?" Notice that each request asks for a specific change in behavior.

Once you've written down your request, plan to bring it up at a time when neither of you is emotionally upset. Be prepared to find that your request may be ignored. Or you may get agreement, but find that your request is forgotten in a few days or weeks. When a direct request is insufficient to engineer change, you'll need to implement the rest of your plan.

2. Praise. As previously described, praise focuses on times when the desired behavior actually occurred in the past. "I really liked it when you _____, could you _____ again?" (Be sure to suggest a specific time.) "It made me feel really good when you _____." "I felt ___(specific positive experience)___ when you _____." "I feel really close to you when you _____." "I'm incredibly appreciative when you _____, and it really makes a difference for me" (followed by a description of a specific experience).

Sometimes praise can be tied to a repetition of your direct request. You describe how good something felt in the past and ask for that same specific behavior in the present.

3. Trading. It's often helpful to write down a specific script for describing the trade you'd like to make. "If you could do _____ _____, I could _____." "I know it's hard for you to _____, but if you could, I'd like to _____ for you." "Let's make a deal. I'd really appreciate it if you could _____, and to show you my heart's in the right place, I'd like to _____ for you."

4. Building in rewards. Building in rewards starts with an analysis of the needs and interests of the other person, then looking for ways to integrate those needs into your request. Be creative. Brainstorm ideas.

A request such as taking more weekend hikes may offer opportunities to meet both people's needs. For example, if your friend is a camera buff or a bird lover, it might be easy to go to areas where photography or bird watching are possible. This part of your plan for change may not always be possible with certain requests. Something simple like "Would you please not read when I'm talking to you?" doesn't contain much opportunity for building in rewards.

5. Verbal and nonverbal appreciation. Getting the other person to try the new behavior once is a big step. Now you've got to reinforce it so it will happen again. Right now plan out what you'll say as well as how you will convey your gratitude in a nonverbal way.

6. Consequences. When all else fails, take a moment to analyze if you are in some way reinforcing the behavior you don't want. What happens after the other person does what you don't like? How do you respond? Is there something you're doing which supports that behavior? Now write down either your self-care strategy or natural consequences that can occur in response to the old, unwanted behavior. "If I can't get your help, I have to take care of myself in some way. I think what makes sense for me to do is _____."

Lisa's Plan for Influencing Change

1. Direct request

"Gail, we spend a lot of time talking about what's happening with your boyfriend. I'd like you to make a point of asking what's going on with me each time we get together. It would feel good if you could pull me into the conversation and make room for my stuff."

2. Praise

"Remember how you asked me all about my trip back to Texas to visit my father? That felt great because I got to tell you a lot of things I might not have said otherwise. I felt invited, like you were really interested."

3. Trading

"If you could ask about me each time, it would make a big difference. I'd even be willing to go to that Salsa club I've been shining you on about."

4. Building in rewards

I can't think of any rewards I can build in.

5. Verbal and nonverbal praise

Tell her, "Thanks for asking, Gail. It really feels like you're interested." Smile and hug her.

6. Consequences

"Gail, I need to feel you're interested in me. If you don't ask me things and take an interest, I'd just as soon do stuff together where we go out to movies and concerts and things where we don't talk that much. Then I won't be angry about long conversations that feel kind of one-sided."

19

Small Groups

Members of the West Coast Sales Department of the Techtrex Instrument Corporation are meeting to discuss next year's marketing plan for their line of scientific measuring devices.

Bill, the department head, is dreading the meeting because the marketing plan calls for increased sales targets next year. The plan was set even though the economy is depressed, no new products are being offered, and his travel budget has been reduced. Bill feels that he has to sell his sales force on an impractical plan.

Joe is the best salesman. He's here to tell how he was tops in sales for the third year in a row. He doesn't care if times are tough—if everyone would just follow his example they could sell hibacis to the devil.

Patrick is a salesman who doesn't believe in working too hard. Life is for enjoyment. He thinks that the marketing plan is a joke—everybody always forgets about that kind of thing three months into the year. Pat is here to crack a few jokes and see if he can get Joyce to go to bed with him.

Joyce is the only woman on the field sales staff. She feels that she has to prove she can do as good a job as any man. Because she is a newcomer, she has the smallest, least productive territory. She's at the meeting to see if she can steal Nevada from Patrick's territory.

Kathryn is the sales department secretary. She's been with Techtrex for years and has seen lots of salespeople come and go. She doesn't understand the marketing plan and doesn't care to learn anything about it. She's here to catch Joe up on company gossip, laugh at Pat's jokes, and bully Joyce about not filling out price quotes and expense vouchers properly.

The meeting is a disaster. Bill hems and haws about the plan without presenting the facts and figures clearly. Joe tells a long, irrelevant story about how he nailed down the Cutter Labs account. Pat and Kathryn trade sarcastic comments about the people in marketing who developed the plan. Joyce explains how the only way to meet the new sales targets is to reorganize their territories. Nobody really listens to the others or makes constructive suggestions. There is no sense of teamwork or common purpose. The meeting breaks up with a vague resolution to "do our best" and "see how the first quarter goes." Each person leaves feeling unsatisfied and irritated.

All these people are actually quite competent and successful in their private lives. They may even communicate adequately with their families and loved ones. But they can't communicate effectively in a small group designed to accomplish a specific task.

Types of Small Groups

The most common type of small group is the social group in which friends get together to enjoy themselves. A seminar is a small group whose purpose is educational. Therapy and sensitivity groups are very specialized small groups organized to improve mental health or generate insight. To function well in these types of groups you need at least some of the basic communication skills covered elsewhere in this book.

Task-oriented small groups are business, committee, club, team, union, charity, or other organization meetings intended to solve a problem, promote a cause, or generate ideas. This chapter focuses on small, task-oriented groups because they require some special communication skills.

Task-oriented groups demand special skills because solving the group problem takes precedence over the needs and agendas of the individuals in the group. Although you may be a great listener, in touch with your deepest feelings, able to express anger and other strong emotions, and dedicated to achieving intimacy through good communication, you may still be a total failure at communicating effectively in a group. Successful group process requires a level of cooperation and accommodation that isn't needed when only two people are talking.

Another reason task groups are challenging is that they frequently operate according to a rigid, parliamentary structure that is very unlike the free-flowing communication you enjoy with friends. The structure is designed to cool emotions, allow minority opposition to be heard, and move the group systematically toward a solution. But often the structure just seems to get in the way. You can't speak when you want to, and when it's your turn the topic has changed.

Task-Group Roles

Members

Members of a task group can be divided into *initiators* and *responders*. Initiators are the ones who speak up first. They initiate discussion by contributing their knowledge of relevant facts, sharing pertinent information or experiences, and giving their opinions.

Responders listen and respond by summarizing and elaborating what they've heard. They evaluate information, criticize proposals, and ask questions.

As the group process unfolds, members switch back and forth between initiating and responding. Neither role is more important and both are necessary for group process to work.

However, the members' roles can get out of balance. When there are too many initiators, the result is a contentious, unruly group that is too divided to make up its mind. When there are too many responders, the result is an overly polite, boring group that is too ambivalent to make up its mind. Maintaining a balance is one of the roles of the leader.

Leaders

Researchers studying group dynamics have come up with long lists of roles and activities carried out by leaders. A widely accepted list devised by Krech and Crutchfield indicates that a leader serves the group at various times as:

- executive (establishing rules, agendas, meeting times)
- planner
- policymaker (establishing broad guidelines and general principles)
- expert
- external group representative (representing the group to the larger world)
- controller of internal relationships (combining and separating individuals, promoting and demoting)
- purveyor of rewards and punishments (praising, criticizing, dispensing values roles)
- arbitrator
- exemplar (providing a good example of how to behave in a group)
- group symbol

- surrogate for individual responsibility (taking responsibility for group decisions)

- ideologist

- father figure (reassuring, praising, protecting)

- scapegoat (taking blame for group failures, absorbing hostility)

Some of these roles are obvious. Others will be more fully explained by the section on leader's rules for task-group effectiveness.

Block to Effective Task-Group Communication

In a task group the purpose of the group has to be paramount over the needs of the individuals comprising the group. The blocks to task-group effectiveness are all related to individuals placing their needs above those of the group.

Aggressors are out to get other individuals in the group. They want to draw blood and scalp their enemies. For example, the manager of the eastern division runs down the achievements of the western division by lamenting missed deadlines. The secretary snipes at the mailroom supervisor by harping on a lost memo. It's more important for the aggressor to win than for the group to succeed.

Defeatists feel that the problem is insurmountable and that there is no hope of a solution. Defeatists are often angry people who express their feelings by sabotaging any progress. For example, an order clerk criticizes a proposed change in the discount policy by asking increasingly far-fetched questions: "What if. . . . What if . . . ?" After introducing several unlikely hypothetical complications, she throws up her hands and cries, "Oh, it's just too complicated. It'll never work." The group has to fail so that the defeatist's pessimism and cynicism will be vindicated.

Stars are onstage all the time. They have to have the best lines, the best ideas, and all the attention. Joe, the star salesman, keeps interrupting a complex presentation of market trends with irrelevant examples of his brilliant sales techniques. It's more important for stars to shine than for the group to succeed.

Storytellers haven't the foggiest idea of the group's purpose because they're so wrapped up in explaining their own personal problems or experiences. They keep lapsing into asides and irrelevant tête-à-têtes. For example, Mable and Joan compare childbirth experiences while the other committee members are trying to form a day-care cooperative. It's more important for the storyteller's story to be heard and appreciated than for the group to succeed.

Clowns are in it for laughs and kicks. They may know the purpose of the group but they don't take it seriously. They may be sarcastic or sexually aggressive. For example, George spends most of the weekly production meeting joking with Adrienne and trying to find out if she lives alone, if she has a boyfriend, and so on. Clowns want to entertain, and whether the group succeeds is irrelevant.

Dominators want to run things more than they want to solve problems. Jack, a computer room supervisor, always has a written agenda for monthly meetings and adheres to it so rigidly that his staff has long ago given up trying to discuss current, fast-breaking problems at the meetings. They let little problems fester until they're big enough to get on Jack's agenda. The computer room typically teeters on the edge of chaos. The dominator gets to be the boss, but group effectiveness is lost.

Ax-grinders relate everything to their pet obsession, whether it has anything to do with the group's problem or not. For example, Betty is such an ardent feminist that she blames everything that goes wrong in the campaign headquarters—garbled instructions, low funds, late pamphlets—on sexism. It's more important for ax-grinders to grind their axes than for the group to succeed.

Rules for Task-Group Effectiveness

Determine Purpose of Group

Before the group gets together, you should get a clear idea of the purpose. Is it to decide whether to fire the receptionist? To discuss a switch to accounting on the accrual basis? To plan your daughter's wedding? If the purpose is to solve a problem, work on stating the problem in as much detail as possible. If you need facts and figures, get them beforehand. Too many groups waste half their time fumbling at a definition of the problem.

Know Your Own Mind

Before you join the other members of the group, consider your own views. What do you really think? Do you want to reprimand the receptionist or hire a new one? Do you think the present cash accounting method is inherently better for the company, or should you switch to the accrual method? Are you willing to pay for a catered extravaganza or would you really prefer that your daughter elope and save you the expense?

Knowing your own mind puts you miles ahead of many people who show up at meetings empty-headed. Most meetings would last only fifteen minutes if everybody showed up with a carefully considered solution to the common problem.

Listen

Since you know what the group is for and what you think, you can afford the time to listen with an open mind to what the others have to say. Are the others clearly aligned behind the same purpose as you? What cross-purposes need to be straightened out before meaningful discussion can take place?

If the other members are all ready to work on the same problem, what do they want the solution to be? Are they cemented into their positions, or are they willing to listen? Really try to understand what each person wants out of this group. You'll start to spot the blockers. They're the ones who want to crack jokes, tell stories, pick fights, boss people around, be noticed, or give up before they start.

Contribute

All this is useless unless you are willing to contribute. Make your opinions known. Provide all the information you have that really forwards the purpose of the group. You can include your wild ideas, your doubts, your hopes. If you've done your homework on determining the purpose and knowing your own views, your contribution will be clear, concise, and appropriate. Try not to be a bully. Take a genuine interest in the collision of ideas. Look for ways of combining and refining the good ones.

Keep Your Cool

Participation in a small task group is one situation in which it may not pay to be yourself. Often your expression of yourself must be tempered to the task at hand. You may have to be nice to people you don't like, attend to incredible bores, endure unfair criticism in silence, and let obvious fallacies pass unchallenged in the service of group harmony and getting the job done. Insincerity and withheld feelings that would be the kiss of death to an intimate relationship may be the breath of life to a business meeting.

Leaders' Rules for Task-Group Effectiveness

You should read this section even if you don't consider yourself a leader. Most groups have more than one leader, and anyone in a group can play a leadership role some of the time. It's more important that the fourteen "leader's roles" listed earlier get accomplished than that a particular person accomplish them. In fact, even the most experienced leader can't perform all of the leader's roles all of the time.

This is good news for aspiring executives and others who yearn to gain power within an organization. Participation in meetings, committees, and other types of small groups will give you chances to perform leadership roles even if you are not the designated leader. By stepping in and effectively performing the functions that the designated leader is neglecting, you can advance the cause of the group and yourself at the same time.

State Group Purposes

This is the first and most important function of a leader. You state the purpose by your opening remarks: "We're here today to come up with a new credit policy." "The purpose of this meeting is to consider three possible health plans and choose the best one." "Thanks for coming here tonight to help plan the rent control initiative."

You should restate the purpose whenever the group wanders off onto another topic. Keep hammering home the reason for this group meeting at this time until everybody who is capable of getting the point gets it. It will help to put the purpose in the form of concrete goals that can be broken down into manageable steps: "Let's start by identifying the one aspect of our current credit policy that most needs changing." "First let's compare the benefits of each health plan, then consider the costs." "We basically need to figure out three things: setting up fund-raising letters, getting endorsements, and finding a headquarters."

As suggestions are made and discussion progresses, keep relating what is said back to the purpose you stated. This will help eliminate secondary and unrelated topics. The best meetings are those that take up one subject or problem and solve it. If you have to have a meeting with several unrelated topics, set up an agenda and stick to it.

Elicit Contributions

If you have a group made up mostly of responders and with very few initiators, you'll have to work to elicit contributions. One way to do this is to set up a brainstorming session. Pick a part of your problem that seems one of the easiest to solve and invite the group members to bring up all the solutions that pop into their heads. At this stage no criticism is allowed, not even the mildest sort of laughter or head shaking. Encourage imaginative solutions or suggestions, even impossible notions. The goal at this stage is quantity, not quality.

With a very recalcitrant group, you will probably have to make a couple of contributions to the brainstorming session yourself, then ask each member in turn to say something. Persist until you have a pool of suggestions. Have someone write them down so that you can keep track.

Now you can invite the group to go over the list of suggestions and throw out those that won't work. Try combining good ideas into better ones. By this time the group should be loosened up and the discussion should have some momentum.

Another skill that's important for eliciting contributions is active listening. Any time a suggestion is offered or a point made by a group member, restate it in your own words. Your brief one-sentence summary will give members the experience of being heard. When you sense that someone has something to say but his or her idea is vague or garbled, focus your attention on that person. Invite him or her to elaborate by asking, "What is it you're saying?" Feed any response back to the person: "So your opinion is that credit customers are not properly screened, is that right?" Ask for clarification and continue to provide feedback as you get more information. Keep your manner supportive. Smile and nod and refrain from criticism or argument.

It's especially important to notice who in the group is hanging back because he or she doesn't agree with the others. These are the people you should draw out with active listening. You probably won't get them to agree with the consensus, but they need to air their views. Chances are good that if you encourage them to state their position, they'll support the majority decision even if they disagree with it. If you allow them to stay silent, they're more likely to sabotage the group's decision later.

Determine Consensus

This is a continuation of the previous rule. As the discussion proceeds, you should relate suggestions to the purpose of the meeting. Point out conflicting positions and suggest compromises. After long, confused exchanges, give a brief summary of the main points.

When the alternatives are clear or a proposal has made and discussed, call for a vote. When the group agrees on a certain line of action, nail down the details: Who is going to do the first step? By when? Who will help? What other groups need to be involved? Ask for volunteers, write down deadlines, and in general ensure that the agreed-upon action will be carried out when the group disperses.

If a meeting is inconclusive, set a time and place for another meeting. Try to end on a positive, concrete note, even if it's just an agreement to meet again.

Keep Order

Conflict is inevitable. It arises eventually in even the most harmonious groups. It's the leader's job to recognize when conflict is getting out of hand and to restore order.

Conflict is getting out of hand when the group stops moving toward a solution to its problem or stops serving its purpose. This can happen when a group has too many initiators: everyone wants to talk and no one wants to listen. The traditional way to handle the situation is to insist on some form of parliamentary procedure. Insist that no one can address the group until recognized, that no one can interrupt a speaker, that motions be formally proposed and seconded, that all decisions be ratified by vote, and so on. These rules can be made as rigid as needed to control a contentious group.

However, most groups are not organized formally enough to use parliamentary procedure effectively. A more casual but sophisticated leadership strategy to handle group conflict is the "content-to-process shift." To do this, a leader draws the group's attention away from the *content* of the discussion and toward the *process* of communication. For example, to "call process" you might say, "I'm finding it very hard to follow these arguments because we're all talking at once. I know there are people here with good ideas, and I'd like the chance to listen to each one without distraction."

This approach is effective because it highlights the *style* of the interchange without attacking the validity of anyone's ideas or position. It is one of the most powerful tools a leader can use to quiet disruption and keep a group in order. Calling process is also a good tactic to use to counter many of the blocking tactics previously discussed. It can show up defeatists for what they are, embarrass storytellers into rejoining the group, and short-circuit the time-wasting arguments of ax-grinders.

Here are some other tactics for dealing with the common blocks to task-group effectiveness:

Aggressors. If you've got a genuinely hostile group member, the best long-term solution is to kick him or her out of the group. If you can't do that, try calling process: "George, you seem awfully critical about this report. Is there a reason for your hostility?" This will probably direct George's hostility toward you as the leader—an effective strategy. In most groups there is a little hostility toward the leader just because he or she has the mantle of power. If you can recognize and accept this fact, you can further the purpose of the group by absorbing the hostility. Hostility has to go somewhere, and if you don't take it, group cohesion will be weakened. The most effective leaders are willing to be the scapegoat from time to time. Such a vent relieves pressure and lets the group get on with business. For example, you can say, "I understand that some of you are mad because the raises didn't go through. I just want you to know that it was largely my fault. I could have pushed harder for the raises, and I didn't. I'm sorry." This kind of approach will get you much farther than trying to lay the blame on someone else.

Defeatists. Active listening and calling process can expose a defeatist's whole mechanism of bitterness and pessimism. But it takes time. A quicker tactic is to treat defeatism as a legitimate option. Whenever the defeatist says "That won't work," you reply with something like, "Thank you, James. We'll note that your opinion is that it won't work and we shouldn't try it." Treat defeatism as a consistent no vote and get on to more positive contributions.

Stars. Give these group members something to do that has a high profile but keeps them quiet. Writing suggestions on a blackboard or large pad is ideal. Insisting on parliamentary procedure sometimes works, as does a simple rebuke like, "Why don't you listen for a while? I think you're missing the point."

Storytellers. Interrupt their stories to tell them the purpose of the meeting. Ask them what they intend to do at the meeting to further the purpose. If they don't intend to do anything, cut their stories short whenever they begin a new one. Exclude them from the group process until they either choose to become productive or voluntarily leave.

Clowns. Try giving them some responsibility. Keep on asking for their opinions and disregard the jokes. Also consider that some joking is necessary to relieve the tension in a group.

Dominators. If you can't exclude a dominator from the group, try delegating some of your leadership roles to him or her. Sometimes a dominator just doesn't have enough to do. If the person turns out to be a poor leader, put him or her in charge of an unimportant subcommittee and make efforts to get him or her out of the group permanently.

Ax-Grinders. Try active listening to expose their favorite topic. Restate the purpose of the group and point out how their pet topic is irrelevant. Call process each time they wander off the track.

Maintain Group Morale

Every meeting actually has two purposes: the specific group goal at the time and the maintenance of the group. The specific group goal changes from meeting to meeting. The goal of group maintenance is constant and unchanging. As a leader, your role is to serve both purposes at once and not operate at cross-purposes by pushing through a solution to an immediate problem while damaging group morale. One purpose is not more important than the other. Often there are two leaders in a group—one for the specific group goal and one to maintain morale.

The best leaders serve both purposes at once. They get the immediate job done in a supportive, uncritical manner. They concentrate on group cohesiveness by taking time to explore minority views and include the more retiring or obstreperous group members. They encourage good interpersonal relations within the group by establishing a good working relationship with each group member.

To maintain group morale, you should always keep in mind the needs of group members. To feel good in a group, everyone needs three things: inclusion, control, and appreciation. Inclusion means feeling that you're part of the group, a member of the "in" crowd. Control means feeling that you have some say in the group, that you will be heard and your views will be taken seriously. Appreciation means feeling accepted and liked.

Choose the Appropriate Leadership Style

Some leaders are authoritarian. They dictate to their group members from the top down. The style is somewhat militaristic, abrupt, and rigid.

Other leaders are democratic. They accept proposals from the group, encourage discussion, and set up a structure for voting. The majority rules most of the time, except when the leader exercises veto power.

Still other leaders are hardly leaders at all, preferring a liassez-faire style. Everyone talks as the urge moves them. The group arrives at a consensus without direction from the leader. There is very little formal structure to a meeting. The leader has no veto power.

You probably have an innate preference for one of these styles over the others. However, effective leaders can utilize each of these styles as needed. None of these styles is inherently better or worse than the others. Choice of style depends on the situation.

For example, suppose you are in charge of six file clerks. You might be totally authoritarian when telling them how to fill out their timecards: there is no room for discussion, just a right way and a wrong way to fill out a timecard. On the other hand, when you meet with the clerks to figure out how to keep the phones covered during lunch and coffee breaks, you might be democratic. You set up a structure in which you tell them that you want the phones answered at certain times and they then discuss and vote on who will go on break first, who will take a late lunch, how doctor's appointments will affect the schedules, and so on. You might veto a hopelessly complicated or unrealistic plan, but your intent is to agree as closely as possible with whatever they come up with.

At the other end of the continuum, you might be discussing the Christmas Party or who should bring what to the potluck lunch: you're totally laissez-faire, since it's inappropriate for you to have more or less say than anyone else in the group.

Thus, the key to choosing the appropriate leadership style for a given situation depends on your sensitivity to the task at hand and the needs of group members and your flexibility to vary your own role accordingly.

20

Public Speaking

The United Way Committee has asked you to address your fellow workers about making donations. The committee chose you because you did so well last year getting contributions from people on a one-to-one basis. As you try to gather your thoughts and prepare your talk, you realize that public speaking is very different from a casual chat on the coffee break.

Effective public speaking requires special communication skills. It is less spontaneous than personal communication, since you have to prepare your message in advance and make sure it is logically organized. Your address is more or less continuous, with little feedback from your passive audience. You have to communicate to a relatively large number of people at once, including some who aren't particularly interested in what you have to say. Often you don't get to choose the most advantageous time or setting for your speech.

All this means that you have to take special care to determine the exact purpose and subject of your speech, organize it accordingly, and deliver it in a style appropriate to your audience and the occasion. it's no wonder you experience some stagefright!

Purpose

The first step in speech writing is to ask yourself, "What is the purpose of this speech?" You'll find that most speeches are intended either to inform or to persuade.

Once you have determined whether your purpose is primarily to inform or persuade, you should refine the purpose by stating it in one complete sentence. For example, the purpose of the United Way speech might be: "This speech is intended to persuade the audience to sign up for the automatic payroll contribution plan." An informative speech about Egyptian pyramids might have as its purpose "to tell about the Pharaoh's god-like position at the center of Egyptian religion, the purpose of the pyramids, and facts about their construction."

It's often helpful to state the purpose of a speech in terms of behavioral goals. What do you want the audience to do at the end of your speech? This is especially important in the case of persuasive speeches, after which you want the audience to contribute money, vote for you or your candidate, or take some kind of personal action such as writing a congressman or volunteering for community service. This way of clarifying the purpose also works well when preparing an informative speech. You can state the purpose like this: "My speech will enable the audience to remember that the Pharaoh was a god, that the pyramids contained everything he would need for eternal life, and how the pyramids were constructed with massive ramps."

Subject

The next step is to outline your subject matter. In general, the less said the better. If you can't sum up your speech's content in one sentence, it's probably too long. Your audience won't remember it all. Many experiments in audience retention have shown that the average audience member can only follow one main point and three subpoints. All the rest is wasted breath. You're better off with a tightly focused, short speech than a long, all-inclusive speech.

Presentation

The purpose and subject of your speech will suggest which style of presentation will be most effective. There are four types of presentation: *Impromptu,* in which you have no time for preparation and must think on your feet; *extemporaneous,* in which you have prepared a speech but not memorized it word for word; *memorized,* in which you deliver a verbatim recitation of your speech; and *manuscript,* in which you read your written speech aloud.

The impromptu speech is the most effective in terms of rapport and spontaneity. However, it is hard to pull off unless you know the subject perfectly, can think and organize while you talk, and don't suffer at all from stage fright. For most purposes, the extemporaneous speech is better. It allows you to be spontaneous in your word choice and phrasing, creates good rapport with your audience, and can be carefully organized beforehand.

The memorized speech usually sounds wooden and mechanical, and should be avoided unless there is no other way to conquer your anxiety or convey very difficult material. The manuscript speech is reserved for formal occasions such as political announcements or the presentation of scientific papers, when the exact word-for-word content is so much more important than style of delivery or audience rapport.

If you do have occasion to deliver a memorized or manuscript speech, remember to make eye contact with your audience. This keeps you in closer contact. In the case of a manuscript speech, looking up to establish eye contact forces you to pace your reading slowly enough for audience comprehension. Mark your place with your finger as you read so you can look up at the end of each long phrase without getting lost.

Organization

The advice most commonly given to beginning speakers remains the best: "Tell them what you're going to tell them, tell them, then tell them what you've told them."

This advice recognizes the two most important facts about speech organization: (1) All good speeches must have an introduction, a middle, and a conclusion. (2) All important information must be repeated at least three times to be retained.

The introduction is one of the most important parts of a speech. It gets your audience's attention, establishes your relationship with them, sets the tone you want to take, and orients them to the subject matter. If you have already stated the content of your speech in one sentence, you have the kernel of the introduction. Most successful introductions include a capsule summary—the "tell them what you're going to tell them" part. It's a good idea to write your introduction last, or at least revise it after you know the full content and tone of the rest of the speech.

The middle of your speech contains the meat. Depending on your purpose and subject, the middle part can be organized in different ways:

Sequential. This is best when dealing with historical material such as the history of the CIO, child development, or how you went bald. It starts in the past and proceeds in sequence toward the present and the future. The connectives are "and then . . . next . . . after that . . . the following year" and so on. This is one of the easiest organizations for an audience to follow and works especially well for informative speeches.

Spatial. This is similar to sequential organization. It proceeds in space rather than time and is good for informing audiences about such topics as the New England Colonies, the voting precincts of the city, European geography, travel stories, and so on. Its simplicity makes it easy to understand. Add a map and a pointer and it's almost impossible to lose an audience with spatial organization.

Structure/Function. This is good when you're describing a complex organism or organization. For example, a talk about how squash grows could be organized according to structure first and function second:

Structure	Function
root	absorb water and nutrients anchor to ground
vine	carry water and nutrients physical support
leaf	catch sun's rays for photosynthesis shade earth
blossom	attract pollinating insects fruit formation
fruit	form seeds for next year's plants protect and nourish seeds

Or the same talk could be organized first according to function:

Function	Structure
intake of nutrients and energy	roots leaves
conversion of nutrients and energy	photosynthesis in leaves
physical support	roots vines
reproduction	blossom fruit seeds

By thinking about a complex subject in terms of structure and function, you can often hit upon a clear way to organize your material.

Topical. Sometimes you have two or three things to talk about that are not closely related by time, place, structure, or function. In this case, you can take up each topic in turn, being careful to let your audience know each time that you are changing topics. For example, a speech to your sales group at work might be broken into three parts: inventory, new prices, and overseas markets. A talk about ecology could be broken down into water quality, landfill, and legislation. This kind of organization is casual and works only when the information is simple and short. It is not to be confused with presenting a long list of arguments or other items—that's a symptom of poor organization and it never works.

Problem/Solution. This is a good way to organize a persuasive speech. You present a problem in detail, then present the solution in such a way that it clearly solves every aspect of the problem. For example, a speech in favor of a school bond initiative could be organized like this:

Problem:

> Overcrowded classrooms
>
> Long school bus rides
>
> Poor performance on standard national tests

Solution: A new school to give us:

> Smaller average class size
>
> Shorter school bus routes
>
> Better education and thus higher test schools

Cause/Effect. This is related to the problem/solution method of organization. You can describe the cause first and then its effect, or you can do it vice versa and trace an effect back to its cause. For example, you could describe the western migration of Americans in the nineteenth century by covering the causes first:

> Economic depression in the east
>
> Homestead Act
>
> Declining fertility of eastern farmland
>
> Pressure of new immigrants from Europe
>
> Discovery of gold in California

Then you could cover some of the effects:

> Development of wagon trains and professional guides
>
> Indian wars
>
> Disruption of sod/buffalo ecology

> Formation of new states
>
> Great age of railroading

As you an see, some effects are in themselves causes of further effects. This is a flexible organizing principle that can throw selected facts into highlight and thrust inconvenient facts into the shadows.

In the conclusion of a good speech, you summarize what you have told your audience. In persuasive speeches the conclusion is also a call to action: a vote, to write a letter, to contribute, to volunteer, or to support a candidate or position. The conclusion is the most important part of a persuasive speech.

The conclusion should also clearly signal that you are through talking. There's nothing worse than a speech that dwindles into embarrassed silence and tentative applause. Conclude with a clear summary, statement, resolution, catch phrase, or call to action that lets the audience know you're finished.

Audience Analysis

Before preparing your speech, consider your audience. Are they all men, all women, or is it a mixed crowd? Are they mostly old, young, or all ages? How much education have they had? Are they rich or poor? Are they conservative or liberal? What are their racial or ethnic backgrounds? What are their occupations? Their attitudes? Their interests? All these considerations are important in choosing appropriate language, examples, jokes, and overall tone.

When the day of the speech arrives, give some thought to your audience's circumstances. Have they just eaten a big lunch? Is it very early in the morning or late at night? Do they have comfortable seating? Is it too hot or cold or noisy? Have they just heard another speaker who bored or angered them? These considerations may make you change the length or tone of your presentation to match or counteract the mood of your audience.

During the speech, watch your audience for smiles, applause, frowns, restless movements, looks of confusion, and people leaving or talking to their neighbors. You may need to talk louder, slower, cut things short, or change your tone.

Style

The basic rule of style is that your language must be appropriate to the audience, the subject matter, and the occasion. You shouldn't talk over your audience's heads, nor should you condescend. You should use correct grammar and standard English when presenting an oral defense of your thesis, and save slang and colloquialisms for proposing toasts to your football buddies.

Public speaking creates some special stylistic problems. A speech differs from a letter or a friendly conversation in that your audience has to be able to remember what you said and follow your train of thought without being able to ask you questions or reread the previous paragraph. You can ensure a good basic speaking style by following these five rules:

1. Use simple terms. Never use a two-syllable word when one syllable will do. The shorter, more common words in the English language have more impact and are more easily understood and remembered. "Now" is better than "at this point in time," and "most voters" is better than "the vast majority of the electorate."

2. Use short sentences. If you have to draw breath before the end of a sentence, it's too long. If a sentence has more than one subordinate clause, it's too long. Before you reach the end of a long sentence your audience has lost track of the beginning. Break long sentences down into several short, punchy sentences. For example, this sentence is grammatically correct, but too long for a speech:

> "In order to run an effective business, you must not only have a firm grasp of the day-to-day and week-to-week operations and cash flow, but also you must project your earnings and expenses several weeks, months, yes, even years into the future and plan your new products, services, and facilities."

This should be broken down into several impactful sentences:

> "Running an effective business is hard. You have to do several things at once. You have to have a firm grasp of the day-to-day operations. You have to watch your weekly cash flow. At the same time you've got to project your earnings and expenses. You've got to plan new products, new services, and new facilities."

3. Repeat yourself. Your audience only absorbs about a third of what you say. Therefore anything important should be said at least three times. You can actually repeat yourself word-for-word in a speech and sound perfectly normal, whereas the same technique employed in an essay would sound silly. Besides verbatim repetition, you should paraphrase your key points. Say them another way. Repeat your main ideas in slightly different terms. It also helps to provide your audience with short internal summaries as you proceed with your talk. It helps them remember where you've been, and gives slow listeners a chance to catch up.

4. Put up signposts. Signposts are transitional words or phrases that alert your audience to a change of direction or remind them of where you are in your presentation. They are the verbal equivalent of subheadings and paragraph indentations in a written piece. Signposts can be subtle or obvious. Generally speaking, the more obvious the better:

"Now we'll move on to. . . . "
"This is the third point I'd like to make:"
"On the other hand. . . . "
"Now!"
"Pay attention, this is where is get complicated."
"First . . . second . . . third. . . . "
"In conclusion. . . ."
"Let me summarize what we've covered so far."
"Another example of this problem is. . . . "

5. Choose personal terms. Refer to yourself as "I" and "me." Refer to your audience as "you." Refer to people in general as "we" and "us." Do this at every reasonable opportunity. It builds rapport by underlining the personal nature of your relationship with your audience. It also makes some positions clearer. Notice how this stilted, vague statement is enlivened and clarified by recasting it in more personal terms:

Impersonal: "It has been argued that the only way to ensure a fair flextime policy is to install time clocks for use by all personnel. However, it is possible that the honor system will work."

Personal: "I've heard that the only way to ensure a fair flextime policy is for all of us to punch time clocks. However, I feel we can be trusted to follow the honor system."

Supporting Materials

Let's say you've clarified the purpose of your talk so that you can state it in one sentence. You can also summarize the content in one sentence. You've resolved to use simple terms and short sentences. In fact, your speech now seems so simple, you're wondering how you'll ever fill up the allotted time. That's where supporting materials come in.

The most important supporting materials are usually examples, illustrations, anecdotes, and jokes. These give flesh to the dry bones of the abstract point you are trying to make. The best examples are concrete—a particular person or group does a particular thing in a particular place at a particular time. Include sensory data about sights, sounds, smells, and feelings to bring the scene to life. But keep your examples brief and to the point. As a general rule, give only two examples to support a given point, then summarize the point again.

Statistics are popular supporting materials. For speeches the best statistics are simple ones that indicate general measures of tendency or dispersion. Precise figures and subtle distinctions serve no purpose in a speech. Your audience will not remember that 34.657 percent of males exhibit 10.587 percent hair loss. They will remember that one man out of three goes bald.

In debates and other types of persuasive speeches, arguments are often supported by opinions, quotations, or testimony by experts or eyewitnesses. When presenting the words or opinions of others, make sure of three things: that you are quoting accurately, that the ideas effectively support your argument, and that your audience respects the authorities you're citing.

Slides, tapes, movies, chalkboards, displays, flipcharts, and handouts are audio/visual aids that can help get your point across. If you choose to use them, be sure to practice beforehand and make sure that you have the materials you need and are familiar with their use. Clumsy audio and visual aids are worse than none at all.

The Outline

The following is an outline of a five-minute speech on divorce mediation, showing examples of most of the suggestions made so far:

Divorce Mediation Speech

Purpose: To persuade divorcing couples to choose mediation over litigation.

I Introduction. Mediation is better than litigation because it:

    A. protects family assets

    B. protects children

    C. provides emotional support for the couple

II Body

    A. Expense

        1. Litigation costs $6,000 to $10,000 in legal fees, eating up family assets.

        2. Mediation costs $500 to $1,500, preserving family assets.

B. Children

    1. 13 million American kids have experienced divorce, and many of them end up losing a parent.

    2. In a mediated divorce parents are taught to take equal responsibility for the children and develop co-parenting skills.

    3. "Divorce each other, but not the kids." (American Association of Mediated Divorce)

C. Emotional Well-Being

    1. Example: Joe cancels all the charge cards on the advice of his lawyer. Jill follows her lawyer's advice and cleans out the joint checking account. In one week they are reduced to screaming at each other.

III Conclusion. Mediation is better because it's less expensive, ensures continued parenting for children, and protects the emotional well-being of the divorcing couple. "Don't hate, mediate."

Notice that the introduction, body, and conclusion of this speech follow the dictum, "Tell them what you're going to tell them, tell them, then tell them what you told them." Also note that the purpose and content of the speech can each be expressed in one easy-to-understand sentence.

The body of the speech is restricted to three points: expense, children, and emotional well-being. These points are supported by statistics, examples, and quotes. The body of the speech is organized on the problem/solution principle: the expense problem, the children problem, and the emotional problem. The same two solutions are examined for each problem: a litigated versus mediated divorce. The conclusion of the speech summarizes the arguments and ends with a call to action: "Don't hate, mediate."

Exercise: Pick a topic that you know a lot about. It can be a hobby, your job, a subject in school—whatever you are very familiar with.

Imagine an audience and a situation in which you could be called upon to talk about your topic for five minutes. Based on that audience and situation, compose one sentence that describes the purpose of your speech.

Proceed to outline your five-minute speech. Make sure you have a clear introduction, body, and conclusion. Organize the body according to a clear principle. Include examples, quotes, facts, and figures where appropriate. The outline should be one or two pages long.

Compare your outline with the example given above. Imagine giving the speech and make any changes to your outline that seem necessary. Save this outline for use in the last exercise of this chapter.

Delivery

The most important part of your delivery is your voice. It must have the correct volume, rate, clarity, and pitch to get your message across.

To get correct volume, deliver your speech to the last row of your audience. If they still can't hear, deliver the speech to the back wall or an imaginary point across the street. If in doubt about your volume, ask the people in back if they can hear. Avoid using a microphone. Your unamplified voice will sound more natural. If you must use a microphone, practice with it beforehand to find the optimum distance between your lips and the business end: too far and you won't be heard, too close and you'll get hisses and feedback.

Most speakers talk too fast. Make a conscious effort to speak slowly. Pause at the end of each sentence. A pace that sounds painfully slow to you will probably sound just right to your audience.

Clarity refers to how well you enunciate and articulate. Pronounce each consonant clearly and crisply. Dwell on your vowels. Don't slur— include every syllable in every word. In public speaking you can't get away with the lazy-lipped habits of everyday conversation.

Vary your pitch from loud to soft. If you're asking a rhetorical question, let your voice rise at the end of the sentence. Let you intonation register amusement, criticism, surprise, excitement, concern.

Once your vocal delivery is adequate, notice what you do with your body, especially your eyes. Good eye contact with your audience is essential. It implies sincerity, interest, intimacy, honesty, and other positive qualities. If eye-to-eye contact rattles you, just look at foreheads. The effect will be the same.

Your gestures and facial expressions should be natural to you and appropriate to what you're talking about. A lot of arm-waving and grinning is inappropriate when delivering a eulogy, but just the ticket for a pep rally. Don't put your hands behind your back or in your pockets. Use them to support what you're saying.

Move your body. Stepping to one side, forward, or back is a good way to indicate that you are about to change the subject. Movement adds welcome variety to any speech. For this reason, it's best to avoid getting trapped behind a podium.

Dealing With Stage Fright

Stage fright is a form of anticipatory anxiety. Your thoughts about having to speak in front of other people trigger a complex of "fight-or-flight" arousal symptoms. You feel butterflies in your stomach, your hands are cold and clammy, your mouth is dry, your heart is racing.

Fear of public speaking is probably the most universal type of anxiety. It has been widely studied and several effective strategies have been developed to combat it. There are things you can do before and during your speech to keep you nervousness at a manageable level.

The Week Before

If you know in advance that you are to deliver a speech, you can use Covert Modeling to prepare yourself to speak without nervousness. First, write out a brief description of yourself delivering the speech well: "I step up on stage and smile at the audience. I walk to the center and take a deep breath. I begin talking in a loud, strong voice. I speak slowly, clearly, pleasantly. As I make eye contact with individual members of my audience, I notice they are paying close attention and smiling. I feel relaxed and at ease. I'm having a good time. I know my material and enjoy sharing it with the audience. When I finish talking they applaud for a long time."

Memorize your description. Sit down in a quiet place where you won't be disturbed. Close your eyes. Take a deep breath and let it out. Visualize the place where you will give the speech: the walls, the chairs, the tables, the colors and shapes. When you have the scene clear in your mind, imagine someone very different from you getting up and delivering your speech. Pick someone you know who is older or younger than you, or of the opposite sex. Imagine that person being a little nervous at first, but then delivering your speech in a relaxed, natural manner. See the smiling, applauding audience. Run through this scene twice, seeing this dissimilar model struggling, then succeeding

Next, imagine an acquaintance your same age, sex, and general appearance giving your speech. See this person being a little nervous, but then getting into the swing of the speech and really doing a good job. Run through the scene twice with this similar model.

Then imagine the same scene with you yourself giving the speech. You're a little hesitant at first, then you gain confidence and start speaking out with authority. You make a few mistakes, but at the end the audience is genuinely pleased and you feel great. Run through the scene, watching yourself deliver the speech, until you feel your confidence increase.

Finally, practice the speech in front of a mirror, as described in the exercise at the end of this chapter.

An Hour Before

Just before your speech it helps to relax your whole body, going through this progressive relaxation procedure twice:

1. Sit in a comfortable position. Pull your feet and toes back toward your face, tightening your shins. Hold for five seconds and relax. Curl your toes, tighten your calves, thighs, and buttocks. Hold for seven seconds, then relax for eleven seconds. Notice the relaxation flooding your legs.

2. Clench both fists, tightening your forearms and biceps in a Charles Atlas pose. Hold it for seven seconds, then relax for eleven seconds. Notice the wave of relaxation that goes through your arms.

3. Arch back as you take a deep breath into your chest. Hold for five seconds. Relax. Take a deep breath, this time into your stomach. Hold seven seconds and relax for eleven seconds. Notice the relaxation in your chest and abdomen.

4. Wrinkle up your forehead. At the same time, press your head as far back as possible, roll it clockwise in a complete circle, and reverse direction. Now wrinkle up the muscles of your face like a walnut: frowning, eyes squinted, lips pursed, tongue pressing the roof of your mouth, and shoulders hunched. Hold for seven seconds and relax for eleven seconds. Notice the relaxation in the many small muscles of your head.

During Your Speech

Before you start talking, take a slow, deep breath and let it out gradually. This is the best quick relaxer, and it reminds you to fill your lungs fully before trying to speak. At any time during your speech you can pause and take a deep breath to relax. It will seem like a natural pause to your audience.

If nervousness threatens to overwhelm you, you can try the Paradoxical Admission. This involves telling your audience frankly, "I feel so nervous I'm sure I am going to blow this whole speech." By admitting your nervousness, you reveal what you want to hide. It is paradoxical but true that revealing hidden nervousness makes it disappear or subside to a manageable level.

Exercise: Deliver your speech into a full-length mirror while you tape record yourself. While speaking, watch your gestures, eye contact, and facial expressions. When listening to the playback, check your volume, speed, clarity, and pitch. Notice where you can use shorter words and sentences, where transitions are not adequately signposted, and where you should repeat yourself or use more personal language. Pretend you know nothing about the subject and see if the speech makes sense.

Deliver your speech again into the mirror with the recorder's microphone as far from you as your most distant listener will be. Correct all the errors you noted the first time. Keep practicing until the speech is as perfect as you can make it. Be careful that you don't speed up too much as you become more practiced.

21

Interviewing

You've been sending out resumes for a month, and you have finally landed an interview for a new job next week. You're getting more nervous by the minute. How can you prepare for what feels like the Inquisition? What questions will you be asked? How are you going to make a good impression on the interviewer? What questions should you ask in order to be sure it's the right job for you?

Your kitchen remodel is half done, and you're tired of cooking in the microwave and washing dishes in the bathroom sink. You and your kitchen contractor have a falling out, and he quits. How you are going to find reliable subcontractors to finish the job?

You supervise an employee who is chronically late. You plan to meet with him to see if you can motivate him to be on time.

You are being interviewed for a job, and the interviewer is a curious fellow who asks you what your sexual prefer-ence is, whether you smoke marijuana, and if you have ever been arrested. You think to yourself, "He's getting pretty personal . . . and what does this stuff have to do with the job anyway?" How do you respond?

You're thinking of opening a day-care program, and you want to interview the mothers in your neighborhood to find out their views on local childcare services.

As these examples illustrate, an interview differs from a casual conversation in that the participants in an interview are meeting with a serious purpose in mind. The person initiating the interview proposes a conversation on a topic of interest to him or her. His or her purpose may be to give information, get information, change the other's behavior or attitude, or reach a decision.

A successful interview takes place when both parties in an interview get what they want. For example, a supervisor motivates her worker to be on time and the worker keeps his job. But people in an interview often have different interests and therefore may be working at cross-purposes. For example, you want to buy the best car for your money, and you answer a classified ad placed by a stranger who wants to unload a lemon. It still may be possible to gratify both sets of expectations: somebody else's lemon, for the right price, may be the car of your dreams. But you will need to know something about automobiles or be able to consult with someone who does, and you will need interviewing skills.

What factors contribute to your getting what you want in an interview? Having more control in the interaction increases your odds of achieving your objectives. Usually the person with higher status has more control, and participants in an interview are typically of unequal status: job applicant meets with employer, patient meets with doctor, student meets with teacher, journalist meets with politician, someone seeks knowledge or help from someone who has knowledge or can help. The subordinate gives up control by letting the other take the lead, listening carefully, taking care not to offend, and in general deferring to the other's status. The subordinate in an interview can still exercise a considerable amount of control by carefully defining his or her goal, preparing questions beforehand, and anticipating the other person's questions.

Whether you are in the role of the interviewer, who primarily asks questions, or the role of the interviewee, who primarily responds to questions, you can learn how to maneuver the conversation to achieve your objectives. Understanding both roles will enhance your ability to gain the other person's cooperation, exchange useful information, and arrive at a mutually satisfying outcome.

An interviewer exerts control in an interview by the questions he or she asks. In a tightly structured *screening interview,* an employer asks a large number of job candidates a standard set of questions for the purpose of eliminating unqualified applicants. His questions probe for specific objective data: facts about a candidate's background, education, experience, and skills. Job candidates who appear best qualified for the position based on a screening interview may then be invited to a more loosely structured *selection interview* in which the employer asks questions intended to gather more subjective information about the candidate's personality. In loosely structured interviews, the experienced interviewer asks broad, open-ended questions, such as "Tell me about yourself," "Why should we give you this job?" and "If you were working for us and X happened, what would you do?" The job candidate's response to such questions reflects his or her priorities, insight, and judgment and gives the interviewer a sense of the inner person.

An interviewee exerts control in an interview by how he or she responds to the questions that are asked. When a job applicant faces a highly structured interview, he or she will do well to respond directly and accurately, emphasizing positive factors and avoiding saying anything that would bias the interviewer in an unfavorable way. In less structured interviews, the interviewee can control the flow of the interview by how he or she answers the questions asked. For instance, in an informational interview a politician may choose not to answer a question or to respond to a question in a way that advances his political views. If an interviewee realizes that the questions being asked will not further personal goals for the interview, the approach to take may be to redirect the conversation. For example, if a job candidate realizes that the interview is almost over and the interviewer hasn't asked questions that allow her to describe her strengths and accomplishments and what she would bring to the position, she must take the initiative to present this curtailed information. It is crucial for the interviewee to define his or her own goals for the interview and be prepared to shape the flow of the interview to fit those goals.

How Do You Interview?

Begin to think about how you participate in interviews by asking yourself the following questions for at least three past interviews. Be sure to include at least one interview in which you had a positive outcome and one interview in which you had a negative outcome.

1. What was your purposes for participating in the interview? Did you have more than one?

2. What was the other person's purpose?

3. What was your primary role? Were you the interviewer or the interviewee?

4. How did the interviewer exercise control in the interview?

5. How did the interviewee exercise control in the interview?

6. How was the interview structured?

7. In retrospect, what do you think of that interview now?

Clarifying What You Want

Knowing what you want simplifies your quest, motivates you to keep searching for your goal, keeps you from settling for something else, and enables you to communicate about your objective with enthusiasm to others. What you want can be ambitious, as long as it is also realistic. You must be willing and able to make your dream come true.

Cindy, who is thinking about buying a car, took a few minutes to imagine what she wanted.

> I see myself driving to school and work in a pale blue economy car that is safe and won't break down. It has a reliable heater, an air conditioner, and a great radio and tape deck. It's big enough so that I can carpool comfortably with my three friends. I feel confident and at ease driving it. My friends and I enjoy its great sound system. I am pleased that it was within my budget of three grand.

Cindy then asked herself what aspects of what she wanted were essential and nonnegotiable.

> It must be safe and unlikely to break down. No major repairs in sight until I graduate and get a full-time job. A heater and radio are musts. It must be comfortable for four adults. I should feel confident and at ease driving it. It must have economical gas mileage. It can't cost more than $3,000.

Cindy finally asked herself what aspects of what she wanted were optional.

> The pale blue color, air conditioner, tape deck, and great sound system would be nice bonuses, but are negotiable.

Set aside a few minutes to close your eyes, take a few deep breaths, and relax. Think about what you want. Imagine yourself having attained your goal. What does it look like? How do you feel? What are you doing? What is the setting like? Are you alone or with others? If you are with people, how are you interacting with them, and how are they responding to you? Use all your senses to fill in as complete an image of what you want as you can.

1. Write down a description of what you want.

_____

_____

_____

_____

2. Are some aspects of what you want essential and nonnegotiable? Write down these requirements.

_____

_____

_____

_____

3. What parts do you feel would be nice to have, but are not essential (and are therefore negotiable)? Write down these bonuses.

_____

_____

_____

_____

Refer back to what you wrote here when you feel discouraged, when you are tempted to get sidetracked into something else, when preparing for an interview, and especially at the conclusion of the interview.

Preparing To Conduct an Interview

Gathering Background Information

Time spent gathering background information about what you want will help you refine your goal and determine who to contact for an interview and what questions you should ask. Your research will typically begin with "impromptu interviews" with family, friends, and colleagues. You have established connections with these people and therefore can afford to "think out loud" with them. Your local library has a wealth of information including books, magazines, newspaper articles, government publications, trade journals, consumer reports, and Better Business Bureau reports.

Strangers are usually very willing sources of information if you let them know the purpose of your inquiry and assure them that you only want a little of their time. An impromptu interview with a stranger may work at a social gathering, but when you want to systematically probe people for their opinions and feelings on a topic, it is best to have a prepared list of questions for them to answer. This type of *informational interview* should not be used to get facts that you can easily glean from library resources; rather, it is used to learn about the "insider's point of view" on the topic of interest to you.

Preparing for an Informational Interview

If you want to make an appointment with a stranger for an informational interview, follow these steps:

1. Write a brief introductory script in which you explain who you are, establish a connecting link, state the purpose of your interview and how much of their time you want, and arrange a time and place to meet or talk on the phone.

   _____

   _____

   _____

   _____

2. Write down five or more questions in the order you want to ask them. Start with an easy one, and save the tough questions for the middle, when the person you are interviewing has warmed up to the subject. If you think you may run out of time, ask your most important question in the middle of the interview and save your least important question for the end, in case you don't get to it.

   _____

   _____

   _____

   _____

3. End your interview with a statement summarizing the important points, thanking the other person, leaving the door open for further contact, and asking if he or she could recommend other people with whom you might talk. While you can also use your conversation to let the person you are interviewing get to know you better, he or she will feel taken advantage of if you use an informational interview to try to sell yourself or a product.

   _____

   _____

   _____

   _____

Jamie is a social worker in private practice who is reevaluating her career options. A friend gave her the name of a social worker employed at a local hospital, and she prepared a script for scheduling an informational interview on the telephone and questions for an in-person interview.

1. Introductory script

    Hello, David Loeb, my name is Jamie Anderson, and I'm a social worker in private practice in town. We have a mutual friend, Alice Samuels, who suggested that I get in touch with you. I am exploring my career options and would like to talk with you for half an hour about your work at the hospital. Is that okay with you? I can come to your office. When would be a good time for us to meet?

2. Five questions in the order that she plans to ask them

    1. How does a typical day go for you when working at the hospital?

    2. What are some of the things that you like the best and the least about your work?

    3. I hear from Alice that your department is planning some new programs. What are these programs going to be like?

    4. I understand that you will be hiring staff for these programs. What will they add to the program?

    5. Alice tells me that the hospital is undergoing a major reorganization. How is this going to affect your department and what you do there?

3. Closing remarks

    Thank you very much for your time and insight into your work. You have been very helpful. I am very excited to hear about your department's plans to develop new programs. May I call you to find out how your new programs are doing? By the way, could you recommend anyone else whom I could talk to about my career options?

Establishing Rapport

Your goal is to get honest responses to your questions from a stranger with whom you are meeting for a very short period of time. In order to get someone to open up and not be defensive, you need to begin the interview by establishing rapport, so that the other person feels that you share some common interests and that you know what you are doing and can be trusted. While every interview is different, there are a few basic rules about how to create rapport.

1. Greet the interviewee warmly. Smile, shake hands, make eye contact, and use his or her name. If the interview takes place in your office or home, make sure that he or she is comfortable.

2. Review the purpose of the interview, why you are interested in this purpose, and how long you expect the interview to last. Be sure the interviewee understands and is in agreement with the structure that you are proposing.

3. Show genuine interest in the interviewee. Asking questions as a way of getting to know him or her.

4. Create a connecting link by bringing up mutual interests, attitudes, friends, and experiences.

5. Pay close attention to how the interviewee responds to you. Adjust your behavior to put him or her at ease and move on to the next phase of the interview as soon as it's clear to you that the person is comfortable with you.

Don't make the mistake of spending too little time on establishing rapport; after all, there is no point in asking questions of someone who doesn't trust you. But remember that you only have a short time in which to get answers to your questions, and you don't want the interviewee to feel you are wasting his or her time by spending too much time building rapport.

Directing the Flow of the Interview: Asking Questions and Responding to Answers

Once the interviewee seems at ease, you are ready to ask the questions that are directly related to your purpose. As you conduct this portion of the interview, remain aware of the time and the interviewee's nonverbal communication. You want to ask all of your most important questions, have your interviewee be candid with you, and not go over the time you've allotted.

The interaction will flow like this: you will ask a question which the interviewee will answer. You will respond to his or her answer with a comment or a follow-up question. Let the exchange go on for some time before you ask your next planned question, since your responses to the interviewee's answers are as essential to gathering the information you need as your planned questions are. You can respond in many different ways:

1. You can signal agreement and encourage him or her to go on with a nod of your head or an "uh-huh."

2. You can probe for more information by asking a follow-up question. ("How do you personally feel about the reorganization of the hospital?")

3. You can summarize the point just covered to be sure that you understand it. This will often cause the speaker to elaborate or clarify his or her point further. Summarizing can also be used as a way to signal closure before moving on to the next planned question. ("Your description of your typical workday suggests to me that you spend at least as much time doing paperwork and attending administrative meetings as you do working with your patients.")

4. You can state your agreement. ("Your saying that what you like best about your job is being a member of a well-functioning team reminds me of my own experience working as part of an inpatient unit. It was very much like a family.")

5. You can change the subject to a related area. ("Members of a family don't always get along. What kinds of conflicts come up, and how do members of your team resolve their differences?")

6. You can change the subject to a new area. ("What kind of patients do you work with?")

As the interviewer, you use your responses to the interviewee's answers to lead the conversation toward your objectives. When you feel that the interaction is not going in a useful direction, feel free to change the subject. The transition can be minimal: "I'd like to ask you about something else now" or "Let's take a minute to explore. . . . " The interviewee expects you to ask the questions and usually will not balk.

Exercise. Write five responses to the following statement of an interviewee.

> The additional staff which we hope to bring on board by the beginning of next year will enable us to serve twice the population we currently see. We also will be able to provide many new kinds of therapy groups and more one-on-one therapy.

Probe for more information: _____

_____

_____

State your agreement: _____

_____

_____

Summarize: _____

_____

_____

Change subject to related area: _____

_____

_____

Change subject to a new area: _____

_____

_____

Closing

Plan how you want to end the interview. The flow of conversation may lead you to choose a different ending, but it is always good to be prepared with a gracious and clear closing statement. You can:

1. Thank the interviewee for his or her time, help, insights, and so forth.

2. Summarize the important points of the interview.

3. Ask for final comments.

4. Stand and offer your hand.

Debriefing After the Interview

It is best to review what happened in the interview while it is fresh in your mind. Write down in more detail than you were able to do during the interview your recollection of what the interviewee said. Be sure to separate facts from assumptions. Ask yourself if the interviewee would agree with what you are writing. If you have some doubt about what was said, you may want to either call the interviewee to confirm or send your written summary for him or her to review. If your purpose in the interview was to change the other person's attitude or behavior, be sure to write down exactly what was accomplished. What did he or she agree to do? What did you agree to do?

After you write down what took place in the interview, take some time to evaluate your own performance. If you were dissatisfied with some parts, how can you avoid making the same mistakes the next time you conduct an interview? Ask yourself the following questions:

1. Did you sufficiently prepare for this interview? What could you have done to be better prepared?

2. Did you successfully put the interviewee at ease so that he or she trusted you and was interested and cooperative in answering your questions? What more could you have done to build rapport?

3. Did you control the flow of the conversation so that your purpose was achieved? How could you have structured the interview differently to accomplish your objective?

4. Did you use the time efficiently? How could you have used the time better?

5. Are you satisfied with how you ended the interview? What could you have done differently?

6. How do you want to follow up on this interview? (For example, you may want to send a letter thanking the interviewee, asking for clarification on points that you are unsure of, highlighting the important points, or stating the results of the interview.)

Interviewer's Checklist

The basic informational interview format can be used not only to gather information, but also to give information, influence attitudes and behavior, or reach a decision. The interviewer defines the purpose of the interview, whether the goal is to get information on a famous person for an article, introduce a new product to a customer, decide whether or not to hire someone or to buy a particular product, solve the problem of a worker's chronic tardiness, or decide with a neighbor how to fix a dilapidated old fence that separates the two yards. In each case, you can follow the same basic steps.

1. Clarify what you want. What is essential? What is optional?

2. Research what you want.

3. Decide who you are going to interview and learn as much as possible about them.

4. Define your specific purpose in initiating this interview.

5. Decide what information you want to convey and the most effective way to present it.

6. List the questions that you want answered in this interview. (Remember to ask questions that can't be answered readily by another source.)

7. Put your questions in the order that you want to ask them.

8. Anticipate questions that the interviewee is apt to ask you and prepare a response to each of these questions.

9. Decide how long the interview will be.

10. Set up the interview.

11. Greet the interviewee, reiterate the purpose and length of the interview, and establish rapport.

12. Exchange information to accomplish your purpose: give information, ask your planned questions, and respond to the interviewee's answers.

13. Bring the interview to a close by thanking the interviewee and summarizing the important points of the interview, any agreements that were made, and what the next step will be.

14. Debrief.

Gus found it helpful to follow the checklist when he had a house to rent out.

1. He clarified what kind of renters he wanted: a nonsmoking married couple with no pets or children, both spouses working full-time and able to easily afford the rent. Must have good references and be willing to stay for at least one year. He decided that it was essential and nonnegotiable that the renters be nonsmoking, employed, have good references, be willing to stay a year, and be able to easily pay the rent. That they be married, have no pets or children, and be working full-time were optional and open to negotiation.

2. He researched the rental market in his area and arrived at a fair and attractive rent. He found that the most common way to rent a house was to place an ad in the classified section of the local paper.

3. Since he would be interviewing strangers who responded to his ad, he decided to use his initial phone contact to learn as much as possible about them.

4. The specific purpose of this screening interview would be to weed out inappropriate candidates and people who were not seriously interested in his rental. Emphasis would be on the

facts. He would invite the best applicants to meet him at his rental property and decide when he talked to them face-to-face whether he liked them as people.

5. He wrote out a paragraph describing the rental and the neighborhood which he could refer to when he was on the phone.

6 & 7. He wrote out a list of questions to screen the callers and arranged these questions in the order that he would ask them.

   a. What is your full name and a phone number where I can reach you in the evening?

   b. Will you be living alone or with others? If others, the following questions apply to them also.

   c. Where are you currently living and why are you moving?

   d. If you decide that you want to rent my place, may I talk to your three most recent landlords?

   e. Do you smoke?

   f. Any pets?

   g. What do you do for a living and who do you work for?

   h. May I contact your employer to confirm your salary and that you are an employee in good standing?

   i. How long do you plan to rent the house?

8. He anticipated the questions that the interviewees would ask him and came up with his responses.

   a. How long is the lease for? (It's open to negotiation. How long would you like it for?)

   b. Is there a garage? (No, but there's plenty of street parking.)

   c. Are the appliances gas or electric? (The heat, stove, and dryer are gas; everything else is electric.)

   d. How close are the schools? (There is a grade school and middle school within walking distance. The high school is three miles away; the school bus for it stops at the corner.)

9. He decided to limit the interview time to ten minutes.

10. He set up the interview by placing an ad in the paper and waiting for his phone to ring.

11. When he got a call inquiring about the ad in the paper describing a house for rent, he introduced himself, asked the name of the inquirer, and explained that he was screening

people briefly on the phone before showing the house. He took time to establish rapport.

12. He gave a brief description of the house and neighborhood. He asked his planned questions, responded to the inquirer's answers, and answered questions.

13. Based on the information he gathered, he made a decision on the spot about whether the person had the essential characteristics that he was looking for in a renter. If he thought that the person seemed appropriate, and the person was still interested in the rental after being screened, he set up an appointment to meet the person at the rental. If he thought that the person was inappropriate, he told the person: "I'm sorry, but I prefer not to rent my place to people who _____. Good luck to you in your search for what you want" or "I already have a number of people interested in renting my house, and I plan to pick one of them. Thank you for your interest and good luck in finding a place."

14. For each person that he screened on the phone, he filled out a card with basic information about them, his impression of them, and the outcome of the interview.

Exercise. To develop your own interviewing skills, use the interviewer's checklist to prepare for and conduct an interview.

Preparing To Be Interviewed

Interviewee's Checklist

1. Define your purpose in being interviewed.

2. Define the purpose of the interviewer.

3. If you are not already an expert on the topic of the interview, do your homework. For instance, if you are applying for a job, research the person or company with whom you are interviewing. What do your prospective employers do? How do they do it? How successful are they? Who is their competition? What factors contribute to their success? How does the job that you are applying for contribute to their success?

4. Based on your research, write down several questions that you can ask the interviewer.

5. Make a list of the important points that you want to communicate about yourself. For example, think of at least three

things that you have done that demonstrate how you can contribute to your prospective employers' future success. Use your education, experience, outstanding accomplishments, skills, interests, personal qualities, plans for your future, and innovative ideas to convince the interviewer of your value.

6. Anticipate questions that you are likely to be asked and prepare well-thought-out responses to each of them.

7. Anticipate objections that the screener is likely to have to you and come up with a good defense. For instance, if you have a pet and are responding to an ad to rent an apartment, you will want to be ready with a response for the landlord who says "Sorry, no pets!" You can be honest about your pet and still say something like "My cat is an outdoor cat; I can't stand animals in the house because of my allergies, and besides, they're so dirty!" You may find that the landlord will soften to you.

8. Plan to make a favorable impression on the interviewer.

9. Think of ways to quickly establish rapport with the interviewer before he or she begins to question you.

10. Practice interviewing by role playing in front of a mirror, into a tape recorder, or with a friend. This will make you more comfortable for the real event and give you a chance to make needed improvements.

11. Be ready to ask for clarification regarding the outcome of the interview. If you are seeking a positive decision and the interviewer rejects you out of hand, ask for feedback. You have nothing to lose, and you may be able to counter his or her objections. If the interviewer seems positive about you but doesn't tell you what the next step in the decision-making process is, ask him or her what it is. When will you be contacted for a selection interview? When can you see the rental property or the used car?

12. If you are clear that you are interested in what the interviewer is offering, say so with enthusiasm. Summarize what you have to offer. If appropriate, make an offer or give the interviewer an opportunity to make one. Push for a decision. For instance, if the interviewer can't make the decision, ask to speak to the person who can.

13. Debrief as soon as possible after the interview.

a. Write down the date of the interview and the basic facts about the interviewer, company, position, or item that you are interested in.

b. What were the main points that you made and the interviewer's response to them?

c. What were the interviewer's main concerns and how did you respond to them?

d. What are the next steps?

e. What did you say that you wish you hadn't?

f. What didn't you say that you wish you had?

g. How do you plan to follow up on this interview? (For example, plan to send a letter thanking the interviewer for his or her time. Review your key points and how they relate to the job. State what you think the next steps should be. Make your letter interesting and relevant. You may want to add something new or challenging.)

If appropriate, make a list of reasons to check back with the interviewer in the following weeks. Ask a question. Send a note giving your thoughts on a question that was left open. Send an article that supports your views. Follow up by asking the interviewer if he or she got the note or article and what he or she thought of it. If you think you did badly in the interview, you may want to call back and ask for a second chance.

Exercise. Prepare for an interview in which you will be interviewed by using the interviewee's checklist.

Making a Good First Impression

First impressions, for better or worse, are very important. Research indicates that an interviewer's negative impression of a job applicant typically forms within the first five minutes of an interview. Once this negative impression is established, 90 percent of the time the applicant isn't hired. If the interviewer forms a positive impression of a job applicant in the first five minutes of an interview, 75 percent of the time that applicant is offered the job. You never get a second chance to make a good first impression.

Although the following ten ways to impress an interviewer are tailored to a selection interview for a job, they apply to any interview situation in which you seeking a positive outcome.

1. Be on time. Be sure that you know when and where you are going to be interviewed. Leave enough time to get lost or caught in a traffic jam and to find your way there early.

2. Know your interviewer's name and use it. People like to hear their own name.

3. Dress appropriately for the position and to please the interviewer. If you are unsure about what is appropriate for the position, a good rule of thumb is to dress professionally and conservatively. This is not the moment to try out a trendy new fashion or make a political statement. Dress in colors and a style that is flattering to you. Be perfectly groomed, from your recent haircut down to your freshly polished shoes.

4. Appear calm, even if you are churning inside. Remember to breathe. Overcome your self-consciousness by making a point to get to know your interviewer. Tell yourself that you are prepared and dressed for success and remember that the interviewer expects and will forgive some nervousness. Keep in mind that if you do blow the interview, the worst thing that will happen is that you will be maintaining the status quo; you won't have lost anything that you already have.

5. Be courteous. Show the interviewer that you are respectful and appropriately friendly. Your nonverbal communication is as important as what you say when it comes to conveying courtesy: give a warm, firm handshake, maintain natural and direct eye contact, wait to be shown where to sit, pay attention to your posture, sit slightly forward in your chair, and so forth. See Chapter 4 on "Body Language" for more pointers on nonverbal communication.

6. Be flexible and tactful. Disagree only if you feel you must. When you disagree, acknowledge the interviewer's point of view and underscore any merit that you see in it before you present your point of view. Keep an open mind. Assume that everything that the interviewer asks you has a purpose.

7. Be honest and consistent. Nothing destroys trust in a relationship faster than a lie uncovered. Even the appearance of deception is usually unsalvageable.

8. Show your genuine interest in the interviewer and his or her concerns. Listen attentively to what he or she has to say and give the interviewer positive nonverbal feedback. Be ready to listen to the interviewer's stories or draw him or her out. Pay attention to the nonverbal feedback that he or she conveys so

that you can adjust your behavior accordingly. For instance, if the interviewer is fidgeting, looking away while you are talking, or glancing at the clock, he or she is ready for you to stop or change the subject.

9. Get the interviewer interested in you. If you simply wait to be asked questions, you won't be doing anything to make yourself stand out from all the other people he or she is interviewing. Say or do something that will break the monotony of the interviewer's day. Share something memorable about yourself. Tell an interesting story.

10. Look for bridges between you. Take advantage of the informal small talk at the beginning of the interview to talk about people and interests you have in common. Leave the interviewer with a good feeling about you. If the interviewer can identify with you in some significant way, you will have won him or her over. The gut feeling that he or she has about you after the interview is more important than the facts that the interviewer may recall about you when the time comes to select who will get hired.

Making a good impression is also important for the interviewer. After all, the interviewee is also forming opinions while he or she is being interviewed.

Anticipating and Responding to Questions in a Job Interview

While a job interview will sometimes contain elements of both a screening and a selection interview, the interviewer's purpose is very different for each of them. Keep in mind that the screening interview serves a gate-keeping function; it is designed to weed out inappropriate candidates based on the facts as presented. Therefore it is wise to be ready to answer the questions put to you honestly, consistently, and succinctly, but not to volunteer information that might bias the interviewer against you.

Selection interviews are commonly used to explore the personality of a job applicant. While the screening interview focuses primarily on the facts, the selection interview tries to uncover the inner person. The interviewer wants to get a sense of what this applicant would be like in the position he or she is applying for. No matter what the interviewer says he or she wants, the final decision is likely to be based on his or her feelings about the interviewee after the interview. This fact makes it essential that the interviewee be prepared to favorably impress the interviewer.

As an interviewee, you are primarily a salesman. Your product is yourself: your assets are your experience, skills, and personality. While your resume can communicate your background clearly, your personality can only come across in the interview.

When interviewing for a job, the interviewer basically has only one question: "Why should I hire you?" The best answer you can give to this question is that you will produce far more value than you will cost. You can demonstrate this with your accomplishments. Whatever question you are asked, try to frame your answer to indicate that you would be an asset in the position for which you are applying. You will rapidly become productive because you learn quickly and don't require a lot of supervision. You will remain productive because you are versatile and flexible and therefore able to adapt to change. You are an enthusiastic, committed, responsible worker who can handle problems and get the job done. You will fit into the company's culture, and you will be a fun and easy person to work with. If hired, you plan to stay.

Find out what the interviewer is looking for. Ask how he or she sees the position that you are applying for. What tasks does the interviewer want accomplished? What characteristics is he or she looking for in the person who fills this position? Shape your description of your experience and skills to fit the desires that he or she has revealed. If you start describing your background before you understand his or her perspective of the job, you are in unknown territory. Tell about your accomplishments in terms of what the interviewer wants done.

Listen carefully to each question. Be sure that you understand the question before you answer. If a question is particularly difficult, take your time before answering. Be sure that the interviewer understands what you intended to say. Take advantage of open-ended questions to demonstrate how you will be an asset if hired. Answer closed questions that call for a yes or no answer forthrightly. If the answer is no, follow it with a positive statement: "No, I don't know Word Perfect, but I do know several other word processing programs, and I think I can pick it up quickly." If you have been dutifully answering all the interviewer's questions and find that the interview is going in a direction that does not allow you to express your accomplishments and how you can be an asset if hired, you must find a way to redirect the conversation.

Know Your Rights as an Interviewee: Illegal Questions and How To Respond to Them

Legislation and changing attitudes have greatly reduced discrimination in preemployment interviews. Inquiries into the following areas are or can be out of bounds in an interview:

1. Race, ethnic background, or national origin

2. Marital status

3. Family makeup

4. Gender and, in some states and cities, sexual orientation

5. Age, unless related to job

6. Weight or height

7. Membership in social clubs or organizations

8. Religious affiliation

9. Arrest record

Some of these areas of questioning are clear cut—any question about color, national origin, or religion is illegal—but most are a little more tricky. While it's legal to ask a woman's marital status, it's considered discriminatory to ask if she wants to be called Mrs., Miss, or Ms., or if she is married, single, divorced, separated, engaged, or widowed. It is also illegal to ask about her spouse, or children, her plans for a family, or her perspective on the ERA. It is legal to ask if a job candidate has ever been convicted of a crime, but it is illegal to ask if he or she has ever been arrested, pled guilty to a crime, or "been in trouble with the law."

In general, employers can ask about a candidate's skills, abilities, motivation, and personality as they apply to the job that the applicant is being interviewed for. Such questions may touch not only on former job experiences, but also on outside interests. For example, it is legal to ask whether he or she belongs to specific organizations in which membership is relevant to the job, but it is illegal to ask for a list of all the organizations to which he or she belongs. It is legal to ask a job applicant if he or she has any impairments that would interfere with their ability to perform the job, but it is illegal to ask if he or she has a disability, has ever been treated for specific diseases, or has been compensated for injuries, or to inquire how much time has been lost because of illness in the past two years. It is legal to ask the applicant to submit to a company physical or provide a doctor's certificate of health after the interview. It is illegal to ask an applicant's age or date of birth or why he or she is seeking employment at a particular age. It is legal to ask if the applicant is old enough to work, if he or she is between 18 and 65 years of age, and, if not, to state his or her age.

If you are uncertain as to whether a particular question is discriminatory, ask the interviewer how it is relevant to the job. If you think that you are being asked an illegal question, you may choose to answer it or not. Remember, though, that just because a question sounds discriminatory to you does not necessarily mean that the interviewer intends to discriminate against you. Many interviewers are unsophisticated and ask whatever pops into their heads. An employer might ask if you are Polish simply because you remind him of a Polish acquaintance; your answer will have nothing to do with whether he is going to hire you.

Some interviewers will appreciate your pointing out when they ask an illegal question. Others will feel threatened by you and not offer you the job. If you do decide not to answer a question that you consider discriminatory, do so as tactfully as you can. You could simply say that you think the question is discriminatory and that you prefer not to answer it. Decline to answer in as nonthreatening a way as possible. For instance, you might say, "I'm certainly willing to cooperate with you in any legitimate areas of inquiry, but it's my understanding that questions that are not job related are inappropriate. I don't think that question is relevant to the job, do you?"

If you think that answering an illegal question is not going to hurt your chances of getting hired, you may choose to answer it, rather than risk offending or scaring the interviewer and blowing the interview. Refusing to answer even an illegal question may give the interviewer the impression that you are hiding something, and filing a discrimination claim that will take years to process is not as satisfying as getting the job now. If you do answer an illegal question, consider the interviewer's underlying concern and answer accordingly. For instance, if the interviewer takes note that you are not wearing a wedding ring, you might decide to say, "I'm not married, but my boyfriend is one hundred percent behind my getting this job." You also may want to gently let the interviewer know that you have some familiarity with the law. For example, you could say, "I believe I read somewhere that that type of question is inappropriate in an employment interview."

If you feel that you have been denied a job because you refused to answer a discriminatory question or because of your answer to an illegal question, you have the option of writing a letter to the appropriate agency in your area to protect your rights. These agencies include the regional office of the Division of Human Rights in your state, your local chapter of the American Civil Liberties Union, or a regional office of the Equal Employment Opportunity Commission. You also may want to discuss your rights and options with an attorney if you are not satisfied with the progress of the investigation.

Bibliography

1. Listening

Barker, L. L. 1990. *Listening Behavior*. New Orleans: SPECTRA.

Wolvin, A., and C. G. Coakley. 1992. *Listening*. 4th ed. Dubuque, IA: W. C. Brown.

2. Self-Disclosure

Jourard, S. M. 1971. *The Transparent Self: Self-Disclosure and Well-Being*. 2nd ed. New York: Van Nostrand Reinhold.

3. Expressing

Cavanaugh, M. E. 1980. *Make Your Tomorrow Better*. New York: Paulist Press.

McKay, M., M. Davis, and P. Fanning. 1981. *Thoughts & Feelings: The Art of Cognitive Stress Intervention*. Oakland, CA: New Harbinger.

4. Body Language

Birdwhistell, R. L. 1970. *Kinesics and Context: Essays on Body Motion Communication*. New York: Ballantine.

Fast, J. 1994. *Body Language in the Workplace*. New York: Penguin.

Hall, E. T. 1990. *The Hidden Dimension*. New York: Doubleday.

5. Paralanguage and Metamessages

Davitz, J. R., et al. 1976. *The Communication of Emotional Meaning*. New York: McGraw-Hill.

6. Hidden Agendas

Berne, E. 1985. *The Games People Play*. New York: Ballantine.

7. Transactional Analysis

Harris, T. A. 1976. *I'm OK, You're OK*. New York: Avon.

James, M., and D. Jongeward. 1971. *Born to Win*. Reading, MA: Addison-Wesley.

Meininger, J. 1974. *Success Through Transactional Analysis.* New York: Dutton.

8. Clarifying Language

Bandler, R., and J. Grinder. 1975. *The Structure of Magic I.* Palo Alto, CA: Science and Behavior Books.

———. 1979. *Frogs Into Princes.* Palo Alto, CA: Science and Behavior Books.

Lankton, S. 1980. *Practical Magic: A Translation of Basic Neuro-Linguistic Programming into Clinical Psychotherapy.* Cupertino, CA: Meta Publications.

9. Culture and Gender

Ellis, A., and G. Beattie. 1986. *The Psychology of Language and Communication.* New York: Guilford Press.

Pearson, J. C., L. H. Turner, and W. Todd-Mancillas. 1991. *Gender and Communication.* 2nd ed. Dubuque, IA: W. C. Brown.

Tannen, D. 1986. *That's Not What I Meant! How Conversational Style Makes or Breaks Your Relations with Others.* New York: Morrow.

———. 1990. *You Just Don't Understand: Women and Men in Conversation.* New York: Morrow.

10. Assertiveness Training

Alberti, R. E., and M. Emmons. 1990. *Your Perfect Right.* 6th ed. San Luis Obispo, CA: Impact Press.

Bower, S. A. 1991. *Asserting Your Self.* Reading, MA: Addison-Wesley.

Davis, M., M. McKay, and E. R. Eshelman. 1995. *The Relaxation & Stress Reduction Workbook.* 4th ed. Oakland, CA: New Harbinger.

Fensterheim, H., and J. L. Baer. 1975. *Don't Say Yes When You Want to Say No.* New York: David McKay.

Phelps, S., and N. Austin. 1987. *The Assertive Woman.* 2nd ed. San Luis Obispo, CA: Impact Press.

Smith, M. J. 1985. *When I Say No, I Feel Guilty.* New York: Bantam.

11. Fair Fighting

Bach, G. R., and P. Wyden. 1976. *The Intimate Enemy.* New York: Avon.

McKay, M., P. D. Rogers, and J. McKay. 1989. *When Anger Hurts: Quieting the Storm Within.* Oakland, CA: New Harbinger.

Tavris, C. 1989. *Anger: The Misunderstood Emotion.* 2nd ed. New York: Simon & Schuster.

12. Negotiation

Fisher, R., and W. Ury. 1991. *Getting to Yes: Negotiating Agreement Without Giving In.* 2nd ed. New York: Viking Penguin.

Scott, G. G. 1990. *Resolving Conflict: With Others and Within Yourself.* Oakland, CA: New Harbinger.

13. Prejudgment

Hamachek, D. E. 1982. *Encounters with Others: Interpersonal Relationships and You.* New York: Holt, Rinehart and Winston.

McKay, M., and P. Fanning. 1991. *Prisoners of Belief: Exposing & Changing Beliefs That Control Your Life.* Oakland, CA: New Harbinger.

14. Making Contact

Brassell, W. 1994. *Belonging: A Guide to Overcoming Loneliness.* Oakland, CA: New Harbinger.

Crowell, A. 1995. *I'd Rather Be Married: Finding Your Future Spouse.* Oakland, CA: New Harbinger.

Kahn, M. 1995. *The Tao of Conversation.* Oakland, CA: New Harbinger.

Markway, B. G., et al. 1992. *Dying of Embarrassment: Help for Social Anxiety and Social Phobia.* Oakland, CA: New Harbinger.

Wasmer, A. C. 1978. *Making Contact.* New York: Dial Press.

15. Sexual Communication

Bach, G. R., and R. M. Deutsch. 1971. *Pairing.* New York: Avon.

Barbach, L., and L. Levine. 1981. *Shared Intimacies: Women's Sexual Experience.* New York: Bantam.

Goldberg, H. 1977. *The Hazards of Being Male: Surviving the Myth of Masculine Privilege.* New York: Signet Books.

Hite, S. 1987a. *The Hite Report: A Nationwide Study of Female Sexuality.* New York: Dell.

———. 1987b. *The Hite Report on Male Sexuality.* New York: Ballantine.

McKay, M., P. Fanning, and K. Paleg. 1994. *Couple Skills: Making Your Relationship Work.* Oakland, CA: New Harbinger.

Wile, D. B. 1992. *Couples Therapy: A Nontraditional Approach.* New York: Bantam.

Williams, W. 1988. *Rekindling Desire: Bringing Your Sexual Relationship Back to Life.* Oakland, CA: New Harbinger.

Womack, W., and F. Strauss. 1991. *The Marriage Bed: Renewing Love, Friendship, Trust, and Romance.* Oakland, CA: New Harbinger

Zilbergeld, B. 1992. *The New Male Sexuality.* New York: Bantam Books.

16. Communicating With Children

Durrell, D. 1989. *Starting Out Right: Essential Parenting Skills for Your Child's First Seven Years.* Oakland, CA: New Harbinger.

Faber, A., and E. Maylish. 1982. *How to Talk So Kids Will Listen.* New York: Avon.

Gordon, T. 1970. *Parent Effectiveness Training: The Tested New Way to Raise Responsible Children.* New York: Peter H. Wyden.

17. Family Communications

Bandler, R., J. Grinder, and V. Satir. 1976. *Changing with Families.* Palo Alto, CA: Science and Behavior Books.

Blevins, W. 1993. *Your Family, Your Self.* Oakland, CA: New Harbinger.

McKay, M., P. Fanning, and K. Paleg. 1994. *Couple Skills: Making Your Relationship Work.* Oakland, CA: New Harbinger.

Newman, M. 1994. *Stepfamily Realities.* Oakland, CA: New Harbinger.

Satir, V. 1982. *Conjoint Family Therapy.* 3rd ed. Palo Alto, CA: Science and Behavior Books.

Watzlawick, P., J. Beavin, and D. Jackson. 1967. *Pragmatics of Human Communication.* New York: W. W. Norton.

18. Influencing Others

Axelrod, R. 1984. *The Evolution of Cooperation.* New York: Basic Books.

Rusk, T. 1993. *The Power of Ethical Persuasion.* New York: Viking.

19. Small Groups

Bennis, W. G., K. D. Benne, and R. Chin, eds. 1985. *The Planning of Change: Readings in the Applied Behavioral Sciences.* New York: Holt, Rinehart and Winston.

Luft, J. 1984. *Group Process: An Introduction to Group Dynamics.* 3rd ed. Palo Alto, CA: Mayfield Publications.

Ouche, W. 1993. *Theory Z.* New York: Avon.

20. Public Speaking

Desberg, P., and G. Marsh. 1988. *Controlling Stagefright.* Oakland, CA: New Harbinger.

Haynes, J. L. 1981. *Organizing a Speech: A Programmed Guide.* 2nd ed. Englewood Cliffs, NJ: Prentice-Hall.

McCroskey, J. C. 1986. *An Introduction to Rhetorical Communication.* 5th ed. Englewood Cliffs, NJ: Prentice-Hall.

Wolpe, J. 1988. *Life Without Fear.* Oakland, CA: New Harbinger.

21. Interviewing

Donaghy, W. C. 1984. *The Interview: Skills and Applications.* Glenview, IL: Scott, Foresman.

Hirsch, A. S. 1994. *National Business Employment Weekly Interviewing.* New York: John Wiley & Sons.

Jackson, T. 1993. *Interview Express.* New York: Times Books.

Medley, H. A. 1992. *Sweaty Palms: The Neglected Art of Being Interviewed.* Berkeley, CA: Ten Speed Press.

Sack, S. M. 1991. *The Employee Rights Handbook: Answers to Legal Questions from Interview to Pink Slip.* New York: Facts on File.

Index

Italicized numbers are used for those pages on which illustrations appear.

A

Absolutes as overgeneralizations, 99
Active listening
    and children, 220
    as dependent on feedback, 16-17
    and making contact, 186, 189
    in interviews, 295
    in leading groups, 258, 260
    paraphrasing and, 15-16
    in sexual communication, 204
    See also Negotiation
Adult, speaking as. *See* Transactional
    analysis
Agendas, hidden. See Hidden agendas in
    communication
Aggressive communication, 124-127, 261
    as defense tactic, 73
    as game, 75-76
    and loudness, 64
    See also, Fighting, fair; Negotiation
Agreement, 151, 157
Analysis of speech presentation, 270
Analyzing communications, 83-85
    See also Transactional analysis
Anger
    covering feelings with, 145
    in incongruent messages, 58, 232,
        239
    and metamessages, 67
    responding passively to, 131
    in sexual communication, 201
    strategy for warding off, 75
    and using content-to-process
        strategy, 138-139
    venting, 126

    See also Fighting, fair; Aggressive
        communication
Antisocial, 123
Argue, John, 67
Articulation, 64, 66
Assertive communication, 125-128, 132
Assertiveness training
    exercise, 127, 129, 135-136, 140-141
    strategies, 131-141
    traditional assumptions and
        beliefs, 122-123
Assessments,
    based on perceptual accentuation,
        170
    exercise on listening blocks, 12-15
    of self-disclosure, *27*, 28-29
Assumptions
    based on parataxic distortions, 174
    and criticism, 132
    erroneous, 115, *169*
    and mind reading, 9
    mistaken traditional, 122-123
    in understanding experiences of
        others, 95
    See also Styles, communication;
        Parataxic distortion
Attitude
    breathing as indicator of, 57-58
    in fair fighting, 147
    metamessages conveying, 67-70
    in seeking solutions, 158
    and self-disclosure, *28*
Authoritarian, leaders, 263
Awareness
    to avoid sterotyping, 111
    exercises, 116-118
    to listening blocks, 14

listening with, 14, 19
place, 40
of nonverbal communication
gestures, 55
rules for gender, 111-116
and whole messages, 39-43

B

Bach, George, 143, 177
Bandler, Richard, 95, 105
Berne, Eric, 75, 81, *91*
Blackmail, 237-238
Blame, 217, 237,
avoiding, 20, 148
form of, 144
and parent, 217, 227, 239
to influence change in others, 124,
144, 148, 217, 237, 245-246
taking, 261-262
when needs denied, 237
See also Children.
Blocks
to awareness, 230
to effective task-group
communication, 256-257, 261
in interviews, 295
to listening, 8-12, 14-15
in meeting people, 182-183
and nonverbal messages. *See*
Nonverbal communication
to self-disclosure, 24-25
to ward off demands and
expectations, 75
Body awareness, 182
Body language, 39, 182-183
See also Nonverbal communication
Boundaries
of males, 114
for children, 216
Brainstorming, 159-161, 260
Breathing
to combat effect of rejection, 182
to counteract stage fright, 277
as nonverbal message, 57-58
and posture as indicators of
feelings and attitudes, 57
in voice exercises, 66
Broken record. *See* Assertive strategies

C

Calling process, 164, 261-262
See also Content-to-process shift
Cause and effect
errors in, 102-103
in speech presentation and
organization, 269-270
See also Speeches, public
Change
denying suggestions for, 11
fair fighting and, 148-149, 150, 151
ineffective and effective strategies
for influencing, 246-249

in paralanguage, 65-67
plan for 250-251
Child, speaking as. *See* Transactional
analysis
Children
affect of withdrawal on, 238
assessment of listening to, 13
consequences and, 217-218
and criticism, 131-134
developing self-esteem, 218
and excuses, 132
and joint problem solving, 220-225
making choices, 226
and need for self-expression, 213,
215
Choice
for children, 226
and imposed limits, 100-101
and rights as adult, 122-123
See also Assumptions
Clarification
and awareness rules of females
and males, 111-116
and children, 215
for effective expression, 45-47, 136
of first impressions, 177-178
of goals, 282, 289-290
in interviews, 282-283, 289
in listening to understand, 16-17,
19, 20, 45
of personal models, 95-97, 105
Clouding, 133-136
Cognitive-behavioral methods used for
anger and conflict, 143
Comfort zone. *See* Spatial zones in
relationships
Commitment
to listening, 5-6, 19, 20
to practice whole messages, 43
Communication styles, influence on.
See Transactional analysis
See also Self-disclosure
Comparing. *See* Parataxic distortions
Compliments, 188
Conflict
as assuming, 143
interpersonal, 84
and negotiation, 155, 156
resolving with children, 220, 225
in transactions, *88-90*
See also Negotiation
Congruence, 19, 45-46, 53-54, 56, 65
See also Incongruent communication
Consequences
and children, 217, 218
negative and positive, 149,
151-152, 249
Contamination in communication, 37-40,
83
Content-to-process shift
as assertive communication
strategy, 138-139
to keep order, 261-262

Coping and hidden agenda, 78
Couples
    reciprocal communication, 20
    sexual communication between.
        See Sexual communication
Covert manipulation strategies, 236-240,
    242
Covert modeling, 276
Criticism, responding to, 131-132
Cultures
    different communication styles
        between, 109
    gestures used in different, 55
    and physical space in
        communicating, 60-61
    types of, 107-108

D

Davis, Martha, 123
Daydreaming, 9-10, 203
Defense mechanism, 22
Defensive maneuver. *See* Hidden agendas
    in communication
Demands, 92, 145-146, 159-160
Delays in reponding, 139
    See also Time out
Deletions 95-96, 231, 239, 240
Denial of feelings in family, 231
Depression, 75, 115, 131
Derailing, 11
Disclosure
    for absolving guilt, 24
    and children, 219
    intimacy and, 21, 187-188
    See also Self-disclosure
Discounting
    in sexual communication, 205
    as sparring, 11
Disorders in family communication,
    231-234
Distance, physical. *See* Proxemics;
    Cultures
Double messages, 46

E

Ego in communication transactions. *See*
    Transactional analysis
Emotions, interpretation of through facial
    expression, 56
Empathy
    asking for, 115
    and assertive communication, 125
    listening with, 17-18, 113, 115
    in negotiation, 156
    See also Listening
Eshelman, Elizabeth Robbins, 123
Examination of communication styles. *See*
    Transactional analysis
Expression
    of appreciation, 112
    assertive, 127-131. *See also*
        Assertive communication

effective, 43-48
facial, 39, 55-56, 182-183
family alliances and, 236
family rules limiting, 229-230
negotiation, 156
need of children for, 213, 215
of observations, thoughts, feelings,
    and needs, 23, 34-42
as partial message, 37
of self, 43
in negotiation, 156
types of, 34-36, 38, 39
See also Feelings; Nonverbal
    communication; Self-disclosure

F

Family rules, 229-230, 231
Fear in meeting people, 179-182, 188
Feedback, 16, 17, 24, 31, 39, 43, 66, 132,
    156, 191, 208, 213, 293
Feelings
    agenda for coping with, 78
    assertive expression of, 128-129
    and contaminated message, 37-39
    denial of in families, 229-231
    disclosed through body
        movements, 55-58
    discounted in sexual
        communication, 205
    expressing, 23, 24, 34, 35, 37, 40-42,
        148
    hidden in metamessages, 70-71
    need to share, 157
    nonverbal cues conveying, 55
    substitution used to express, 232
    toward physical image, *29*
    and whole messages, 36
    See also Self-disclosure
Fighting, fair
    attitudes for, 147
    definition, 143-144
    rules for, 147-150
    See also Blame; Negotiation; Time
        out
Filtering, 9, 18

G

Games, 75-76*91*
Gender, 109-115
    See also Cultures; Awareness
Gestures
    hidden agendas and, 77
    as illustrators and regulators, 55-57,
        74, 77, 109, 125
    self-disclosure and, 21
    threatening, 149
    used in giving speeches, 275, 277
    See also Nonverbal communication;
        Social kinesics
Goals in interviews, 282-283
Goals in work, *28*
Grinder, Richard, 95, 105

Groups, 254
Guilt
    and disclosure, 24
    making others feel, 124
    in manipulating, 237, 240

H

Hall, Edward T., 58, 107
Harris, Thomas, 83-84
Hidden messages. *See* Metamessages
Hidden agendas in communication
    functions of, 73, 78-79
    list of 74-77
    and straight messages, 47

I

Icebreakers, 183-185, 189
Illustrators. *See* Nonverbal communication
Immediacy in communication, 44
Impressions, first, 108, 167-*168*, 171, 177,
    293, 294-296
Incongruent communication, 58, 232-234,
    239, 241
Independence, 114
Initiators, 255
Interpretation, 93, 214, 233
Interview
    goals, 289
    going to and conducting, 279, 283
    illegal questions asked in, 297-299
    preparing for, 284
    self-evaluation of, 288-289
    See also Scripts
Intimacy, 21, 23, 34, 35, 64, 73, 157, 188

J, K, L

Johari Window, 22
Judgments
    and first impressions, 167
    making while listening, 9
    negative, 9, 180
    See also Listening; Prejudgments
Krech and Crutchfield, 255
Labels, 168
    global, 48, 101
    negative, 9, 126, 179-180
    See also Judgments
Language patterns
    interfering with understanding,
        95-98
    and mind reading, 103
    to understand individual models,
        95
Leaders in task groups, 255-256, 257-264
Letting go, 225
Limits, imposed, 100-101
    See also Choice
Listening
    active, 5, 15-17, 185-186, 190, 213,
        260. *See also* Active listening
    assertive, 129-131
    blocks to, 8-11, 12-15

    to children, 211-213, 215
    commitment to, 19
    as a complement, 5-6
    empathy in, 17
    and filtering, 9, 18
    and half-listening, 6, 7, 9
    and identifying with experience, 10
    intention in, 6-7
    and mind reading, 5, 8, 9
    and paraphrasing, 15, 16
    personal model and, 94
    and the probelm solver, 10
    pseudo, 6-8
    real, 6-8, 15-17, 258
    and reciprocal communication, 20
    and intention, 6, 7
    and self-awareness, 39
Luft, Joseph, 22

M

Martyrs, 239-240
McKay, Matthew, 123,
Meditation, 184
Meeting people, 182-185
Mehrabian, Albert, 53-54
Metamessages
    attitudes and feelings
        communicated in, 67-69
    definition, 63
    verbal modifiers used in, 68-69
Mind reading, 5, 8-9, 94, 102-104, 105,
    233, 234-236, 240, 241
Models, personal
    challenging limits of, 99-100
    communication of, 95
    distorted, 102, 105, 106
    exercises on clarifying language of,
        96-105
    generalization of, 101
    as interpretation, 93-94
    understanding of other, 105
    See also Interpretation

N

Name calling, 219
    avoiding, 20
    and blaming, 144
    and children, 217, 227
Needs, expressing, 20, 34-42, 126-131
Negative thought, 180
Negotiation
    active listening in, 156
    and calling process, 164
    clarifying goals in, 282-283
    and fighting, fair, 133
    negative tactics in, 164
    proposal and counter proposals in,
        154
    in sexual communication, 206
    time-outs from, 153-154
Nonjudgment and children, 217-218, 222
Nonverbal communication

barrier of, 57-59, 182, 277,
breathing. *See* Breathing
body movements, 54-57
congruence of, 53-54
facial expression, 55-56
gestures, 54-56, 56-57, 74, 77, 109
as illutrators and regulators, 55
interviews and use of, 295
methods of, 53-60
posture, 39, 55, 57, 77, 136
and self-disclosure, 21
signals, 151, 208
Nonverbal signals. *See* Nonverbal
    communication

O

Observations, expressing, 40-42, 55-56
Openness, listening with, 18
Options, listing in negotiation, 158-162
Order. *See* Content-to-process shift
Organization
    of public speeches, 267-268

P

Paralanguage
    definition, 63
    elements of, 63-65
    See also Verbal communication
Paraphrase
    defined, 15
    in listening, 14, 15-16, 113
    in sexual communication, 204
Parataxic distortions
    assumptions made in meeting
        people, 174-176
    example of, 167
Parent
    as critical, 131
    speaking as, 81-84
    See also Transactional analysis
Parenting, effective
    and respect, 226
    skills for, 211-226
    See also Listening
Partial messages, 37, 39-40
Passive communication, 124-127, 131
Perceptions
    family rules on, 230
    limits of, *168-169*
    and stereotyping, 171-172
Perceptual accentuation, *169*, 170
Pitch as affecting communication style,
    63, 65, 66, 67-68
Pity as manipulative strategy, 237
Placating
    in families, 238
    as listening block, 11-12
Place awareness, 40
Posture. *See* Nonverbal communication
Prejudgments
    illusions in, 176-177
    in listening, 9

types of, 167, *168*
    See also Impressions, first
Presuppositions, 104, 105
Probing in understanding criticism,
    134-136
Problem solver, 10
Problem solving, 115, 143, 161, 212, 215,
    220, 225
Projection and mind reading, 103
Proposals and counter proposal, 150,
    154-155
Proxemics
    definition, 58
    intimacy, *59*
    spacial zones, 58-*59*, 60-61
Pseudo-listening
    and half listening, 6-7, 9-10
    reasons behind, 6-8
Put-down, 10-11, 67, 70, 124, 126, 133,
    180, 200

R

Real listening, 6-8
Reciprocal communication, 20
Regulators. *See* Nonverbal
    communication
Rejection
    and criticism, 131
    and defense manuevers, 73, 75
    fear of, *25*
    mind reading, 94
    parental, 82
    reframing, 180-182
    See also Listening
Relationships, 7
    making and keeping, 5
    intimate, 23
    See also Sexual communication
Relaxation, progressive, 277
Resonance as affecting communication
    style, 63-64, 66
Role play of communication styles,
    125-126
Roles
    in task-group meetings, 255, 256
    communication style determined
        by. *See* Transactional analysis
    in job interviews, 280-281
    See also Blocks; Transactional
        analysis
Rules
    effective expression, 43-49, 259-260
    effective task-group
        communication, 257, 264
    to fair fighting, 147-150
    to keep communications clean, 92
    of parent, 82-83, 229, 230, 231

S

Scripts
    for change, 151-152
    for interviews, 284-285

Self
    parts of, 22-23
    understanding, 23
    disclosing. *See* Self-disclosure
Self-awareness
    of observations, thoughts, feelings,
        needs, 39-43
    of nonverbal cues, 54
Self-care when needs denied by others,
    249
Self-consciousness, 180, 182, 207
Self-depreciation
    and fear of strangers, 179
    as setting tone for discussion, 108
    See also Cultures
Self-disclosure, 186-191
    assessing, 27, 28-29
    blocks to, 24-25
    and children, 219
    in content-to-process shift, 138
    example, 189-191
    and intimacy, 187, 188
    and parts of self, 22, 23, 25-27
    practice in, 30-31
Self-esteem, 18, 35, 77, 114, 157, 218, 222
Self-interest, 6, 134
Self-knowledge, 23, 25-26
    See also Self-disclosure
Self-worth, 47, 156, 226
Sexual communication
    anger in, 201
    enhancing, 207-209
    fears, 200
    guidelines for effective, 196-199,
        203-208
    guilt as factor in, 199
    problems in, 195-196
    through metamessages, 68
Sex life, evaluation of, 28-29, 202-203
Shyness, 179, 182
Social kinesics, 54-55
Social rules, 186
Social settings
    behavior in, 111
    physical distance in, 60, 183.
    responding assertively in, 127
Spacial zones in relationships, 58-59,
    60-61, 109, 183
    See also Proxemics
Sparring, 10-12
Speech. *See* Paralanguage; Metamessages
Speeches, public
    control of pitch and resonance in
        giving, 64
    cause and effect in, 269-270
    presentation and organization in,
        266-270
    state fright, 265-266, 276-278
    supporting materials used in,
        272-273
Stage fright, 265-266, 276-278
Stereotyping

based on membership, 170-172
    cultural, 107
    gender, 111, 115
    and self-fulfilling prophecy, 171-172
Styles, communication, 12, 124-126
    See also Transactional analysis
Sullivan, Harry, Stack, 173-174
Support
    expressing of, 48-49
    and parent, 92

T

Tannen, Deborah, 109
Task-group communication
    blocks to, 256
    free-flowing communication in, 254
    rules of initiators and responders
        in, 255
Tavris, Carol, 143
Thoughts
    expressing, 30, 34-35, 128-129
    negative, 179-180
Threats, making, 146, 162, 237-238
Time out, 139, 140, 149-150
    as assertive strategy, 139-140
    rules for, 149-150, 151
Transactional analysis
    ego state of parent, child, or adult,
        speaking from, 81-83
    exercises in identifying ego states,
        84-85
    as influence on communication
        styles, 81
    kinds of, *87-91*
    See also Rules
Triggers
    anger, 146
    in listening, 13-14

U, V

Ulterior transactions, *91-92*
Value judgments, 34-35
Values, personal
    distorted, 102
    imposed, 101
Verbal communication
    icebreakers, 183-185, 189
    and paralanguage and
        metamessages, 63-71
    regional difference in, 64
Verbal modifiers and meaning, 68-71

W

Whole messages, 36, 38,
    and partial messages, 37
    practicing, 40-43
    self-awareness of, 39
Withdrawal, 239-240
Words, interpretation of, 93-96
Wyden, Peter, 143

Communication Skills Tapes

Based on *Messages: The Communications Skills Book*, these audiotapes bring specific personal communication skills into focus and provide tools for improving relationships and personal effectiveness. **$11.95 each.**

Assertiveness Training

Making Contact

Effective Self-Expression

Sexual Communication

Becoming a Good Listener

Fair Fighting

The Tao of Conversation

by Michael Kahn, Ph.D.
November 1995, **$12.95**

This eloquent exploration of the art of conversation shows readers how to talk about things that really matter in ways that encourage new ideas, deepen intimacy, and build effective and creative working relationships. Author Michael Kahn exposes the underlying themes of our conversations and the reasons that participants may end up angry, alienated, or hurt and suggests ways to raise any conversation to a higher level of real communication.

Other New Harbinger Self-Help Titles

When Anger Hurts Your Kids, $12.95
The Addiction Workbook, $17.95
The Mother's Survival Guide to Recover, $12.95
The Chronic Pain Control Workbook, Second Edition, $17.95
Fibromyalgia & Chronic Myofacial Pain Sybndrome, $19.95
Diagnosis and Treatment of Sociopaths, $44.95
Flying Without Fear, $12.95
Kid Cooperation: How to Stop Yelling, Nagging & Pleading and Get Kids to Cooperate, $12.95
The Stop Smoking Workbook: Your Guide to Healthy Quitting, $17.95
Conquering Carpal Tunnel Syndrome and Other Repetitive Strain Injuries, $17.95
The Tao of Conversation, $12.95
Wellness at Work: Building Resilience for Job Stress, $17.95
What Your Doctor Can't Tell You About Cosmetic Surgery, $13.95
An End of Panic: Breakthrough Techniques for Overcoming Panic Disorder, $17.95
On the Clients Path: A Manual for the Practice of Solution-Focused Therapy, $39.95
Living Without Procrastination: How to Stop Postponing Your Life, $12.95
Goodbye Mother, Hello Woman: Reweaving the Daughter Mother Relationship, $14.95
Letting Go of Anger: The 10 Most Common Anger Styles and What to Do About Them, $12.95
Messages: The Communication Skills Workbook, Second Edition, $13.95
Coping With Chronic Fatigue Syndrome: Nine Things You Can Do, $12.95
The Anxiety & Phobia Workbook, Second Edition, $17.95
Thueson's Guide to Over-The Counter Drugs, $13.95
Natural Women's Health: A Guide to Healthy Living for Women of Any Age, $13.95
I'd Rather Be Married: Finding Your Future Spouse, $13.95
The Relaxation & Stress Reduction Workbook, Fourth Edition, $17.95
Living Without Depression & Manic Depression: A Workbook for Maintaining Mood Stability, $17.95
Belonging: A Guide to Overcoming Loneliness, $13.95
Coping With Schizophrenia: A Guide For Families, $13.95
Visualization for Change, Second Edition, $13.95
Postpartum Survival Guide, $13.95
Angry All The Time: An Emergency Guide to Anger Control, $12.95
Couple Skills: Making Your Relationship Work, $13.95
Handbook of Clinical Psychopharmacology for Therapists, $39.95
The Warrior's Journey Home: Healing Men, Healing the Planet, $13.95
Weight Loss Through Persistence, $13.95
Post-Traumatic Stress Disorder: A Complete Treatment Guide, $39.95
Stepfamily Realities: How to Overcome Difficulties and Have a Happy Family, $13.95
Leaving the Fold: A Guide for Former Fundamentalists and Others Leaving Their Religion, $13.95
Father-Son Healing: An Adult Son's Guide, $12.95
The Chemotherapy Survival Guide, $11.95
Your Family/Your Self: How to Analyze Your Family System, $12.95
Being a Man: A Guide to the New Masculinity, $12.95
The Deadly Diet, Second Edition: Recovering from Anorexia & Bulimia, $13.95
Last Touch: Preparing for a Parent's Death, $11.95
Consuming Passions: Help for Compulsive Shoppers, $11.95
Self-Esteem, Second Edition, $13.95
I Can't Get Over It, A Handbook for Trauma Survivors, $13.95
Concerned Intervention, When Your Loved One Won't Quit Alcohol or Drugs, $11.95
Dying of Embarrassment: Help for Social Anxiety and Social Phobia, $12.95
The Depression Workbook: Living With Depression and Manic Depression, $17.95
The Marriage Bed: Renewing Love, Friendship, Trust, and Romance, $11.95
Focal Group Psychotherapy: For Mental Health Professionals, $44.95
Hot Water Therapy: Save Your Back, Neck & Shoulders in 10 Minutes a Day $11.95
Prisoners of Belief: Exposing & Changing Beliefs that Control Your Life, $12.95
Be Sick Well: A Healthy Approach to Chronic Illness, $11.95
Men & Grief: A Guide for Men Surviving the Death of a Loved One., $13.95
When the Bough Breaks: A Helping Guide for Parents of Sexually Abused Childern, $11.95
Love Addiction: A Guide to Emotional Independence, $12.95
When Once Is Not Enough: Help for Obsessive Compulsives, $13.95
The New Three Minute Meditator, $12.95
Getting to Sleep, $12.95
Beyond Grief: A Guide for Recovering from the Death of a Loved One, $13.95
Leader's Guide to the Relaxation & Stress Reduction Workbook, Fourth Edition, $19.95
The Divorce Book, $13.95
Hypnosis for Change: A Manual of Proven Techniques, 2nd Edition, $13.95
When Anger Hurts, $13.95
Free of the Shadows: Recovering from Sexual Violence, $12.95
Lifetime Weight Control, $11.95
Love and Renewal: A Couple's Guide to Commitment, $13.95

Call **toll free, 1-800-748-6273**, to order. Have your Visa or Mastercard number ready. Or send a check for the titles you want to New Harbinger Publications, Inc., 5674 Shattuck Ave., Oakland, CA 94609. Include $3.80 for the first book and 75¢ for each additional book, to cover shipping and handling. (California residents please include appropriate sales tax.) Allow four to six weeks for delivery.

Prices subject to change without notice.